UNDERSTANDING
DEATH

THE MOST IMPORTANT EVENT OF YOUR LIFE

UNDERSTANDING
DEATH

THE MOST IMPORTANT EVENT OF YOUR LIFE

By John S. Hatcher

Bahá'í
PUBLISHING
Wilmette, Illinois

Bahá'í Publishing
415 Linden Avenue, Wilmette, Illinois 60091-2844

Copyright © 2009 by the National Spiritual Assembly of
the Bahá'ís of the United States

12 11   4 3 2

Library of Congress Cataloging-in-Publication Data
Hatcher, John, Dr.
  Understanding death : the most important event of your life / by John S. Hatcher.
    p. cm.
  ISBN 978-1-931847-72-8 (pbk. : alk. paper) 1. Death. 2. Death—
Religious aspects—Bahai Faith. 3. Hatcher, John, Dr. I. Title.
  BD444.H38 2009
  297.9'323—dc22
                          2009024257

Cover design by Robert A. Reddy
Book design by Patrick Falso

Dedicated to Norma and Amrollah Hemmat

CONTENTS

PREFACE

I'm healthy enough—decent blood pressure, relatively sound organs, no history of heart or lung disease, but with the help of computer research, I've traced those males from whom I am directly descended all the way back to the fourteenth century, and thus far, only one has lived into his eighties. My grandfather died at seventy-four. My father died at seventy-six; my brother at seventy. I had a first cousin who visited me with his wife at age seventy-nine. He seemed fit, strong, humorous, and indomitable. I thought surely he would make it, but he died unexpectedly from some anomalous disease six months later.

So at sixty-eight, I feel as if I am frantically trying to live each day to the fullest because I simply don't know how many more days are allotted to me. For sure it's a finite number, and anything short of infinity is scary. But the laws of probability are starting to weigh on me. Five years, ten at most—that's probably the best I can hope for. Now I no longer have to use my imagination about what the persona feels in Shakespeare's famous sonnet "That Time of Year," especially in that last quatrain:

> In me thou see'st the glowing of such fire,
> That on the ashes of his youth doth lie,
> As the deathbed whereon it must expire,
> Consumed with that which it was nourished by.

That very life force that has impelled me down the corridors of my brief time, that has snatched me from my magical and matchless childhood in Greensboro, North Carolina, is now all too rapidly eating away my remaining days, months, and years. And my deathbed is indeed composed of all those recollected times I dream about each night. And if a mind as great as Shakespeare's was made nervous by this fact, then why should I be ashamed to confess it?

My brother often said he couldn't wait to get to the other side. He was not very much of this world. He lived his life barely touching the ground. He was mostly intellect, and only occasionally did he own stuff or let stuff own him. Most of his life he and his family lived in apartments. He never worked in a garden or cared about the mahogany furniture and other relics passed down from the deceased generations. He never cared much for family stories or histories—he liked to think of himself as a self-made man, at least in regard to the important accomplishments.

For him, life's journey was headed inexorably to the celestial abode, and sometimes, perhaps weary with the pain of this life, he actually embraced the thought of its surcease. I remember him asserting this as early as his mid-twenties, and I remember trying to accept his declaration as a sign of fearlessness, certitude, or detachment, but in no way could I relate to it on a personal level. For me such statements seemed a denial of the joys of this life, which for me are no less divine creations.

Not that I am unaware of the dark side of this "dust heap," as 'Abdu'l-Bahá calls this life on occasion. I appreciate that according to the Bahá'í teachings, among the most prized attributes one can acquire in this life is detachment from the things of this world:

Abandon not the everlasting beauty for a beauty that must die, and set not your affections on this mortal world of dust (Bahá'u'lláh, Hidden Words, Persian, no. 14).

Abandon not for that which perisheth an everlasting dominion, and cast not away celestial sovereignty for a worldly desire. This is the river of everlasting life that hath flowed from the well-spring of the pen of the merciful; well is it with them that drink! (Bahá'u'lláh, Hidden Words, Persian, no. 37)

Set not your affections on mortal sovereignty and rejoice not therein. Ye are even as the unwary bird that with full confidence warbleth upon the bough; till of a sudden the fowler Death throws it upon the dust, and the melody, the form and the color are gone, leaving not a trace. Wherefore take heed, O bondslaves of desire! (Bahá'u'lláh, Hidden Words, Persian, no. 75)

Yet among all these exhortations to become detached from the things of this world—whether precious objects, sensual passions, or pride and power—are equally important laws and ordinances commanding that we disdain asceticism and monasticism, that each of us acquire a profession or occupation, and that we demonstrate and refine our spirituality by means of establishing a regimen of righteous actions:

Holy words and pure and goodly deeds ascend unto the heaven of celestial glory. Strive that your deeds may be cleansed from the dust of self and hypocrisy and find favor at the court of glory; for ere long the assayers of mankind shall, in the holy presence of the Adored One, accept naught but absolute virtue and deeds of stainless purity (Bahá'u'lláh, Hidden Words, Persian, no. 69).

Guidance hath ever been given by words, and now it is given by deeds. Every one must show forth deeds that are pure and holy, for words are the property of all alike, whereas such deeds

as these belong only to Our loved ones. Strive then with heart
and soul to distinguish yourselves by your deeds. In this wise
We counsel you in this holy and resplendent tablet (Bahá'u'lláh,
Hidden Words, Persian, no. 76).

The Bahá'í writings often cite the principle of moderation as a guide-
line for every sort of endeavor: "It is incumbent upon them who are
in authority to exercise moderation in all things. Whatsoever pass-
eth beyond the limits of moderation will cease to exert a beneficial
influence" (Bahá'u'lláh, *Gleanings,* no. 110.1). And yet it would seem
that these two sets of guidelines—the one exhorting us to detach
ourselves from the things of this earthly life and the other exhorting
us to become active in the world—are not intended to establish two
extremes between which is a middle path of moderation.

As I hope I have explained clearly and extensively in my book, *The
Purpose of Physical Reality,* our participation in those activities and
objectives that are of merit both to ourselves and to others do not admit excess. We cannot be *too* virtuous or perform *too many* righteous
deeds. But as I try to make plain in that same book, the objective of
our life's activities is to practice in symbolic or metaphorical forms the
inner qualities we possess, or which we wish to acquire. In this sense,
Bahá'í community life is a laboratory wherein we are challenged to
develop those qualities that will enhance our own character and create
an environment that will be conducive to others accomplishing the
same objectives.

My brother understood this, practiced this principle in his life's
work, and left behind a chorus of those whom he had inspired to do
the same. Nevertheless, I suspect that at seventy years of age, having
accomplished most of what he had set out to do, he was not disap-
pointed when he lay down for a nap that afternoon in November of
2005 and awoke in the realm of the spirit.

I, however, am not ready to leave this life. Most of the time, I love what I do, and I love this time in my life. I am retired after teaching at universities for forty-five years. I love this old house out in the country with its cozy wood-paneled rooms, the stone fireplace, and a view of the pasture from each window.

I love my small farm, my animals, my plants, and the little pond in the yard. I particularly love working the front loader on my Kubota L3130 tractor. It's as if the hefty toy Tonka truck I had in my sandbox has come to life with me inside it, and I am able to lift huge limbs or mounds of soil with the flick of a lever.

In the morning I write, and in the afternoon I work outside. In the evening I set a fire in the winter or watch the stars in the fall and spring. For me, at least for now, this is paradise enough. I can be as drab as dust inside at my writing desk, and within five minutes of stepping outside into the field, I am at peace. I am at home in this world with its trees, fields, birds, chickens, my dog, and my tools (whether manual or motorized).

I love my wife, and she loves me and all that I love, and daily works her garden until it bursts forth in rows of edibles and blossoms. The cows come when I call, and Teddy, a runt bull who has been with me since his mother was slain by a truck, loves when I brush him and scratch him around his horns and ears. I love the Sandhill cranes and their raucous call and the whispered swish of their wings in the evening when they fly overhead returning to the swamp after feeding in our fields.

I love the silly ibis with their impossible beaks and the egrets' deft scamper following behind the tractor to peck up juicy bugs when I till the field or top the pasture grass with my bush hog. I love the fish leaping in the pond snapping the flies, and I love to watch the burn pile after I coat it with kerosene a couple of times a year. I watch the scraps of dead tree limbs start a joyous blaze to celebrate the raw beauty and power of fire, the infinite colors of flame eating up chicken bedding, scraps of lumber, and defunct fence posts. Afterward, there remains only a small heap of ashes, and in a few days I begin another burn pile.

For a couple of weeks each spring, a pair of bluebirds perch on the fence outside my office window, and for about a week a flock of transient robins heading up to Georgia and North Carolina rest in our oaks. The sassy fox squirrels scurry around all year long from limb to limb among the same trees in the side yard, dashing in circles, screeching to a halt, then doing a full back-flip for no apparent reason I can discern.

Several months of the year the same kestrel waits atop the lightning rod at the corner of the fence scouring the field for his moveable feast. There are wrens, sparrows, finches, fly-catchers, swifts, ospreys, hawks, doves, crows, majestic giant blue herons, and an occasional bald eagle.

Down the road at the next farm, there are a bunch of peacocks that were brought up decades ago from Key West at the behest of old CW Cone, the now deceased rancher who built this house. Sometimes the gauche colored peacocks perch in the oak that the hurricane brought down two years ago. Like sentinels they roam daily up and down the road warning us of every passing truck they think is invading their territory; their piercing calls sound ever so much like a small child screaming, "heeeelllp! Helllp!"

A few years ago such a call would have startled me, and the morning birds would have interrupted my sleep. Now I find all this background noise quite pleasant, whether it is Scrappy the rooster heralding the sun, the horse across the pond whinnying for oats, the braying donkey supposedly scaring away the coyotes, or the steady lowing of cattle from all directions.

On summer nights I may hear a hoot owl or the coyotes' call from the clump of trees atop the hill that was a battlefield in the Seminole wars. When we walk beyond the pasture into the trees, we find the bare-bone remains of a calf that a pack of coyotes managed to separate from its mother. Death is all around us here, but it's expected.

I have come to like the people, the small town folk who have lived here for generations, families that have farmed or raised livestock here. They share each other's pain and loss. They know everything I do through some network of communion from which I am mostly excluded. I never see them looking because when I'm outside my eyes are focused on the earth.

I suppose they notice what the "professor" is doing with CW's old house as they rumble by in their pickups. For the first three years, they probably expected me to give up doing things for myself, thinking I would hire someone to work for me the way CW did. They are more cordial now that I bought a used tractor, a twenty-year-old pickup, built new fences, fixed the old pump to irrigate the garden, and constructed a chicken coop that has withstood two hurricanes.

Of my neighbors, I know that one is on chemo again. I know that another is recovering nicely from his bypass surgery, that still another is adjusting to the death of her husband who got lung cancer from working in the mines. One friend who is my age is starting to become aware that his arms aren't as well muscled as they were just a couple of years ago. But he still works twelve-hour days in the fields, on his tractors, or tending his cattle.

Perhaps Old CW has infected me with a bit of his own perspective about life out here. He was rich. He owned all the land from here to Zephyrhills. He could have lived anywhere he wanted or built some palatial estate in town, but he chose instead to remain in this old ranch home because he had built it himself in 1953 before he had so much.

Over the years he added to it according to the proclivities of each succeeding wife. He paneled it with tongue-in-groove boards fashioned from the felled cypress trees in his fields. He had a huge fireplace built in the den with fieldstones dug up from plowing these same pastures, and early on CW determined that he would stay in this place until he died because he loved it so.

And he did. His life's journey ended five years ago in a room near an outside door where they placed him partly so they could haul him out more easily. He was a big man, a large man, a man of substance. And though in the end he slept with a shotgun at his side, had two nurses, a cook, and a foreman to do his bidding, he did things the way he wanted, and not many people get to do that. At the estate sale, hundreds of town-folk came to buy something of his or just to see how the notorious CW had lived. "I don't think this is so nice," I heard one woman say. "My place is fancier than this."

I sense that CW is pleased with what we have done to preserve what is fine and noble and beautiful in this house and outside it. We have changed only what was needful, and I think he is pleased that I have come to know this house and its convoluted construction as well as he did, maybe better.

I think he's at peace. I pray that he is, because he left us this special place where I have spent so many days surveying the pastures and trees in any direction I look. He has left me a place to write and think and do a thousand tasks I have never done before. He has left me a place where I too am more or less at peace, even though I am never still and even though I am starting to count down the years. I frankly wouldn't mind living out my days here—not at all.

Though I am retired, I am writing, farming, and working harder than ever before. My one concern is that "I always hear / Time's winged chariot hurrying near." Yes, Marvel's one good poem does its work on me, even as it seduced whatever fair young thing he plied with that wonderful gambit. Because it's undeniably true! We're all going to die!

Go ahead. Say it out loud once. Doesn't it sound like the line out of a World War II battle movie with John Wayne as the tough but loveable sergeant? On the screen or the TV, it doesn't worry us. We know the hero will survive unless the director has pulled a fast one on us—certainly we would have read that in the reviews. So no matter how dire it looks for those fictional characters who represent us on some emotional level, we know at heart that everything will turn out OK.

Now say it again, but calmly, factually: "We are all going to die." Is there any doubt that this is true, an integral part of life, every single life? In Chaucer's "Knight's Tale" in his magnum opus *The Canterbury Tales*, old Egeus, the father of Theseus, tries to console his son when a plan to bring about justice has gone awry. The bright young knight Arcite has died when his horse bolts, thereby totally bungling the agreement that whoever won the tournament would win the fair young Emily, though she is an independent sort and doesn't really want either one of them. So the old man Egeus, who "knew this world's mutability, because he had seen it change, both for good and ill, joy after woe, and woe after felicity," says to his son Theseus who has arranged this entire scheme: "Just as a man never died . . . Who did not live on earth for a while, So no man ever lived . . . in all this world, who at some point did not die. This world is but a thoroughfare full of woe, and we are pilgrims passing to and fro. Death is the end to every worldly sorrow."

Perhaps we might not consider this a really *great* consolation for Theseus, who is trying as ruler to bring about justice on earth. But certainly it is accurate, or is it? This deep uncertainty about death causes Shakespeare's Hamlet to refrain from slaying himself as he desperately seeks to end the anxiety and depression that consume his psyche. If he is to be believed, Hamlet refrains from self-slaughter not because he fears the possibility of nonexistence. To him, ceasing to exist would be preferable to his present condition of emotional pain, dark depression, rage, turmoil, and confusion.

What he fears, in other words, is not death, but the possibility of an existence after death in which he might remain just as bewildered, confused, and alone, but without the ability to respond in any way— he might be eternally doomed to remain just as he is. Therefore, his "dread of something after death, / The undiscovered country from whose bourn / No traveler returns. . ." impels him to conclude that it would be best simply to "bear those ills we have / Than fly to others that we know not of." Why should he take the chance of leaping into another reality that might be worse than the one in which he presently abides?

Ultimately Theseus doesn't accept this solution either—that death is the end of our suffering and dismay—at least not as a sufficient consolation. After a few years of mourning Arcite and reflecting about life, death, and injustice, Theseus summons a parliament to announce what he has figured out about how to respond to the untimely death of the young knight, as well as to death in general. First he recites the principal axiom he has concluded about the length of life for each creature on earth: "The Creator hath established in this wretched world below a certain (number of) days and duration for everything that is engendered in this place, beyond which set day no one may pass, although one can cut short those days."

After enunciating this principle about predestination, he gives examples of how this axiom applies to various parts of creation, ending, appropriately, with the example of men and women, who may die in youth or in old age, regardless of whether they be a king or a page. He concludes that since none of us has the ability to know what our allotted time may be, nor can we alter this predetermined decree, we might as well not gripe about what we cannot control or what we believe to be life's injustice. Instead, he suggests, we should "make a virtue of necessity" by doing the best we can with that time we have.

The contrary of this attitude, he goes on to say, is willfulness and doesn't accomplish anything at all.

Theseus's thoughtful conclusion sounds very much like the first lines of the "serenity prayer" attributed to Reinhold Niebuhr: "God grant me the serenity to accept the things I cannot change; courage to change the things I can; and wisdom to know the difference." Perhaps these axioms are the best we can come up with.

But what if they aren't? What if there is a logic and consolation to this perplexing uncertainty about our lives that will enable us not to blunder around so blindly in an attempt to fashion something that makes sense, some course of action that will enable us to endure, to have an impact on reality or, at the very least, to be remembered?

If life is confined to the stuff between being born and dying, and if the paradigm imposed on us for successful living—the "Good Life"—is ultimately a chimera, a mirage, then a second problem we face regarding our own mortality, once we become aware of it, is how to plot a course for ourselves that has the greatest meaning, or at least some meaning.

This response is especially true if the various afterlife paradigms seem mythical, far-fetched, or nonsensical. But before we venture out on our own, it would obviously be the better part of wisdom first to see how others have responded to this challenge. And because our first awareness of our own mortality occurs in our childhood and youth, we might find some value first in assaying what some of the great minds have to say about those first images of death and mortality and the power of those childhood visions to shape our life's purpose.

John S. Hatcher, Professor Emeritus
University of South Florida
2009

1

THE ART OF DYING GRACEFULLY

Caius is a Man
Man is Mortal
Caius is Mortal

What prompted me to write this book is that I am dying. I don't have a terminal disease, but I am, like Caius, a man, and an aging one at that. And thus far in the history of human beings—at least on planet Earth—this classic (and classical) syllogism has proved invariably accurate. So far every one of us has met the same fate, though we don't dare discuss it much because it's so . . . defeatist.

Consequently, at age sixty-eight, the laws of statistics and probability dictate that I would do well to focus my attention more acutely on that point of transition, that "milestone" that I will most surely experience before many more years have passed. The problem is that the term *death* has such a negative and final connotation that I am loathe to use it. Like most others, I prefer euphemisms like "pass," "pass on," "pass away," "ascend" (a bit presumptuous on my part), or "kick the bucket" (more in keeping with my present country environment). But I have chosen for our purposes to employ the term "milestone" because I have come to believe that we continue to exist after our body gives out, as I hope to demonstrate later on.

So I have taken it upon myself to write this book—for myself more than for you—to explore and hopefully to demystify this natural and inevitable milestone in all our lives. My objective is partially to deal head-on with a subject that is rarely discussed dispassionately and frankly, even though it is, so far as we know, a rather important climax to (or milestone for) everything we undertake in this, the physical portion of our lives. For even though I believe that our consciousness and individuality continue beyond this milestone, I cannot in all honesty say that I am ready and prepared for that transformation or that I am without anxiety or fear at its inexorable approach.

A SUBJECTIVE PERSPECTIVE

This brings me to an important forewarning to the reader. Because it is primarily my own death I will be discussing, I will be speaking from an unabashedly subjective point of view. This is not a matter of my being an expert on the matter, but, then, I suppose I am as much an expert on aging and dying as any other mortal human, except for those who have already died or possibly those who have had a near-death experience, and I will certainly use their observations as a part of this discussion.

Psychologists, gerontologists, and oncologists could help us make better academic generalizations about what the aging and dying among us go through, and I will include their comments as well if it helps. But I'm not really interested in generalizations about what it feels like to get old, to be old, or how old people act or live or die. I have not entitled our conversation "Understanding Death" because I think I have come up with sage advice about how to do it well. Rather, it is my hope that this discussion will help me come to terms with this next stage of my life.

According to all the standards that I once held, I am old. What is more, almost every month another of my former colleagues at the university dies off. I see old friends at a funeral, and a few months later I'm at their funeral. When I survey the obituary page, I notice that the mean age of those who have "passed on" is about my age or close to it.

I certainly don't intend for this to be an elegy or lament about the abominable treatment or status of the elderly in our society. I am not a social reformer per se, and I still feel spunky enough to handle most things that come my way. But I would rather deal with the fact that even though every one of us is on "death row" awaiting one and all the same fate, we never seem to have an open, honest, and forthright conversation about this fact. We somehow think we can ignore this elephant in the room.

But the elephant will not leave. To repeat a passage I cited in an earlier book, *The Purpose of Physical Reality*, "Death is a subject that is evaded, ignored, and denied by our youth-worshipping, progress-oriented society. It is almost as if we have taken on death as just another disease to be conquered."

THE QUEST OF OUR SAFARI

I know we cannot capture or slay the elephant of death, and who would want to? He's peaceable enough. He does nothing specifically to interrupt all that we would do in our lives. We can move around him, arrange our furniture so that he's hardly noticeable, perhaps hang a nice tapestry across his back or place some flowers in his trunk. My now deceased friend Gertrude Ridgell used to collect elephants, had them on every surface in her living room—porcelain, crystal, or clay. Perhaps now I understand why. Familiarity does not always breed contempt. Sometimes it makes us fearless.

So wouldn't it be nice if, instead of trying to ignore him, we tried to understand him, tame him, and make him our friend and companion? I realize that many will consider this quest somewhat ludicrous or unnecessary. Death is what it is, and all our speculation, study, and talk will not change what it is. In fact, our pursuit reminds me of a passage from literature that touches upon this notion of who can claim to be an expert about death.

I should warn you that as a retired professor of literature, I will make these allusions from time to time, not to demonstrate my breadth of knowledge, but simply because in some areas of living, more of my experience comes from having lived life vicariously through great works of literary masters than from any exotic life I might have lived. Big game hunting, for example, is strictly for Hemingway types.

In any case, this passage is from Chaucer's "Friar's Tale" about a corrupt summoner who is going about the land trying to elicit bribes, mostly from the impoverished, in return for not issuing them a summons to the ecclesiastical court to stand trial for some sin he will accuse them of having committed. As he travels, he encounters a fiend from hell, an emissary of Satan who is gathering souls. The summoner in his hubris challenges the fiend to a contest to see who is the better trickster.

Without going into needless detail, the summoner gets tricked himself by a sly elderly lady, loses the bet, and is doomed to hell. A bit unperturbed, the summoner, who had earlier asked the fiend eagerly what hell is like and how it operates, is now angry that he has lost the bet, even more so than that he has lost his soul, since he had pretty well abandoned it long before. So the fiend consoles the summoner, saying, "Don't be angry. . . . You shall be in hell with me tonight where you shall learn more about our operations than a Master of Divinity."

My point in this obscure allusion is that since each of us would like more than anything to know about death and the afterlife, we,

4

too, might ply philosophers, theologians, and spiritualists with end-less questions about what they think the milestone of death is about, but the fact is that after our own "passing," each of us will also come to know more about the afterlife "than a Master of Divinity." We will all become experts when our time comes—possibly tomorrow, possibly this afternoon, given the possibility of a sudden and unexpected departure from physical reality.

Nevertheless, let us plod ahead as best we can to see if we can come to understand this implacable quarry because ours is a worthy quest, as relevant to our present lives as any task could be. I would not be writing this if I did not feel we could discover some worthwhile methods of coming to terms with death—some respectable answers to the essential questions about aging, death, and the afterlife. I also suspect we can discover insights that are not the usual pat answers, not the illogical or baseless myths with which we have been plied our whole lives. This is not to say that our conclusions need disparage or disdain the best of what others have discovered in their own journeys into the jungles of theology or philosophy to track down that enigmatic beast that sometimes emerges in the dark of night to startle us from the quietude of sleep.

MAPPING THE JOURNEY

Our investigation, like our lives, will proceed according to a series of milestones, turning points that section out the sequence of our lives, or at least the "normal" paradigm we have devised for those of us who endure to old age.

We will begin with our prenatal experiences in the uterine world where, though alive and kicking, we don't seem to have much control over our destiny. We do seem already to have a fully developed personality, or so I have observed as my own children emerged at their second major milestone of birth, the first being conception itself when whatever we become is set in motion "like a fat gold watch," as Sylvia Plath calls the newly conceived child in her poem "Morning Song."

Next we will discuss the primal stirrings of life during childhood, or at least as childhood should be. We will then examine our awakening from that special time of grace when we are mostly oblivious to our own transience, until that point when we first become aware of our own mortality. In particular we will take note of some of the theories proffered about the power and importance of this time when, according to some, we are newly emerged from the realm of the spirit and are attuned to the sacred verities of life. We will consider to what extent these early notions of life, nature, and self become a repository we revisit and draw on for the rest of our lives.

And so we will proceed from milestone to milestone until, at last, we try to assess the wisdom we have accumulated through the years. We will talk frankly about the degree to which our lives can become shaped more by our desire to reject our mortality than by positive forces, and that we are we impelled more by anxiety, fear, and consternation than we are by love, the desire for knowledge, and the pursuit of truth. Related to this assessment will be our examination of some attempts to bring about a degree of reassurance, consolation, and peace of mind in spite of our awareness of our own mortality as well as the fears we harbor for our children and grandchildren.

Finally, we will discover how the teachings of the Bahá'í Faith in regard to life, aging, dying, and the afterlife might offer consolation and resolution for the most difficult questions we will encounter along the way, especially those that concern our own mortality. In fact, we will discover how some of the more cogent arguments about aging, death, and the afterlife discussed by great minds of the past have set the stage for the very enlightenment that is now available through the authoritative Bahá'í texts.

WHY BAHÁ'Í?

The reason we will often consult the Bahá'í texts and teachings regarding life in relation to death and to the afterlife is in large part because I am a member of the Bahá'í Faith. I have been since 1959, my sophomore year at Vanderbilt when I converted from the Methodist Church after studying the Bahá'í religion rather intensely for three years.

But please don't worry about my trying to convert you or convince you I am right or that the Bahá'í Faith is the single valid source of salvation or of consolation about being mortal. I intend to examine various opinions, beliefs, and theories about death even though I approach this subject personally convinced that there is an afterlife, that our conscious self continues to exist after our bodies malfunction, and that this afterlife experience will be tailored to our individual situations. After all, since no two people have had the exact same life experience, it only makes sense, especially if we assume God is as reasonable as we are.

However, you may be assured that though I approach this subject as a person of faith, I am no less affected by the process of aging and possibly no less intrigued by or apprehensive about approaching death than most other people. True, I am comforted and sustained by my beliefs, but I am still in need of this discussion, even as I suspect most people are. For while I am constantly amazed by the depth of logic set forth in the Bahá'í writings about the reality of human existence, I am no less curious by the prospect of what will happen to me when my body no longer exists, though I have to confess I am less concerned than I might have been when it was unwrinkled, taut, and mildly attractive.

Perhaps I am not supposed to admit all this. The writings of my own faith assert unambiguously that any exact knowledge about the process of the continuation of our lives is purposefully withheld from us so that we can go about fulfilling the purpose ordained for our earthly existence. The Bahá'í writings imply, even while assuring us that death is "a messenger of joy" and a point of release from the constraints of physical limitations, that this bewilderment, this awe and wonder are likewise purposeful, and that the details about the afterlife are veiled from our exact knowledge for a very specific reason: "If any man be told that which hath been ordained for such a soul in the worlds of God, the Lord of the throne on high and of earth below, his whole being will instantly blaze out in his great longing to attain that most exalted, that sanctified and resplendent station (Bahá'u'lláh, *Gleanings*, no. 81.1).

In short, one reason we are not told by the Prophets or Manifestations of God more exact information about the afterlife is that if we knew how wonderful that reality is, we would not be able to restrain ourselves from "crossing over"—a euphemism for suicide. In this same passage, another reason for this veiling of the afterlife is implied—we need to focus on preparing ourselves for that next stage of existence by developing those spiritual faculties and capacities that we require if we are to navigate in a metaphysical environment:

> The nature of the soul after death can never be described, nor is it meet and permissible to reveal its whole character to the eyes of men. The Prophets and Messengers of God have been sent down for the sole purpose of guiding mankind to the straight Path of Truth. The purpose underlying Their revelation hath been to educate all men, that they may, at the hour of death, ascend, in the utmost purity and sanctity and with absolute detachment, to the throne of the Most High. (Bahá'u'lláh, *Gleanings*, no, 81.1)

Notice that in this same statement, Bahá'u'lláh, the Prophet and Founder of the Bahá'í Faith, has implied another obvious but worthy observation regarding our inability to learn what comes next: we have no context for understanding an environment that has no physical properties, no frame of reference for comprehension.

We would have the same problem trying to explain to a child in the womb the properties of this world, were we able to converse with the unborn child: "You'll really like it here. There are trees, bicycles, and furry animals." It would be impossible to describe such objects to someone who has no context for comprehending shape, size, color, or any other attributes of physical reality.

But as soon as the child is born into this new reality, all the senses, arms, legs, opposable thumbs, and other tools it has been developing for nine months suddenly enable it to learn firsthand the benefits of all that was occurring in the uterine world. The importance of developing physical faculties is now readily apparent without any need for explanation.

LIFE ON DEATH ROW

Assuming I die from "natural causes"—whatever that means—I could endure another five or ten years. But it seems that as I approach age seventy (my biblically allotted three score and ten) the chance of my meeting the same fate as my now deceased colleagues increases incrementally by the hour. Actuarially speaking, if a doctor were to tell me in somber tones, "John, I am afraid you have only ten years to live," I would be an idiot not to be delighted—seventy-eight years is longer than almost all of my male progenitors have lived so far.

But recalling as I do how quickly the *past* ten years have gone by, as well as what most men look like at seventy-eight, I would probably respond, "Hey, that's not very long at all! I'd better get to work, finish all my projects, and, most important of all, get back into shape!"

And so that's what I'm doing with this book—getting to work and getting into shape. I write in the morning and swim laps or do farm work in the afternoon. And I am going at a pretty feverish pace because I think each of us, while equal in the sight of God, is endowed with some special contribution to make to our collective project of fashioning a better world. And long ago I decided (correctly, I hope) that an important part of my task in this world is to ask important questions, and then attempt as best I can to discover sensible and convincing answers. My end product may not always redound to the common good, but at the very least I receive some personal benefits and I am able to placate my guilt by laboring under the illusion that I am advancing human knowledge about reality.

But if we are entirely honest about this matter, we should confess that it would be best for us not to wait until age sixty-eight or even fifty-eight or forty-eight to contemplate those parameters that define us, these milestones in our segmented lives that lead us to this end time, this "End of the Line," as the Traveling Wilburys sing it. Let us pretend that the doctor has told our mothers, "Sorry, Mrs. Hatcher, but your child as an American male human being will probably not live to see his eightieth birthday." Is that not also a death sentence? Are we not all, each one of us, given a decree to take our place on death row as soon as we're born?

From a Bahá'í perspective, our individuality begins at conception when the soul emanates from the spiritual realm and assumes an associative relationship with the human body. However the soul—from which all our essential human powers and faculties derive—is not dependent on the body. The body is the horse and the soul is the rider. That is why we might say that our first birth into reality takes place in our mother's womb, and that first nine months is our first life experience. And the more we learn about that existence, the more complex and important we find it to be.

Likewise, the more we come to know about the uterine life, our gestation in preparation for our second birth (the first birth being conception), the more we realize that what's going on outside the womb world has a tremendous effect on the life inside—love, prayer, praise, cooing, and other external influences will also have a lasting impact on how well we are prepared for the stage of our existence that follows our second birth into this physical realm.

Even though our physical life is usually much longer and more complex by comparison, the formative or foundational stage of our development establishes for most of us a lot about our attitudes and possibilities after our birth, even if, as the Bahá'í writings assert, our personality is present from the beginning. We are unique at conception, and our *qadar*[1] (measure or capacity) has already been meted out by the Creator, though it will be up to us to discover our special gifts and then fulfill our potential.

So it is, the Bahá'í writings affirm, that we in this second stage of our lives should be focused on preparation for our third birth, our entrance into the spiritual world. Put more accurately, even as we gradually become accustomed to doing well in our fleshly suit, we should gradually become more intent on preparing to disrobe and cast it aside. The notion that we are essentially physical beings is a grand illusion, because in truth, we are essentially spiritual beings associating for a brief span with a physical temple by means of the intermediary of what I like to call the "bear suit" that is our body.

By the way, "bear suit" is an allusion to my favorite poem about the body-soul duality, "The Heavy Bear" by Delmore Schwartz. This analogy between the body and a clumsy sort of circus bear gives such a fine insight into our lifelong (at least during our physical

---

1. The concept of *qadar* is that the Creator metes out a special "portion" or "measure" of talents and capacities to each of us, and we spend our lives studying ourselves to discover what hidden gifts have been bestowed within us, be they as simple as kindness or as complex as justice.

life) struggle between our spiritual/intellectual aspirations and our sensual/physical drives. One part of the poem presents the idea axiomatically as follows:

> That inescapable animal walks with me,
> Has followed me since the black womb held,
> Moves where I move, distorting my gesture,
> A caricature, a swollen shadow,
> A stupid clown of the spirit's motive . . .

We can train the bear, restrain the bear, dress him in his "dress-suit," but he will always screw up most of our vain attempts to be eloquent, elegant, and refined:

> —The strutting show-off is terrified,
> Dressed in his dress-suit, bulging his pants,
> Trembles to think that his quivering meat
> Must finally wince to nothing at all.

As regards to Schwartz's observation that he (we) will indeed "finally wince to nothing at all," I now notice in the mirror that daily more and more of my own bear suit has winced, drooped, wrinkled, or gone grey.

In other words, in the same way (though unwittingly and through no inherent virtue or will) we developed the essential tools for this life while in our mother's womb rather than simply enjoying the floating warmth, so it is in this life that we are exhorted to recognize and develop, only this time through our own free will, those spiritual faculties and capacities that will enable us to be successful both in this life and, even more particularly, in that stage of our existence we endure after we and our "heavy bear" go our separate ways.

It is precisely in this context that Bahá'u'lláh states ironically—He frequently employs irony and humor to emphasize a point—that if our sole purpose and desire was to be successful in this second stage of our life, if this is what we wanted to aspire to or look forward to, then we should have done it while we were living in the first stage of our existence in our mother's womb. During that stage of our existence, our physical life really was in the future. But as soon as we are born, we are receding from this life:

> Say: If ye be seekers after this life and the vanities thereof, ye should have sought them while ye were still enclosed in your mothers' wombs, for at that time ye were continually approaching them, could ye but perceive it. Ye have, on the other hand, ever since ye were born and attained maturity, been all the while receding from the world and drawing closer to dust. Why, then, exhibit such greed in amassing the treasures of the earth, when your days are numbered and your chance is well-nigh lost? Will ye not, then, O heedless ones, shake off your slumber? (Bahá'u'lláh, *Gleanings,* no. 66.4)

We need not be believers in the Bahá'í Faith to recognize the unassailable logic of this axiom—that as soon as we are born, we are dying, that no matter what we aspire to become or to acquire, we are, as ordinary human beings, destined from the beginning to see ourselves depart this mortal coil and become bereft of all the material wealth, power, and prestige we may have amassed.

True, we may leave behind a park bench, a road, or a building that for a while may bear our name. Hopefully we will leave behind progeny who will recall us with affection and respect. Possibly we may live a life so spectacular it will be recounted for decades or centuries, whether we become a saint, a tyrant, or a serial killer. But in time our life and our deeds will be forgotten, and all our energy invested in trying to leave a lasting impression will be futile in terms of physical reality, other than the infinite ripple of our spiritual actions on the lives of others.

Does it not make perfect sense, the Bahá'í writings argue, that we should therefore spend a decent amount of time in this life considering what will become of us afterward, especially since the life to come is infinite? Indeed, does it not make sense that we should not delay in this focused reflection about our continuity beyond this life? After all, here I am doing it at sixty-eight, though obviously I have thought about all this before, and so have you. Heck, if we are honest about it, we've been aware of our own mortality almost our entire lives!

So let us go then, you and I, on this fearless mental and spiritual excursion, this adventurous exploration. In fact, let us begin without delay since we never know for sure how soon the next milestone will arrive.

2

A DIALOGUE
IN PLATO'S WOMB

Universal beings resemble and can be compared to particular beings, for both are subjected to one natural system, one universal law and divine organization. So you will find the smallest atoms in the universal system are similar to the greatest beings of the universe.

—'Abdu'l-Bahá, *Some Answered Questions*

Most of us would consider our first major milestone to be birth, but we should acknowledge that a great deal of important stuff happens before we get to that milestone in our life's journey. After all, getting started at point zero is a pretty amazing event. Love, passion, biology, and divine emanation converge in an instant, or shortly thereafter. What an amazing beginning, fusing all these diverse components together to form a human being!

A plant from a tiny mustard seed or a mighty oak from an acorn are impressive, but to engender a being with the capacity for abstract thought and sufficient free will to focus that thought on solving problems, creating art, devising machines, or discovering physical and metaphysical laws—that's certainly even more astounding!

THE PROCESS OF CONCEPTION

There is an old saying about the fact that a woman cannot be somewhat pregnant. And yet, from the standpoint of human biology, as well as from the perspective of Bahá'í beliefs, the creation of a human being is a process, not an event. In this sense, the term *conception* when it is used to designate the creation of human life is likewise a process, as opposed to fertilization, which is one part of that process. In fact, even fertilization is not as simple as we might imagine—it is not merely a matter of a sperm penetrating an egg.

From the Bahá'í point of view, human life begins when the soul emanates from the metaphysical realm and associates with the fertilized ovum during the process of conception. But in some cases, the completion of this process might take several days. In the creation of identical twins or triplets, for example, the process of the fertilization of a single ovum first occurs, and then later that single ovum divides to create two or three distinct and separate human beings, albeit genetically identical.

Consequently, we are forced to conclude that the completion of the process of "conceiving" these separate human beings occurs only after the fertilized egg has gone through certain biological processes and then divides. Until that point, the twins or triplets are potential but not actual realities. We can assume, in other words, that the associative relationship of the souls or the personhood of these human beings does not begin until there is a distinct physical being established with which the separate emanating souls can associate.

This fact leads us to another related conclusion—we can make a distinction between the process of fertilization and the beginning of the associative relationship between soul and body, a difference that is more "seminal" than semantic. A brief examination of the process involved demonstrates that a certain degree of rigor in delineating the sequence involved in these processes can prove useful, especially in terms of the Sullivan triplets, whose story we shall soon begin.

CONCEIVING THE SULLIVAN BOYS

Mike and Lucile Sullivan lay peacefully asleep, a smile upon their faces. But their quietude belied a remarkable series of events that had just begun inside Lucile. A sperm had just penetrated an *ovocyte* by passing through the *corona radiate* layer. Suddenly, a molecule on the head of the sperm became bonded to a protein in the *zona pellucida* layer of the *ovocyte* causing an *acrosome* reaction!

The acrosome "exploded," releasing special enzymes that helped the sperm penetrate the zona pellucida of the ovum by degrading the layer itself. This was very important for the sperm because now the cortical reaction could occur and prevent any other sperms from penetrating this special ovum.

Quickly the ovum and the sperm began to fuse together as one. The sperm's tail, the former source of its rapid propulsion, began to degenerate, along with its mitochondria. The sperm had become transformed into a pronucleus, a male pronucleus trapped inside an egg! But it was not alone. Across the way inside the ovum was a female pronucleus. Mutual attraction was instantaneous!

They gravitated toward each other, closer and closer together until they reached the very center of the ovum. Suddenly the DNA of the male pronucleus replicated as did that of the female pronucleus. The membrane of the male pronucleus then began to melt away as did hers, and, as if by magic two spindles began to form, collecting the male and female chromosomes that were no longer separated by membrane, two spindles exactly the same.

But this was not all. Soon these two spindles experienced cytokinesis—they split into two diploid cells, each with its own cytoplasm and membrane. Yes, mitosis had occurred! They had become bonded into two separate but equal and identical nuclei. Their male and female distinction had ceased. They had become two diploid cells, two cells sharing the same attributes. Fertilization had occurred! They were officially a diploid zygote!

Lucile slept softly and turned onto her left side while Mike snored gently. But inside her uterus, all was not so placid. The diploid zygote had only gotten started. Quickly two became four, four became eight, and eight became sixteen—there seemed to be no stopping the geometric progression of these cells. And yet they assumed two distinctly different tasks by dividing themselves into two groups.

Some of the cells stayed very close together, almost like a compact little ball. Other cells joined together, flattened themselves out, and secreted fluid to make a sort of aquarium-like structure with the tight little ball of cells in the middle. The cells that formed the outer layer, the trophoblasts, would in time help form the placenta, the protective sac surrounding the embryo, and the ball of cells in the middle, the embryoblasts, would become the embryo itself.

Life inside Lucile's uterus was hardly routine. Next, the outer layer of trophoblasts attached itself to the endometrium of the uterine wall. But about an hour later a most remarkable transformation occurred that would alter the lives of the Sullivans forever. The zygote—the entire group of embryoblasts—suddenly and spontaneously divided into three exactly equal groups, each an exact replica of the other because the one zygote had transformed into monozygotic triplets.

Each of the three had become complete as each stem cell in each group had become fused into a single being. Even more remarkable, a distinct personality or consciousness suddenly associated with each one of these three! Personhood itself had emanated from somewhere entirely outside the realm of Lucile's uterine universe, and the result was the creation of the three Sullivan boys!

After four weeks of hearing Lucile throw up every morning, Mike was beginning to wonder if becoming a father was going to be quite the wonderful adventure he had longed for. Lucile was even more wary of the sudden changes she was experiencing as she contemplated forty more weeks of nausea, discomfort and becoming larger and larger.

When she emerged from the bathroom, a wet cloth on her forehead, she saw Mike sitting on the end of the bed shaking his head. "Having fun yet?" he asked.

"Not so far," she said.

Mike stood up, walked over to her and placed his hand on her stomach. "It's our little baby!" he said with a smile. She dropped the wash cloth, laughed and gave Mike a large hug.

"Then why does our baby feel so much like a case of the flu?" she said jokingly.

Weeks later an examination revealed that Lucile and Mike did not have *one* little baby, but *three* little babies signaled by three different heartbeats! They had not yet learned that the three heartbeats belonged to three tiny boys, the Sullivan boys.

But the Sullivan boys were there, all right, and they were growing and changing every day and every week. And if this was an unexpected adventure for Lucile and Mike, it was even more exciting and daunting for the boys themselves.

By the fourth week, the neural tube closed. The arm buds formed! Various organs appeared, along with a most beautiful curly tail! By the fifth week, the Sullivans grew to twice their size, from an eighth of an inch to one quarter of an inch. Moreover, the eyes, the beginning of their noses, the leg buds, and the little hand paddles on the arm buds all began to develop.

From week six on, there was no stopping them. They doubled in size again and again. By the eighth week, they reached another milestone—they were officially designated as "human fetuses," no longer "embryos," something that made little difference to Lucile and Mike who already considered these tiny beings quite human and quite a blessing after all.

In the evenings, Mike and Lucile worked on changing what had been their office into a sweetly decorated nursery arranged for a crib in each available corner and an extra large changing table. After distracting themselves with these happy tasks, they would stand back at the doorway and imagine three tiny babies all fast asleep. Then they would plop down together on the couch and imagine going from two years as a couple to the rest of their foreseeable future as a family of five.

Meanwhile, the boys now had all their organs, their arms, legs, feet, hands, and even fingers, though these were still webbed. During the next three weeks, the Sullivan boys grew to over three inches in length. Three weeks following that, they would double again to six inches, though half of that length was head, with eyes, nose, mouth, and even a bit of hair.

Because they all had unique personalities right from the beginning, let's refer to the Sullivan triplets by name: Harry, Roger, and Sammy. It was about this time that Harry started to make a sucking motion with his mouth, and though their eyes were not yet open, Roger and Sammy would later say that this really bothered them, until, reflexively, they found themselves doing the very same thing.

FLOATING, KICKING, AND SPECULATING

It was on a Thursday morning during the thirteenth week that Lucile called Mike on his cell phone as he was overseeing the planting of a row of bird-of-paradise plants for a family two blocks away. "Mike," Lucile said in a somewhat nervous voice, "can you come home for a minute?"

Mike was frantic. "What's wrong?" he said to Lucile who was waiting at the front door. "Are the kids all right?" He knew she had just come back from her appointment with the obstetrician and he feared that some problem had been discovered.

"No, no. I'm all right and so are the boys!" she said, as she took him by the arm into the living room where they sat down.

"Thank goodness!" Mike said. "I was so afraid that . . . BOYS? What boys?"

"We've got three boys, Mike. The ultrasound showed it clearly today." She handed him copies of the confused images of the three tangled triplets.

"See, there and there and there?" she said pointing to the proof.

"Good Lord," said Mike. For some reason he had pictured three little girls in the cribs, three little red-headed girls as sweet and cute as the baby pictures of Lucile. "Good Lord," he said again, repeating a phrase from a children's book he had heard his sister reading to her little boy: "Boys mean noise!"

"Exactly!" said Lucile. "Should we try for twins next so you can have your own basketball team?" Then she cried—she didn't know why—and so did Mike. The speculation and suspense was over.

One evening about a month later as Lucile and Mike were watching a television show, inside Lucile's womb Roger said, "Harry, can you see anything, anything at all?"

"Eyes won't open yet," said Harry. "But have you tried jerking your legs out in a kicking motion—you can sort of move around a bit if you do. I find it quite exciting!"

"Yes," volunteered Sammy, "and there's punching, too. If you ball your hand up into a fist, you can punch the edge of the universe itself!" And both Harry and Roger tried it and realized that's what they were kicking when they weren't accidentally kicking each other.

They then began to notice that sometimes when they did the kicking and punching thing, they could hear a noise, a squeal and some laughter coming from outside the universe.

At first each thought the noise was coming from one of the other brothers. "Harry, was that you just now?" asked Sammy.

"What, you mean the noise?"

"Yes, that squealie noise. It sounds happy enough, but sometimes it scares me."

"It's not me."

"It's not me either," said Roger. "Do you suppose it's some sort of mystical force in the universe? Maybe it's the goddess of kicking?"

"And punching," Sammy added.

"Could be. Could be," said Harry. "Perhaps it gets angry when we punch the sides of the universe."

"Perhaps it's the ruler of the universe!" posited Roger. "Perhaps when we kick and punch the universe, we are hurting or insulting the ruler of the universe!"

"I tell you what," said Harry, who now considered himself to be the more robust of the three, "let me give the universe one of my best shots!" And he kicked with his right leg as hard as he could. Sure enough, they heard Lucile utter a muffled, "Wow!"

"There it went," said Roger. "I guess my theory is correct. The universe and the ruler of the universe are one and the same."

"I wouldn't go *that* far," said Sammy. "I mean, all we've really proved is that the ruler of the universe is affected by kicking the sides of the universe."

"He's right," said Harry. "Sammy always gets it right, doesn't he?"

"Yeah," said Roger, "I suppose he does, but his conclusion wouldn't have had much value without my posing the theory in the first place."

EVIDENCE OF ANOTHER REALITY— MUSIC FROM ANOTHER WOMB?

Around the twenty-third week as their brains and nervous systems began to develop very rapidly, the three Sullivan boys began to open their eyelids, and while it was mostly dark, they could sometimes get a faint outline of each other. Though curled up as they were, they spent most of the time looking at their toes.

"Toes are really neat," said Harry late one evening.

"I suppose," said Sammy.

"How about the fingers!" said Roger. "Why this opposable thumb is incredible. Look at this. I can grab hold of my cord thingy and give it a nice yank!" And with that he pulled his umbilical cord so that the entire placenta shook.

"Do you mind?" said Sammy. "That really bothers me. It makes the whole universe shake."

"Sorry," said Roger, who had grown to have great respect for Sammy's intellectual prowess. "What are you doing?"

"I was just thinking," he said to Roger and Harry, "without this firm cord attached to our stomachs, we could really move around a lot more easily. I mean, I really get tired of untangling these things."

"Hey, don't go fooling with the cord," said Harry.

"Why not?" said Sammy.

"Just don't! That's all."

"You've done it yourself, haven't you!" said Sammy with a smile.

"So? What if I did!"

"Well, what happened?"

"Yeah, Harry," said Roger. "Tell us!"

"Look, all I did was put a sort of kink in it, you know? Just to see what it would do if I stopped all the stuff from coming in and going out."

"And. . .?"

"I fainted."

"Fainted? Really?" said Sammy in amazement.

"Yep. So don't try it. I mean, I thought I was dying, you know?"

"So what did you do?"

"Well as soon as I got woozy, I let go and a few seconds later everything was OK again. But apparently this cord connects us to the universe, maybe even to the . . ."

"Maybe even to the ruler of the universe?" Sammy added.

"Exactly," said Harry.

"Well, I have to say that I just don't buy this ruler of the universe stuff," said Roger. "I mean so far we've seen nobody else but us three, right? And that noise we hear when we kick and punch the sides of the universe might just be some sort of echo or something."

Suddenly, the three were interrupted by a noise they hadn't heard before. It was not a squeal, nor the base thuds they had heard at other times, and not the sense of motion that they had long ago gotten used to as just one of the physical laws of the universe.

No, this was different. This was loud and melodic with different sorts of sounds. Some were deep and sonorous, while others were high pitched. Then, toward the end of what seemed like hours, there came a chorus of voices in unison.

"How peculiar," said Sammy.

"No," said Roger, "it sounded more like 'Hire a Lawyer!'"

"I think it was actually 'Alleluia!' but what difference does it make," said Harry. "Whatever the words were, one thing is clear. There's either another universe, or else there's some sort of life outside the universe!"

"Speaking of which," said Sammy. "I hadn't wanted to mention this because I know you guys get bothered with all my speculation about things, but for some time I have had the feeling that the universe is shrinking."

"Hey!" said Roger. "Me too!"

"Or," said Harry with a very pregnant pause, "perhaps we are getting bigger and bigger!"

"In either case," said Sammy, "something has to give, or we're going to be in *big* trouble!"

"How so?" said Roger.

"He's right," said Harry. "Either the universe has to expand, or else we're going to be smashed together."

"That's not good!" said Roger in an obviously frightened tone. "That's not good at all!"

"What if we grow so much that we make the universe explode?" said Harry.

"Look, let's just calm down," said Sammy. "There's nothing we can do about it now. Anyhow, the music has stopped. Perhaps it was just a glitch in the universe."

"That wasn't any glitch, and you know it," said Harry.

"I'm scared," said Roger. "I don't mind telling you that I'm scared. Why do things have to change? I mean, I was happy when we just swam around and kicked a little."

"It must be another law of the universe," said Sammy. "As soon as we start to relax a little, things start to change!"

THE FLOODGATES OPEN IN THE "END DAYS"

Days and weeks passed, and nothing got any better. They could hear the music at regular intervals now, almost as if the ruler of the universe was piping it in just for them. Not that the music was unpleasant. Actually it was quite beautiful. But it also seemed very serious and, for the three Sullivan brothers, such seriousness seemed to portend some impending disaster, some further alteration in their lives, possibly the end of their lives, or even the end of the universe itself!

While the music was playing, they weren't so nervous. The music was inspiring, uplifting, and even seemed to offer hope. But when the music wasn't playing, they would speculate about what it meant, especially as they became more and more cramped and it became obvious to all three that some major transformation was about to occur. It was unavoidable, what with space contracting and the three of them expanding. It was a mathematical certainty, or so Sammy said.

Roger feared that they were doomed. He was sure of it. Surely if the universe collapsed, their cords would go with it, and they would be without any of the fluid that kept them alive—Harry had proved that. And Harry, though clearly the bravest of the three, was not much more positive. "Look," he would say sometimes to console his brothers, "at least we've had a good life together, haven't we? We've had everything we needed, and we have lived a really long time. We've watched ourselves evolve from little creatures that weren't even aware of themselves to really sophisticated beings with arms, legs, fingers . . ."

"And toes, Harry. You always liked the toes, remember?" said Roger.

"Yeah, and toes," Harry smiled. "And let's not forget that opposable thumb!"

"That's why I want to continue living!" said Sammy, not at all consoled by Harry's pep talk. "I really enjoy all this . . . just . . . existing, you know? Just moving around and then stopping and thinking about stuff. I find it really rewarding, especially when we discover laws of the universe—that's my favorite thing of all. I will really miss it."

"And I'll miss our conversations," said Roger in a glum tone.

"Hey," said Harry, patting Sammy on the back, "How are you going to miss it if you don't even exist?"

"Geez," said Sammy. "That's even worse! I don't want to disappear! Sure, I'm glad we've had a nice long life full of surprises—fingers, toes, the whole thing. But that makes me want to have more, to be more, to learn more. I mean, what sort of ruler of the universe would create us just so we could become so special, could learn all this stuff just so we could end up becoming nothing? Does that make sense to you?"

"He's right, Harry," said Roger. "It doesn't make sense."

"Well, perhaps it somehow makes sense to the ruler of the universe," said Harry.

"Look," said Sammy, "If the ruler of the universe made us, then the ruler has to be at least as smart as we are, right? I mean isn't that logical?"

"Sure," agreed Harry. "I see what you mean."

"OK, then. Would you create beings that become more and more complex, smarter and smarter and smarter, just to let them explode and become nothing?"

"Of course I wouldn't," confessed Harry, "but then . . ."

"But nothing!" said Sammy. "If there is a ruler of the universe, then there's got to be a plan for us, a plan that makes sense."

"Unless the ruler of the universe enjoys watching stuff explode!" said Harry, now growing a bit nervous himself.

"Hey, let's not talk about exploding," said Roger drearily. "Exploding does not sound like fun at all. Maybe we should never have kicked the side of the universe after all."

"Well, perhaps we can start all over again," said Harry. "I mean, we came this far, didn't we? Why couldn't we just start the whole thing over again?"

"And just how do you propose we do that?" asked Sammy.

"I don't know," said Harry. "I was just trying to make Roger perk up a little."

Suddenly it seemed that for a moment the universe contracted! "Hey, did you feel something change?" asked Sammy.

"Yeah," said Roger, "as if the universe sort of squeezed us."

"Maybe it's a nice friendly hug," offered Harry.

Suddenly there was another squeeze, and it was clear at once to all three that this was no hug, or if it was, it was a great big bear hug, not a cuddly expression of endearment. The three became frightened, even Harry. "Join hands!" he hollered as a grumbling, deafening noise began.

"This is it!" shouted Roger. "Just as I feared—it's the end of everything!"

"No, no, there's still hope," said Harry. "Just hold on to each other!!"

"My hand is . . . my hand is slipping!" screamed Sammy. "I don't want to die!"

All three felt a quick jolt and then a shifting as the fluid in which they had floated their entire lives suddenly began to swish toward some lesion in the universe. "The universe, the universe has been rent asunder!" screamed Sammy, as his hand slipped out of the grasp of Roger's hand. "Aaahhh!" screamed Sammy as his head suddenly shifted toward the great cleaving in the universe, which began to collapse around him as if he had been devoured by some monstrous python.

"Harry! Haaarrryyy! Can you still hear me?" cried out Roger with incredible difficulty. "Sammy's gone! He's done for! The universe has sucked him out! All I can see are his legs! He's kicking like crazy! I think the universe must be eating him head first!"

"O great ruler of the universe," said Harry who now could see only Roger's legs, "I do not know who or what you are or even if you exist, but if you hear me, please assist us in this, our time of utmost grief and peril!"

"What did you say?" said Roger, barely audible amidst the squeezing and rushing.

"Oh my God! Oh my God!" screamed a high pitched voice in great agony from outside the universe as the universe squeezed ever more tightly.

"Think that was Sammy?" asked Roger. "The universe must be eating him for sure!"

"Not his voice!" yelled Harry, struggling to wrench himself free from the constricting universe, or at least to shift himself into a more comfortable position.

"Think he's dead?" asked Roger.

"There's always hope!" said Harry.

"You think so?" said Roger, appreciating some reassurance, even though the contracting universe began to exert such force that he felt his own head being forced downward and the universe squeezing him ever tighter. "It's got me, Harry! It's eating my head! Grab my toes if you can!!"

"No can do, Roger. My arms are pinned to my sides!"

"It's been swell, Harrrryyy!" said Roger in an ever fainter voice. Then he was heard no more. Harry, alone and afraid, was occupied with trying to extricate himself from the ever more powerful forces of the universe propelling him irretrievably downward. He had no time to bid adieu to his brother, no time to think or reflect.

His senses reeled as the universe sucked him ever down the dark channel toward what he instinctively sensed was certain disaster, death, or perhaps something much, much worse than his imagination could fathom, and he silently uttered one last plea to the ruler of the universe to spare him, to love him, even as he had grown to love Sammy and Roger.

3

RAISING A WILLFUL FETUS

It is evident, therefore, that man is ruler over nature's sphere and province. Nature is inert; man is progressive. Nature has no consciousness; man is endowed with it. Nature is without volition and acts perforce, whereas man possesses a mighty will. Nature is incapable of discovering mysteries or realities, whereas man is especially fitted to do so.

—'Abdu'l-Bahá, *The Promulgation of Universal Peace*

What the analogical tale of the Sullivan boys lacks in literary merit, it makes up for in its capacity to introduce us to our own perspectives about death. The analogy is hardly original on my part. Frequently in the Bahá'í writings we find a useful analogy between human gestation in the womb and our formative development during our physical existence.

The most obvious point in such a comparison is that the entire purpose or focus of each period of development is preparation for transition or birth into a more expansive, more complete, and more complex form of existence. What is perceived to be death is, in fact, but a glorious birth. Equally important in this analogy is the fact that all activity and development within the microcosmic universe at each stage of our development is often erroneously perceived to be suited exclusively to that phase of development rather than as preparation for some future purpose.

MILESTONES OR MILLSTONES?

Our perspective in the progress and development of our lives is obviously extremely important in all this. In fact, Bahá'u'lláh states that true knowledge is the ability to discern the end in the beginning, to understand the end result of present action. In other words, if we could appreciate their future usefulness in our later efforts at more complex calculations, we might be more enthusiastic about the present drudgery of memorizing multiplication tables. Likewise, if the Sullivan boys could have known that their apparent death was actually the beginning of an infinitely more exciting stage of their lives, they would not have been nearly so apprehensive about what was happening to them.

Obviously we are all in a similar situation with regard to our perspective about what we perceive as our own death. If we were assured that we don't die but continue to exist and that our afterlife will be a fulfillment of all we have worked to achieve in this life, then we might be totally fearless about the prospect of that milestone, that point of transition. We might comprehend the underlying meaning of the Bahá'í scripture that states, "I have made death a messenger of joy to thee. Wherefore dost thou grieve?" (Bahá'u'lláh, Hidden Words, Arabic, no. 32).

Another benefit from viewing our lives as a preparation for another stage of our existence—of being able to discern the end in the beginning—would be that we could better understand what tools we need to develop capacities in this life that will equip us to prosper in a spiritual environment. Were we able to gain this perspective, we could also alter our view about what we consider "milestones" in our present life. As it is, we most often establish for ourselves materially and socially oriented goals that we consider the doorway to some important point of completion, a point in our lives where we will have established the foundation for future material or physical happiness and contentment.

And yet because these objectives are not based solely on what seems satisfying in the context of this initial stage of our existence, our sense of achievement at each milestone is short-lived and ultimately unsatisfying. We soon tire of our present accomplishments. We then establish further material or socially-based objectives, which again leave us unsatisfied and discontented. And so it goes—this insatiable desire to discover ultimate meaning in the confines of a physical environment where no *ultimate* meaning exists.

That's the whole nature of milestones—at least I have found it so in my own life. Sometimes the points of transition we long for the most end up having relatively little impact. So we end up waiting for the next milestone to bring fulfillment until, before we know it, we are sixty-eight, retired, and scurrying around trying to invent new milestones (other than death) because our vocation and our society have left us with no further objectives. These are the wonderful "golden years" when we are supposed to relax, to do nothing but bask in the delight of life without the obligation to accomplish specific tasks or responsibilities. The problem is that doing nothing is simply not all that delightful.

I remember contemplating the various milestones en route to attaining my PhD in literature. I remember thinking that I probably would never make it to that final destination. It seemed that there were just too many hoops to jump through, too many chances to fail. Also, I just wasn't confident that I was capable of attaining such a lofty status. But I did sincerely believe that if I ever did accomplish that seemingly insurmountable achievement, my ascent would be complete. I could relax, enjoy teaching, have a family, and be fulfilled. I might smoke a pipe, lean against the mantle piece, and say very wise things to my children as they sat in a semicircle in rapt wonder at their "professor" father.

I remember the afternoon I received my degree and was "hooded." I was twenty-seven. I had now taught at universities for four years. I was married, had two children, and a job waiting for me in Florida. Was I not in bliss? Had I not fulfilled all I had striven to accomplish and become? I strolled by myself around the apartment complex where we lived. I felt as if I had come up for air after having held my breath for three years, years in which every moment was accounted for, was devoted to one thing and one thing only. And I began to weep.

I wasn't sure why I was weeping, whether from relief or release or from something more subtle. I suspect it was a combination of complex emotions. This was a moment that, in retrospect, I had worked to attain since I began the first grade. And now at grade twenty-one or twenty-two, I was done. And yet I was the same person. I had not emerged into another reality. I was not elated or fulfilled. I was totally exhausted and now had absolutely nothing to look forward to. I had not had time to think of any further milestones. This was it. My life was . . . fulfilled, or was it simply finished?

THE HAPPINESS CHART

Without anyone talking about it, there was permeating the atmosphere of America as I was growing up a cult of competition to which almost everyone belonged, even though we were not always aware of it. The motto or credo of this cult went something like this: "You're only as happy or successful as the number of people who are less happy or less successful than you."

Not that this cult has died out or the credo become altered in the least. Recently I was looking for a local place to buy some firewood, having burned up all of the scrap wood in my fields. I was surprised to find a place that advertised delivering firewood cut to your specifications. But what really caught my attention was the main banner teaser that read, "Your friends will be soooooo envious!"

Of course, I am not blind. I know that we polish our cars for that reason, buy houses, clothes, and a myriad other things for that reason. That's why we love to read about the tragedies of the well-to-do in grocery store magazines, because we are largely incapable of feeling existential delight. We rejoice only in relation to others who are attempting the same thing. So once I finished my PhD, on some level I think I was weeping because of the relief of no longer having to compete, or so I assumed.

At the time, obtaining tenure was not as rigorous a process as it is now—more a matter of time-serving than publications and papers. Consequently, having endured the "third degree," one was virtually assured of a job somewhere. And having gotten the job, one was virtually assured of getting tenure in due course so long as one produced a semblance of academic activity.

Alas, such serenity and peace of mind was not to be. I soon found myself determined not merely to endure, but to prosper as an academic. I would not merely stir the waters a bit; I would be the best in my field. Yes, somewhere along the way I had contracted a terminal case of the American disease of *competition*, whether in sports or in anything else. My brother was the same, though I don't know where we became infected and afflicted with this syndrome. Certainly it was not from our parents who were happy with anything and everything we did and who themselves were generally content with life as they had fashioned it—a decent American middleclass existence.

But the point is that when we develop the full-blown competition syndrome, we appropriate from society, or else invent for ourselves, milestones at every point in the road—short term, mid-term, and long term, as well as at intervals in between. What is worse, once contracted, the competition syndrome is an autonomous pathology sufficient unto itself to ruin our lives, especially when it forms the excruciating symbiotic relationship with the HIITF (happiness-is-in-the-future) syndrome. What is more, when these two disorders became conjoined with the cancer of materialism that developed around the end of the nineteenth century, the western world found itself plagued by the most cruel disease ever devised, a sickness that now has become epidemic throughout our global community, the illusion that material comfort is commensurate with internal felicity.

The result of this epidemic has been the emergence of several generations largely incapable of living in the moment. Our focus has forever been on future milestones, each of which holds the promise of making us finally happy, complete, and successful, even if by somebody else's standards.

NATURE'S MILESTONES

In our lives there are natural and authentic milestones, such as birth, maturation, graduation, marriage, having children, having grandchildren, getting a tractor, and so on. Some of these are ostensibly arduous and frightening before they take place, but they actually become for us moments of fulfillment and transformation in our lives. At least they have the potential to be; they aren't inevitably so.

For someone born with significant physical deformities or a congenital neurological illness, birth itself may mark the beginning of a period of hardship and suffering, though if one has never had the opportunity to know any other sort of existence, such a life might not seem quite so tragic. Likewise, any of the propitious milestones we devise or recognize and accept after birth—such as reaching maturity—can be rendered instantly null and void by a major accident or tragedy.

Superman (Christopher Reeve) had it all—wealth, good looks, a fine mind, a beautiful wife, and lovely children—only to fall while taking a jump with his thoroughbred horse. Because of this accident, he ended up a quadriplegic hooked up to a machine that had to breathe for him for the rest of his life. For him, all of his previous milestones, every one of them, suddenly paled in comparison to this one. And yet he emerged from this apparent end to his life—or at least an end to the "good life"—an incredibly noble soul and probably more loved and loving than if his life and his milestones had followed the expected paradigm society had devised.

The same observation might be said for the renowned professor, Randy Pausch. A few years ago, nobody outside the narrow confines of academic research into virtual reality knew who he was. And yet he had knocked down his major milestones like ten pins, or, as he put it in his book *The Last Lecture*, he had achieved his childhood dreams one by one. He was like a rocket ascending, having become esteemed in his academic field, having found the woman of his dreams, having married her, and together with her, having produced three lovely children. In his mid-forties, he was surely an emblem of all the good life has to offer—handsome, athletic, funny, popular, and a good husband and father.

In the fall of 2006 Pausch was diagnosed with pancreatic cancer. In the fall of 2007, he was told he had about six good months to live. That September he delivered his famous "Last Lecture" on the topic of "Really Achieving Your Childhood Dreams." The video of the lecture spread like wildfire on the Web, inspiring and touching the hearts of millions. By May of 2008 *Time* magazine named him as one of the hundred most influential people in the world. Two months later he died.

Again, was the milestone of contracting pancreatic cancer the beginning of the end, or the beginning of the most important influence this bright young mind and luminous spirit would ever have or could ever have had? Certainly it is true that his lecture would have been on a different subject had he not just discovered his pancreatic cancer was terminal. It is also certainly true that Pausch's notoriety and acclaim would never had wielded such influence had he not had the opportunity to look at the milestone of death face to face, had he not carefully and courageously analyzed what his relatively brief life had meant.

His lecture challenged all of us to examine our milestones and not simply to accept those that society has devised for us. He then observed that, having determined what we ourselves want to achieve, we should pursue these dreams with a vengeance. In this sense, he blazed a trail by daring us to recall those most cherished goals we devised as children, as dreamers when we were as yet immune to goals imposed on us by social norms or parental expectations.

DEATH AS A MESSENGER OF JOY

But for now let us set aside those who have nobly managed to make a virtue of necessity in this life. Let us instead return to the example of the Sullivan brothers from the previous chapter whose untimely death turned out to be the beginning of their "real" lives. In particular, let us recall their preoccupation with and speculation about the strange changes they were undergoing, especially those appendages they were developing to prepare them to be successful in a reality they had never experienced nor could they have even imagined.

From our point of view on the other side of the "second birth" of the Sullivan brothers when they left the uterine world and entered into this world, we might find their emotional plight somewhat silly and amusing. But were the three children at this prenatal stage of development actually able to have the sort of cognition and conversations we depicted in our fable, then surely their fears would be warranted and not silly at all.

And were we their parents and able to converse with them, we would desperately seek some means of reassuring the boys that their concerns, though natural and understandable, are needless, that what they perceive as death is actually the beginning of a more joyous stage of their lives. As their parents, we would want to tell them that we eagerly await their presence, that we are ready to receive them, to guide and protect them, and to love them unconditionally. We would attempt as best we could to explain that their experience in this world is infinitely more glorious and empowering than their limited experiences in the confinement of the womb.

At the same time, we can appreciate that even if we could have talked to them beforehand, our disembodied voice might have done little to assuage their fears or instill in them any confidence in our reassurance. How could they possibly take the word of beings they could neither see nor feel? What evidence would they have that the voices they are hearing are actually those of their parents or that this encouragement is based on reality and not some sort of deception? They might understandably wonder why, if their parents truly exist and have so much to give, do they not demonstrate some more direct evidence of their existence, their goodness, and their love?

Perhaps we can also derive from our fable a better appreciation of why the first response of a child newly born is to scream as loud as it can, to cry out in shock, gasping for that first breath of air, but also screaming for help, for reassurance, for something to hold onto. From peaceful darkness, quietude, and security, they are suddenly encompassed with blinding light, a panoply of noises, various voices, and what seems to be the infinitude of space. From being fed passively through the lifeline of the umbilical cord, they must gasp for breath and suckle for nourishment. From being surrounded by warm fluid, they are naked, exposed, free falling.

Then, almost as suddenly as they have been snatched from the security of the womb and before they have sounded out more than a few notes, the Sullivan boys are bundled again, embraced by the warmth of the universe-mother, caressed and cherished, and sucking that special blend of nutrients from their mother's breasts, an action the child has practiced for some time, though hardly knowing why.

No, this is not death, not being devoured by the python ruler of the universe. They have been loosed from the constraints of a reality so confined, so incomplete that almost instantly the child is transformed, content, cuddled. Now there is something more to grasp than an umbilical cord. Now all the appendages that had before seemed clever but useless assume a value the boys could not possibly have fully appreciated before.

Where they saw almost nothing but darkness before, now their eyes begin to adjust to a world of colors, shapes, and immeasurable wonder. Where once they heard only muffled voices or faint strains of music, now they can detect with clarity a choir of human voices coming from all directions. Where once they could stretch their arms and legs only with great effort in the confinements of the uterine universe, they can now move with ease and use their hands to hold on. Where they had thought they had seen the last of each other, they now enjoy a felicitous reunion that will endure through the years, the decades, and the many milestones to come. From a world in which nothing made complete sense, the Sullivans now find themselves in a world where all their constant growing and changing suddenly makes perfect sense. Indeed, what the Sullivan boys had conceived of as a terrifying end to their existence has turned out to be but a milestone in a journey that has really just begun in earnest.

DIALOGUE WITH WILLFUL FETUSES

In light of this information we would wish to impart to our prenatal children, let us revise our fable a little. Let us presume that Lucile and Mike can communicate with their boys, even as we presume that the Prophets of God—what the Bahá'í writings call Manifestations of

God—as emissaries from the realm of the spirit are trying to do by explaining to us the relationship of our present physical existence to the continuation of our life beyond the physical stage of our existence.

Let us also presume that it is about the fifth or sixth week into the lives of the Sullivan boys and that Lucile and Mike can listen to them and, should they want to, converse with them by means of their Fetocom 500, which has two sets of earphones and a tummy-mike. In addition, let us assume that the Sullivan boys have been endowed with another power unavailable to most embryos—the power of free will. While they feel the inherent urge of their bodies to do certain things—grow arm buds, leg buds, develop the rudimentary beginnings of what will become their senses—they have the power to decide whether or not they will accede to these urges at each stage of their development.

Of course, we also must presume that these decisions are not as simple and obvious as they might seem to us, because unlike ordinary human embryos, the Sullivan boys are keenly aware of the persistent effort and strain that growth demands from them. Thus far, all three have stuck with the program. And while to us they would look like some half-inch armless, legless sea creature with a large head and an equally long pointy tail, the Sullivan boys look pretty darn smart to themselves and to each other.

Thus far Lucile and Mike have not made themselves known. The boys are doing great on their own, and as their parents, they don't want them to feel that they are being too "parental." Lucile and Mike can listen in on their conversations, and sometimes they have to exert a lot of restraint to keep from laughing at the boys' comments as they compare tails and talk about what it feels like to be grown up.

"Grown up?" chuckled Mike. "Would you listen to that?"

"Mike, be quiet. They're going to hear you!" whispered Lucile.

"Oh, Lucile. Don't always be such a worrywart. The tummy-mike isn't even plugged in."

"What was that?" said Sammy.

"I didn't hear anything," said Roger.

"Well, I did!" answered Harry. "It was a deep sort of chuckle or chortle sound."

"It's probably nothing," said Roger.

"Yeah? Well, if it happens again, I'm going to complain," said Sammy.

"Complain?" said Harry. "Complain to whom?"

"I don't know," Sammy answered. "I'll just complain; that's all."

"So, what's it going to be today, fellas," said Roger. "I personally feel like growing my arm buds a bit and possibly lengthening the leg thingies."

"Arms and legs—sounds good to me," said Harry. "What about you, Sammy? Arms and legs sound good?"

"Let's just take a day off. Every day it's the same thing—grow a little here, stretch a little there. Inside it's the organs. Outside it's the appendages. I mean, when does it all end? Don't you guys ever say to yourself, 'Hey, what's wrong with the way I am? I'm strong! I'm fit! I'm beautiful! I've got this long tail!'"

"He's got a point, Harry," rejoined Roger. "We could take a couple of days off—just swim around for a while."

"I don't know. I personally feel like I've really accomplished something after a day of growing. I mean, sure, it's tiring. I know that. But I sometimes get this feeling that we're becoming something . . ."

"Like what, Harry? You're always saying that," Sammy interjected.

"I know I am, but I really do have this feeling that there's some purpose in what we're doing here, some reason we're growing all this stuff. I mean, for one thing, I actually enjoy having more appendages and watching them grow longer and, frankly, I really like the feeling of my eyes getting bigger and my nose starting to change shape, things like that."

"Me too," said Roger in a cheery voice, trying to break the tension he felt between Sammy and Harry. "Heck, it's all great to me."

"Maybe you're right," Sammy conceded in a low voice, "but some days . . . I don't know, I just wonder what the purpose is, that's all."

Lucile and Mike were worried that night after listening to Sammy's disparaging comments about growing and developing. "What if he convinces them not to grow!" said Lucile as she stroked her stomach in bed that night.

"Hon, they'll be fine. You shouldn't worry. I mean, kids are resilient. Sure, they get discouraged. I remember when I was just a third-string linebacker and the coach came to me and said . . ."

"He said, 'Sullivan, can you just *stand* there and not get sucked in on the end-around reverse,'" interrupted Lucile, mocking Mike's voice. "And from then on you were first string."

"Well . . . yeah, I was, as a matter of fact. But look, Lucile, you may think it's funny, but that was a big deal to me, a real milestone in my—"

"I know, I know," said Lucile. "You've told me fifty times how that changed your whole life. But you know me—I think all that competitive stuff is ultimately useless. I mean, what it really did was leave you with bad knees and bridge work, which you need to get fixed, by the way."

"Yeah, yeah. But you know, Lucile, I still remember when I laid out that wide-out as he came full speed in the open and tried to juke me out of my shoes. Man, he didn't—"

"—get up for ten whole minutes. Go to sleep, Mike."

It was one evening a week later when Mike and Lucile listened to the boys and heard something that let them know it was time to intervene. They had tried to let the boys make their own decisions. They had hoped and prayed that all three would make the right choices, do the "right thing," as Mike would say. "They're Sullivan boys!" he would reassure Lucile. "They've got the right stuff!"

But one evening as they monitored the conversation of their offspring, they reached the collaborative decision that they needed to take a more proactive role, even in this early stage of bringing up the Sullivan boys.

It began as Mike and Lucile were settling down to go to sleep. They said their prayers together as usual, then adjusted the earphones into the Fetocom and gradually turned up the volume. As they listened in, they discovered that Sammy's doubts had increased. He didn't see the value of investing so much energy in developing organs and appendages that seemed to have no apparent value or usefulness in their cozy uterine universe. What was worse, Roger, who had originally gone along with Harry, was becoming convinced that Sammy might be right, that it was just as easy to remain curled up contemplating his tail as it was worrying so much about developing his nose, ears, and internal organs. Sammy had also persuaded him that if their arm and leg buds got a whole lot longer, they would just get in the way. "At some point there's just not going to be enough room here for all these arms, legs, umbilical cords, and stuff. We're going to be a tangled mess!" Sammy had said.

Mike, who originally had so much confidence that the boys would come around to appreciating the obvious value of the entire gestational process, was the first one to suggest that he and Lucile could no longer rely on the boys to make the right decisions without a little help. "Before you know it," he said, "Harry is going to have some doubts. You know he will," he whispered to Lucile.

Lucile's eyes were red and moist as tears welled up. "You're right. I know you are right. It's just that things were going so well, and now this. What should we do, Mike?"

"I don't know exactly, but somehow we've got to convince them that if they don't develop as they should, they will be unable to enjoy this life. I'm particularly concerned about the legs and arms—I had already imagined Harry as a quarterback, Roger as a center, and Sammy as a receiver. Boy, what a team they would be!"

"And the fingers," added Lucile. "I just know that Harry has it in him to be a pianist like my father—he's so sensitive and articulate."

"We don't want to scare them, though. That would be worse than doing nothing at all. Somehow we've got to convince them that we have only their best interest at heart."

Before Mike and Lucile got out the Fetocom, they consulted about exactly what sorts of things they should say: how they should introduce themselves, how they should have coequal parts in the dialogue, how they should be careful not to be coercive or overbearing.

They would do their very best to create in their beloved boys a desire to develop so that they might be prepared for their birth into the "real" world of expansive skies, flowering hills, sunrises, moonlit nights, and walks in the forest. They could tell them about how some day they could have families of their own and professions in which they could contribute to the betterment of humankind. Mike even agreed that bringing football into the discussion at this early stage might just confuse things.

They put the earpieces on and placed the tummy-mike on Lucile.

"Helloooo, little ones," whispered Mike softly.

"Helloooo, dears," said Lucile even more softly. And they waited. But they heard nothing. So they repeated their greeting a bit louder, and then a third time a little louder still.

"Enough!" said Sammy at last. "We heard you the first time! We just can't figure out where the voice is coming from! Who are you?"

"What do you want from us?" said Harry.

"Hello," said Roger happily. "Are you in our universe or in another universe?"

"We're your parents," said Lucile eagerly, but gently. "We're your mother and father, your creators."

"Our creators?" questioned Harry. "I don't remember being created. Do you, Sammy?"

"Of course not," said Sammy. "This is craziness. Roger, are you playing another trick with those silly voices of yours?"

"No! No, honestly, fellows. It's not me. I promise! But I think they sound really nice, don't you?"

"Boys," said Mike in his deep bass voice—

"Whoa!" said Sammy. "Did you hear that one? That one sounds big. I'm not sure I like this one bit, guys!"

"Boys, I am your father. Your mother and I simply want to help you a little. We think you've done a great job so far, but . . . well, we heard you talking about . . . slowing down, you know . . . with the growing thing."

"True enough," said Sammy. "We need a break, that's all. Besides, we're beginning to wonder—at least I am—if all this growth is worthwhile. It takes a lot of work, you know, growing stuff, especially the arms and legs.

"But how do we know that you are who you say you are? If you're our creators, how come you never said anything to us before?"

"We wanted to," said Lucile. "I wanted to tell you every day how much we love you and look forward to seeing you, but we didn't want to interfere when you were doing so well on your own."

"You are going to see us?" said Roger. "What do you mean you're looking forward to *seeing* us?"

"Boys, we wanted to talk with you tonight because we felt that it's time you understood that all your growth has a purpose. You see, all three of you will in time enter the world we're in, and then we will see

46

you firsthand. Then we'll be able to teach you directly, and hold you and hug you and . . ."

"And throw a football, if you like," Mike joined in.

"Look," said Sammy, "It's all well and good for you to *say* that there's some other sort of world besides this one we live in, but we can't see it or touch it. How can we be sure it exists? For that matter, how do we even know you are who you say you are? How do we know you're not simply trying to trick us?"

"Yes," said Roger, "Perhaps you're hungry and want to gobble us up!"

"What?" said Harry. "Gobble us up? We don't even know if they have mouths, for goodness sake. Look, whoever you are, is there some way you can explain to us the purpose for all this growing? Unlike my somewhat less ambitious brothers here, I happen to enjoy a good day's growth. But are you trying to tell us that there is some long range plan for us, some destiny beyond swimming about in this gelatinous fluid?"

"Exactly," said Lucile. "Your life in there is really very brief and limited compared to the afterlife in this world where we are, and where you will also be before too long. And even though it may seem like growing legs, arms, organs, eyes, noses, and mouths is all rather pointless, without them, you will be totally unable to enjoy this life or take advantage of all there is to accomplish here."

"You will be totally powerless," added Mike in a somber but sympathetic tone. And he went on in a somewhat awkward but loving attempt to explain the joys of running, playing, and seeing strange animals. He concluded, "I just wish you could understand how very much we love you guys and just how much we want to give you. We're really going to have great fun together. I promise!"

"This stuff you want to give us," said Roger, "it feels good, does it?"

"Better than anything you have ever experienced in your world," said Lucile.

"It's really quite nice in here," said Sammy. "Are you sure?"

"Please, please, listen to what we are saying to you, boys," said Mike. "I promise you that our only motive is to help you, to help you and to love you. But if you don't develop those appendages and organs and senses, then we won't . . ."

"You won't *love* us?" said Harry.

"That's not what I was going to say," said Mike. "We will always love you. Our love is unconditional, endless, unchanging. I was going to say that if you don't do your part, then we won't be able to communicate that love to you. The love won't have a way to reach you. Do you understand?"

"Look," said Harry. "This is all very new and strange to us—I'm sure you can appreciate that. Let us talk privately among ourselves and we'll get back to you on the whole thing. Is that OK with you two?"

"That's all we're asking, boys," said Lucile. "Remember, we do love you so and want only what is best for you. Please keep that in mind as you consult with each other. We'll talk to you tomorrow night at this same time, OK?"

The three Sullivan boys agreed, but were totally exhausted and decided they needed to get some rest before they could possibly have an animated conversation about this bizarre intervention in their otherwise peaceful, albeit ever-changing existence.

Early the next morning the boys were awakened when Lucile got up to make some coffee, and they began immediately to reflect on all that had happened the night before. Sammy was naturally distrustful about the two voices actually being the voices of their creators, noting that any force or any part of the universe could have said the very same words. "What proof do we have?" he queried.

Roger was willing to accept that the voices might indeed be those of their creators, but he was puzzled about this "love thing," as he called it. He wondered what was so mysterious and important about it. "They did sound sincerely concerned for us," he noted. "What's more, whether or not they created us, their advice might still be true. I mean, what if we enter some other world and we have decided not to grow all these organs and attachments, and we're helpless?" He went on to express how scary it sounded, especially the part about how even the love of their creators could not reach them if they refused to develop.

They both turned to Harry who had been quiet until now. "I'll confess that I stayed awake most of the night thinking about all this," he said.

"I thought your tail was drooping a bit," said Sammy.

"Anyhow, what I concluded was this—and, of course, I don't mind the growing as much as you two—but I figured that first of all these voices, these master embryos or whatever they are, have no reason to trick us, right? I mean if they are as large as they sound and are in a world bigger than this one—because they certainly aren't in here or we'd be able to see them or touch them—then chances are they know stuff we don't. Doesn't that just make sense?"

"Makes sense to me," Sammy said.

"I see what you're getting at," added Roger.

"So I personally think it would be the better part of wisdom for us to do what they say, to grow and prepare for the big change they talked about, just in case it really does happen."

"Nothing ventured, nothing gained," said Roger.

"We have nothing to lose but our tails," said Sammy with a laugh.

"So, we'll talk to them this evening, then?"

"Sounds good," said Sammy and Roger in accord.

All day Mike and Lucile could talk about nothing else. Neither went to work, and Lucile took two lukewarm baths in aromatic salts in the hope that she could somehow influence the boys with the soothing waters or they could feel somehow the love that words alone could not adequately express. She then put on a Mozart violin sonata as she reflected on the plight of her young boys.

Mike was no less preoccupied. He paced, then sat and meditated. He felt incredible responsibility for the well-being of the boys. It seemed to him that their entire destiny lay in his and Lucile's hands, and yet they could hardly force the boys to make the right choice, because that would be no choice at all, and he certainly had no way to force them to make the best decisions.

Never before in his life had Mike realized the power of free will, and never before in his life had he ever felt so utterly powerless himself. He was a man of action who always had what he thought to be a good solution to any problem. Yet here he was at the mercy of three beings that could fit in the palm of his hand.

He went into the bedroom and sat beside Lucile who was resting after her second bath. "It's amazing, isn't it," he said to her, taking her hand. "They are so small, so tiny compared to you and me. And yet nothing we can do or say can force them to accept our guidance, even though we obviously know what they need to do, what is best for them."

"Funny you should say that," Lucile said with a smile as she stroked Mike's hand, which was now on her tummy. "I was thinking much the same thing, except I was reflecting about how the most important power in all of reality is love, and yet as necessary as love is to everything else that exists, it can never be given without someone to receive it!"

Then she turned to him in tears and touched his cheek. "O Mike, what if they refuse? What if they are born without the ability to understand our love, to receive it and . . ."

"And return it?"

"Yes, that too. Of course that, but it's not as if we *need* their love—we got along fine before they were conceived. But now that they do exist and are from us, I just love them so much!"

"I know. I know. I feel as if we have given a ransom to fate, as if our own happiness is no longer in our control."

With great trepidation Mike and Lucile got out the Fetocoms that evening. They tried to relax so that they wouldn't sound too nervous, too harsh or demanding. They agreed that the tone of their voices should be as neutral as possible so that whatever decision the boys reached, it would be their decision.

They knew it had to be that way, because this was not one decision only—it was a turning point! The boys would have to maintain a daily commitment to continue striving and growing. Their very lives were at stake, if only they could understand that.

What gave Mike and Lucile heart was that even if the boys refused, were hesitant, or less than enthusiastic, they would never give up trying to urge them on the right path. Their love was indeed unconditional, and even if they failed to get through this one evening, there would be other evenings. And even if the boys agreed, they would always need reassurance, guidance, and love, always more love.

4

DEATH AND HUMAN ONTOLOGY

In the treasuries of the knowledge of God there lieth concealed
a knowledge which, when applied, will largely, though not
wholly, eliminate fear. This knowledge, however, should be
taught from childhood, as it will greatly aid in its elimina-
tion. Whatever decreaseth fear increaseth courage.
—Bahá'u'lláh, *Epistle to the Son of the Wolf*

So did the Sullivan boys make it through the first major milestone
OK? Did they decide to align their will with the hopes and wishes of
their parents? Did they agree at each successive stage of gestation in
the world of the womb to grow everything they would need to have a
felicitous experience in physical reality?

First we must remember that since each of the identical triplets
has a distinct personality, an individual soul and character, we cannot assume they will have a uniform experience. That fact alone is a
noteworthy observation, inasmuch as it would seem to defy the axiom
that emerged during the early twentieth century—that nurture, not
nature, determines the outcome of individual aspirations. And if
"human nature" includes the animating force of the spirit emanating

from the human soul, then the Bahá'í view of human reality would be totally at odds with this materialist view, a view that still maintains its grasp on most professional assessments of human nature.

WHAT IS HUMAN LIFE?

If we are going to discuss death in any meaningful way, we must first discover what we mean by "life." After all, death has no meaning without life and living. In fact, if we approach the matter logically, death may seem to loom before us impervious to all we might desire to become, but in another sense, it's really not there at all. It is a figment of our imagination, just as evil has no essential reality, nor does cold, darkness, or weightlessness. These concepts all describe a type of nothingness, and nothingness does not have any essential reality—it has no essence or properties. Nothingness is simply the absence of something, whether it be stuff or energy—both of which Einstein asserted are interchangeable.

My point is that if we want to create cold, we can simply take away heat. If we want to create evil, we simply take away all available goodness. If we want darkness, we remove all sources of light. Similarly, if we want to create death, we simply remove any source of life. Of course, there are various sorts of life—molecular, plant, animal, human, and whatever kinds of life lie concealed from us in the metaphysical realm, assuming this placeless place exists.

In any case, human death is not so hard to define, or is it? Clearly human death is the absence of human life, but what exactly constitutes human life? If we believe that the true source of our humanness is metaphysical, then the absence of signs of physical vitality may not mean that the human essence or personhood is dead.

Even determining death from a purely materialist perspective is not so easy, especially not from a legal point of view. Is a person dead when all signs of life of an autonomous sort cease, life without the assistance of machines? And if we include machine-aided life in this equation, what machines are we talking about? I certainly would not feel particularly "vital" right now without my prosthetic hips, and I trust nobody will try to repossess them.

In legal terms, which effectively define medical terms so long as lawsuits and malpractice insurance exist, death is presently defined as the point when someone flat-lines—all meaningful brain activity ceases. Some systems may be able to function without machines, but the body cannot feed itself nor do most other activities we most commonly associate with distinctly "human" activities, and yet in terms of our definition above, death is the cessation of life.

So while the essential reality of death may indeed be the absence of life, death in terms of human existence is a condition well worth a more exact description, even if our definition has meaning only insofar as we can describe what we mean by "life." And in human terms, we are obviously not talking about just any sort of vitality or energy. After all, decomposition is also a process driven by energy. In other words, by "life" we mean a quality of vitality in which those faculties and attributes peculiar to human reality are working at some meaningful and measurable level.

As we consider human ontology (the nature of human reality), even at the stage of incipience—or most especially at the stages of our beginning—we leap unavoidably into the churning morass of ideologically and theologically loaded issues: abortion versus the right to life; the right to privacy versus the public good; the right to have control over one's body versus society's obligation to protect rights of those unable to protect themselves; euthanasia versus laws against suicide. These are just a few of the weighty related disputes that involve confrontations between science and morality.

The logical implications of this ontological issue—what is human life—affect the right to abort a fetus that is deformed or mentally deficient, and the logical extension of any answer to that question is the matter of the right to abort a fetus of an undesired sex, race, size, or whatever other attributes we are gradually learning to predict according to amniocentesis and other prenatal testing. Presently, the rights of a woman to decide the fate of an *embryo* (first eight weeks) or *fetus* (post eight weeks) or *child* (viable fetus) are determined by the laws of the land in which the woman resides.

For the most part, the rights of the unborn child have evolved in the United States since the famous January 22, 1973, Roe v. Wade decision by the U.S. Supreme Court stating that a woman can abort her pregnancy at any time until "the point at which the fetus becomes 'viable.'" Decided on the basis of the constitutional right to privacy (part of the Due Process Clause of the Fourteenth Amendment), this ruling asserts that what a woman does with her own body is her own business until her body contains another "viable" human body, at which point the unborn child assumes rights of its own.

This thirty-five-year-old ruling has been, since its beginning, highly controversial and divisive because of obvious flaws in the language of the ruling. But the problem in the language of the ruling derives from the problem inherent in questions we are in the midst of considering—not when does life begin, but at what point can a living entity that is destined to become a mature human being take on the attributes, capacities, and, thus, the rights of a human being.

The two terms that cause most of the contention regarding this ruling are "point" and "viable." The word *point* is particularly awkward because time does not stop, not in this life. Once set in motion through fertilization or conception, there is no vacillating, even if there are explicit milestones where, as we continue to evolve, we can also reflect on how far we've come.

In short, the idea that there is a "point" in the process of gestation other than fertilization or conception, which we have already observed are processes themselves, is to presuppose that there occurs some specific biological event or transformation from one state or stage to another. Even the distinction between the terms *embryo* and *fetus* is merely a useful invention for embryological discussion, not an actual point of biological change. Like all other human development, the development of the human being from conception to death is a continuous and relentless process.

Obviously the second troublesome word in the language of the landmark Roe v. Wade decision is *viable,* a word that the Supreme Court itself thought necessary to put in quotation marks to indicate the need for definition and clarification. The court was doubtless aware that such a term would constantly struggle to attain any final and universally agreed upon definition. According to the court, the term *viable* was intended to designate the point at which a fetus could survive outside the womb—around seven months in 1973 when the ruling was devised.

But here we have room for even more ambiguity. With rapid advances in medical science, this "point" has now evolved into a variable period of time that presently can be anywhere from twenty-two weeks (less than six months) and 500 grams in weight (a bit over one pound), all the way to a somewhat standard time of twenty-eight weeks (seven months) and over two pounds. In other words, that original *point* in time is now a period of time that is a month and a half in length. At one end of this period is a medical procedure; at the other end the same procedure is the heinous crime of infanticide.

A third predicament, allied to and derived from this range in the *viability* of a given fetus is also relatively obvious: the legal system, somewhat in league with the medical profession, is determining at what point humanness occurs based on the parameters of a technology that is changing almost daily. Put simply, instead of defining human rights effectively, the court decision actually blurred any useful distinction between a woman's right to a common medical procedure and the punishable crime of murdering an unborn child. Or from the point of view of the life in progress, the ruling infringed on the subjective rights of a biological essence in the process of evolving by rendering these rights subordinate to observations that are purely circumstantial, unscientific, and convenient for everyone except the evolving human being.

But our language here is beginning to sound too ideological and slanted. Let's see if we can posit the entire problem with little or no implicit bias or loaded terms. When Sylvia Plath in her poem "Morning Song" says to her newborn child that "love set you going like a fat gold watch," she is at that point in the verse conveying a sense of procreation as a mechanical act relative to the creation of her child. She goes on to describe the child as being *from* her but not *of* her.

Only later in the poem does she begin to feel an emotional connection to the being she has helped create, especially as she responds in the middle of the night when the child cries out its morning song calling for nourishment. Then, while holding the infant as it nurses, she seems to experience the joy of bonding that derives from her growing awareness that this new creation is actually a human with whom she can share her love:

> Love set you going like a fat gold watch.
> The midwife slapped your footsoles, and your bald cry
> Took its place among the elements.
>
> Our voices echo, magnifying your arrival. New statue.
> In a drafty museum, your nakedness
> Shadows our safety. We stand round blankly as walls.

I'm no more your mother
Than the cloud that distills a mirror to reflect its own slow
Effacement at the wind's hand.

All night your moth-breath
Flickers among the flat pink roses. I wake to listen:
A far sea moves in my ear.

One cry, and I stumble from bed, cow-heavy and floral
In my Victorian nightgown.
Your mouth opens clean as a cat's. The window square

Whitens and swallows its dull stars. And now you try
Your handful of notes;
The clear vowels rise like balloons.

The child is no longer merely a "new statue" in a "drafty museum." Between the second and third stanzas, the mother, from whose point of view the poem is narrated, begins to undergo an altered perspective.

At first disdaining the presumed instinctive intimacy and affection she is supposed to feel as a new mother, she expresses a sense of detachment, distance, even derision about her pregnancy and the child's birth. Beginning with the third stanza, however, time slows down and the speaker focuses on a single evening.

The mother, half asleep, is somewhat soothed by the sound of the breathing child—the baby is still there, still OK. Then as soon as the first cry emanates from the child's sweet mouth "clean as a cat's," she gets herself up, stumbles in to nurse the child, and, in the last stanza, studies this new life as the whitening window indicates that the morning sun is rising and a new day has dawned—an obvious but effective symbol.

For this mother, the child's transition from a "statue" or "gold watch" to a loving and lovable human being occurs once an intimate relationship and personal routine becomes established. Biological viability has little to do with her altered perception of what had been for her a mere biological inevitability and what has now become for her a precious child with whom she can communicate and share affection.

But while this may be an especially memorable night, a sort of epiphany for this mother, her affection for the child will continue to be a work in progress, not a single point of transformation. This is not an abrupt shift that takes place at a single point in time, though certainly a radical alteration in her perspective is taking place. But what the poet has offered are two snapshots of a relationship in motion, not two different relationships.

Another aspect of the complexity and intricacy in determining the "viability" of a human being is that the court decision in no way implied viability without external assistance or artificial aid. The fact is that of all mammals, the human being is doubtless the least viable without continued external and artificial aid. For while some complex mammals may train and safeguard their progeny for months or years, it could well be argued that the human being does not achieve true viability, at least to the extent of some sort of autonomy, until it can take care of itself and becomes responsible for its own livelihood— normally life around the age of maturity or later.

In other words, neither science nor the courts have devised, nor will they ever be able to devise in the future, any point other than conception at which a human being becomes distinctly human—and therefore deserving of human civil rights. Once the whole process is set in motion with fertilization and conception, there is no pause, no sudden transformation, no point or series of points at which this evolutionary growth is anything other than a human being in the process of developing, a process in which the human being achieves physical maturation around fifteen years of age and peaks at about age twenty-one or so, and then spends the entirety of the remainder of physical existence attempting to achieve mental and spiritual maturity.

THE GHOST IN THE HUMAN MACHINE

Isn't it nice not to have to continue the implicit debate we have just set in motion with the last few paragraphs? We do not need to picket abortion clinics or make speeches about a woman's right to determine what happens to her own body. We can simply conclude that the debate on the subject is likely to continue until there is some consensus about when a human being becomes a human being.

And from what we have thus far observed about this process, such a conclusion can never be reached so long as the criteria by which this decision is made are based solely on the parameters of an ongoing physical process that has absolutely *no* milestones of ontological change—it never changes from one sort of being to another. That embryo, even when a few cells old, even when it looks like a shrimp or rodent, is the only growing bunch of cells that will invariably become a human being. Conversely, a human being is all the embryo can become, much as it might rather be something with fewer problems—like Molly, my collie dog, for example, who snoozes quite peacefully on my sofa in front of the fireplace.

What we cannot avoid in our discussion about what constitutes human life—especially since we have defined death as the absence of it—is whether or not being human involves anything other than the random assemblage of the modular parts of the human body, especially the more intricate parts of the central nervous system. Obviously our laws, for example, assume our brains are more than mere computers, because we hold people responsible for their actions by virtue of their ability to determine what course of action is most closely aligned with social norms, expectations, and limitations (something a computer could do). But we also hold human beings responsible for willfully following that path.

In many cases we hold them responsible even when such a path is not necessarily a course of action that best befits self-interest, at least in terms of ordinary sorts of comfort and felicity. For example, if someone is the head of a household and is penniless and sees his or her children hungry and without proper clothing, our society does not excuse this person for breaking the law by stealing the necessities of life, even if to help others.

THE SUBTLETY OF HUMAN WILL

I discuss this subject of human will at length in *Close Connections: The Bridge between Spiritual and Physical Reality* (pp. 169–233), and I do not wish to rehearse all of that discourse here. But the essential conclusion I reach after examining the findings of some high-powered scientists, who have distinguished themselves by winning Nobel prizes and such, is first that there is a clear distinction between what the brain can do and what the mind can do, particularly regarding human will.

Human will is by definition a metaphysical force. Like gravity, it cannot be examined as a force *per se*; only its results can be measured. A materialist explanation for human reality is that all we are, or all we can become, is merely the result of the function of the modular workings of the human brain, the most complex system in existence. However, as I explain in *Close Connections,* the most complex computer ever devised or that it is ever possible to devise, can do no more than it is designed to do. It has no inherent sense of well-being or willful desire except that which we humans design it to have, in spite of what science fiction would have us believe.

As human beings, however, we have the capacity to make decisions and carry them out based on nothing more than what we wish to do, and what we wish to do, however influenced by a myriad external forces and inherited predispositions, may change from moment to moment. If we have learned nothing else about human nature, it is that we have the capacity to defy the deterministic forces that would usurp our desires and powers to act freely, to become what we decide to become rather than to follow the path of least resistance (what a deterministic model would conclude).

For example, we may begin a course of action to acquire vast sums of wealth, only to undergo some transformative emotional experience that causes us to take action against material self-interest, to dedicate ourselves to assisting others, to incrementally reform our own normative perspective about life, and to effectively reinvent ourselves and our purpose in life.

A strict materialist cannot accept this process as the result of anything other than random brain function or else the illusion of authorship, as Wegner theorizes in his book *The Illusion of Will*. To allow for the existence of some spiritual or metaphysical power (such as human free will) would be to attribute to us a capacity not derived from or dependent on modular brain function.

Similarly, a strict materialist is forced to view events like the Princeton projects described in *Margins of Reality* in terms of quantum physics, even as Jan and Dunn end up doing in spite of the fact that they prove scientifically that human will can affect the outcome of physical events. They do not deny that human will has such a power; rather they posit the theory that the effectiveness of will on physical or phenomenal reality can be explained by the laws of quantum physics. There's no problem with that, but the question remains: What power within us sets the quantum mechanics in motion to cause the physical effect? What is the cause behind the cause?

These same conclusions would apply to all of Dossey's work that measured the effects of prayer on the outcome of physical events, whether the healing of the sick or the thriving of plants. The corner into which many materialists have painted themselves, in short, effectively diminishes their own accomplishments as nothing more than the chance results of brain activity over which they themselves have had no control. Consequently, they belie their own theories by accepting honors and awards for their work. If all they have accomplished has resulted deterministically from random brain activity, genetic predisposition, or environmental upbringing, then in what sense can they claim credit or personal achievement?

NEW PHYSICS AND OLD PROBLEMS

Einstein faced the same problem with the theory on gravity. He could not accept that there was in nature (the physical universe) an inherent force of attraction. Unless the cause of such a force could be explained or justified by scientific law, he argued, this attraction was merely some other event being observed from a perspective that gave the appearance of inherent mutual attraction of masses—simultaneous action at a distance. The long-term result of his ruminations was to devise a theoretical alternative to Newtonian physics, part of New Physics, which has now been surpassed by Newer Physics.

The same problem occurred, as I also discuss in *Close Connections* (pp. 125–152), with the problem of explaining light as waves. For light to be transmitted in waves, there would have to be an ether or plenum, some refined "sea" of materiality through which the waves could pass. Instead, Einstein and other "new physicists" devised or discovered the concept of light as particulates, as photons, the proof of which for the everyday nonscientist is the photoelectric effect that, for example, allows elevator doors to reopen when we stick our foot or arm in the space between the closing doors.

However, the plenum is being rediscovered. In fact, every particle we have thus far discovered seems not to be some final discrete building block of matter, but is itself a composition of even smaller particles. Of course, there is the Super String Theory (SST), which hypothesizes that all the unexplainable stuff can be explained by infinitely various and vibrating particles of string-like design that have temporarily been employed to represent a rather large X (an unknown variable to explain everything that can't otherwise be explained).

The point is that science is in the process of discovering what the Bahá'í writings asserted over a hundred years ago—that every thing (every existent part of physical reality) is composite. Or stated more plainly, there is no final building block of matter, because matter is infinitely divisible, even as matter is obviously also infinitely additive. I observe in *Close Connections* that as we proceed in either direction (toward bigness or smallness), reality begins to emulate the properties of spiritual reality by becoming infinite.

Of course, in neither direction does physical reality end up transmuting into spiritual or metaphysical realities. But because these twin expressions of reality available to us (physical and metaphysical) are the "exact counterpart" of each other, the ability of physical reality to emulate the attributes of metaphysical reality is a primary means by which we can apply what we know about one reality in order to discover things we do not know about the other.

Getting back to the subject at hand, then, if we as human beings are something more than or other than the workings of an intricate and complex physical machine, if our personhood, humanness, or self-consciousness really is more than the sum total of billions of neurons patched together in networks and lobes and other components of a vast modular system, then that essence that we are must, perforce, be more than or other than a physical event or process, however much its nature may be communicated through or associated with physical processes. In short, our essential self must be ontologically metaphysical in nature and therefore nonlocal.

Certainly this is not a new idea, that the brain is an intermediary between our real self, our soul or metaphysical personhood, and the body with which we associate during our formative years in physical reality. In fact, it is an ancient idea. It is the idea that our soul is our essential reality from which emanates our spirit, the animating energy or force of our essential self, whether that essence is expressed as self-awareness, as all manner of mental exercises, as reflection, as meditation, as will, or as judgment.

What is new is that an increasing number of very reputable scientists are acceding to the axiom of Ockham's razor that the simplest explanation is usually the most accurate explanation—the shortest distance between the two horns of a dilemma. These scientists generally conclude that the brain is most likely a transceiver for a nonlocal source, whatever one might choose to call that source, and this is a conclusion that derives in part from the increasing acceptance of the holonomic brain theory.

The holonomic theory suggests that the segments of the brain are not as specialized as previously thought. A neuron is a neuron, and a bunch of neurons doing one specialized job can, if necessity requires it, take on another totally different job. So it is that science has discovered that memory is not resident in discrete portions of the brain. For example, the recollection of your first date is not contingent on the health of a few thousand neurons specifically dedicated to that momentous event. Of course, nowadays, that event is probably retained on someone's cell phone and the entire episode may well be posted on "My Space," "Facebook," or "YouTube."

I do not mean to suggest that a PET (Positron Emission Tomography) scan does not reveal what portions of the brain are specifically active during certain emotional states, physical activities, or thought processes. The point is that the lit up and colorized pictures of the brain's activity during these events are not necessarily the only places that can assist or enable these events, nor are these locales necessarily the origin of the event. The PET scan merely shows what part of the brain is being used at a given moment to transmit or receive information. Furthermore, should these active parts of the brain become injured or otherwise compromised, the activity could still take place by means of employing some other portion of the brain, if not instantly, then over time.

We can discern this capacity of the brain to "rewire" itself (sometimes with the help of outside training) in cases of aphasia when someone who has had a stroke learns to talk again, not because the neurons injured by the stroke have become fixed—once a neuron dies, it remains dead—but because other neurons can be trained to do what the deceased neurons formerly did.

Everybody knows this—if they haven't witnessed it in person, then they've probably learned about it on one of the plentitude of TV shows where temporary amnesia becomes a convenient part of the plot. But think about the reality of this recovered memory. If the capacity to speak or recall events was not resident in some portion of the brain, where was it? If the vast vocabulary you possess still exists (only you have to relearn how to speak it) where did the vocabulary reside while you were being retrained?

Here it would be helpful to revisit the Bahá'í theory of the brain as an intermediary between the metaphysical self and the body, not because I am a Bahá'í or because I am trying to promulgate Bahá'í beliefs, but because I find it to be the most reasonable explanation for what I have studied and what I personally have experienced as regards the three fundamental components involved: the mind, the brain, and the body.

The theory has many ramifications, but simply stated, it asserts that the human reality derives from a metaphysical essence that employs the human brain as a transceiver. The mind allows the human body with which it associates to represent the character and capacities of that metaphysical essence of human reality. I have found that as I get older, this analogy feels much more palpable. My "essential self" (part of which is my memory and mind) seems to be doing OK, but that transceiver is showing glitches. Likewise the body acting out my true self is sometimes sadly out of step.

I still remember my childhood in Greensboro, North Carolina as if it were yesterday, even as I do my first date. And yet when I look in the mirror in the morning, I behold a physical presence that really does not do me justice. This can only mean that while my mind has been learning and developing, my body has been aging. The conclusion I have reached is that my real self, my essential reality, is working as best it can through the intermediary of a brain that has been frequently jostled and a body that has been skillfully sutured together by some of the world's best orthopedic surgeons.

THE NON-LOCALITY OF THE CONSCIOUS SELF

We are going to discuss physical deterioration at greater length later when we talk about aging as a tool for our development and preparation for death, but for now let us turn to a few ancillary axioms related to this assertion about the nonlocality of consciousness and the other faculties and powers of the essential self.

First, we cannot deny that if I hit you on the head really hard, you may end up *non compis mentis*—you may not be able to think straight. Does this not prove that your mind and your sense of self are dependent on a healthy brain and body? And if this is true, how can we simultaneously assert that the essential self is independent of illness of body, mind, emotion, or any other sort of physically related dysfunction?

Here is where certain analogies prove very helpful. For example, analogies of the brain to a periscope, to a TV receiver, or to a computer can prove extremely helpful in beginning to understand how there can be an indirect relationship between our essential self and physical reality. Obviously our body is the major means by which we express to the outer or physical world who and what we are through our words and actions, through our demeanor and comportment. Conversely, our body and its senses constitute the major means by which our essential self receives feedback about who we are and how we are doing, so long as the associative relationship between the "self" and the body endures.

For example, we can view and talk to a friend through computers, even if the friend is thousands of miles away. If suddenly the face of our friend starts to become distorted with squiggles and lines, we do not conclude that our friend has undergone some physical transformation: "Jane, your face! Your face just mutated! What can I do to help you?" What you can do, of course, is to fix the internet connection or else take your computer to the shop, or tell Jane to do the same thing. In short, you have relative confidence that it is the associative relationship with Jane through the computer that has been botched up, not her face.

Fortunately for us, this is precisely the same conclusion that is warranted when we get old and see our own face get squiggles and lines in the mirror. We know there's nothing wrong with the real us, and, unfortunately, we know that most likely there's nothing wrong with the mirror, no matter how much we may wish it were so.

But what if we are getting feedback about our real self that we find disturbing? What if we feel depressed (an all too common condition in our contemporary environment)? Naturally we know that one of two things is occurring. Either something is disturbing us and we can try to discover what it is and fix it, or there is some dysfunction in the biochemical system in our brain that replicates in emotional physical sensations what is going on in our essential self (our soul and spirit).

In extreme cases of disparity between our emotions and reality, there may be some obvious illogical or dissociative response to reality. We may hallucinate and believe that we see people or hear voices that are not really there. What we then hope for is some means of fixing our personal neurological communication system, through surgery if a tumor is causing our brain to malfunction or through medication if there is some problem with treatable malfunction of neurotransmitters, such as the common cause of much clinical depression—a too-rapid re-uptake of serotonin.

The point is that what we can be assured of, as can our friends, is that there is nothing wrong with the "essential" self, even if the cause is some form of dementia resulting from an incurable deterioration of brain function, as in cases of Alzheimer's. Our sense of "self" and of reality has been distorted by improper feedback, by a malfunction in the system that functions as the intermediary between our essential self and reality. With proper medical help, this back-and-forth communication may be restored to transparency and health. But regardless, it is an axiomatic fact (at least from the Bahá'í theory of the essential "self") that the spirit, the soul, the real "self," is in no way impaired or injured by this faulty communication:

> Know thou that the soul of man is exalted above, and is independent of all infirmities of body or mind. That a sick person showeth signs of weakness is due to the hindrances that interpose themselves between his soul and his body, for the soul itself remaineth unaffected by any bodily ailments. Consider the light of the lamp. Though an external object may interfere with its radiance, the light itself continueth to shine with undiminished power. In like manner, every malady afflicting the body of man

is an impediment that preventeth the soul from manifesting its inherent might and power. (Bahá'u'lláh, *Gleanings*, no. 80.2)

The question then arises as to what happens when the communication system or the brain-transceiver is irreparably damaged so that not even distorted information about reality can be sent or received. Is the essential self still unaffected, or once this occurs, is the associative relationship severed? While the answer to this question gets us way ahead of ourselves in our examination of life's journey, we can hardly sidestep the question if we are to define adequately the parameters of what constitutes human life.

So long as the essential self associates with reality by means of, or through the intermediary of, the body and brain, then our emotional sense of "self" is affected. If we are depressed, even if because of faulty brain chemistry, we cannot function well physically, mentally, or spiritually. If we are delusional, our human powers are likewise compromised and diminished. If we are so traumatized or dysfunctional as to be catatonic or if we are afflicted by a disorder such as autism, then to outward appearances, our lives might seem to be little more than dislocation, solitude, and misery.

As we will discuss later, this same relationship remains constant for illnesses that produce severe dementia so that all outward traces of self seem to evaporate and the subjective sense of self is likewise a blur, or muddled, or available to us only in bits and pieces. Doubtless the subjective experience of this association with a dysfunctional transceiver is troubling. Daily life may be experienced in botched images or disconnected words and phrases, as if we were on some hideous ride at a fair, except that we are unable to stop and get off.

Here again, we will discuss more completely the impact of and consolation for such circumstances in our later examination of illness, suffering, and dying. For now, let us observe that however discomfiting and confusing such conditions may be and whatever psychical pain must be endured, these conditions are merely temporary. For as soon as the associative relationship between the essential self and the body-brain temple's miming of the self is severed, all encumbrances between the self and reality are likewise severed. However, no permanent effect on the "essential self" occurs.

While we can deal more fully with some of the other axioms that derive from the assertion of an associative relationship between our "self" and the human temple through which that self operates during the period of our lives as physical beings, we can hardly leave this discussion of the first major "milestone" of being born without taking some position about when human life effectively begins. This is especially important if, as we have noted, contemporary medical and legal opinions are not going to offer us any definitive answers.

We have talked all around the question and have cited the inadequacy of contemporary attempts to discover workable answers, but we have actually arrived at some inescapable answers. First, we seem to have concluded that there is not much alternative to accepting the thesis that at the heart of our humanness is a thinking, contemplative, intelligent, willful essence that is not, strictly speaking, physical in nature. Whether we categorize this essential self as being the soul, the spirit, the mind, or the self's consciousness, it is clear that this being that expresses itself through our physical body-brain mechanism can exist independently of the mortal expression of that self. However, we have also noted that so long as the associative relationship exists between these two realities (the one metaphysical and the other physical or metaphorical), it is impossible for us, except in rare moments of reflection, to sense precisely which is which.

Second, if this "self" is essentially metaphysical in nature, then it must be ultimately impervious to and independent of all the ills, maladies, dysfunctions, and abuses that the body may undergo. This does not mean these misfortunes are not meaningful. Neither does this observation imply that our "self" is not affected by these experiences. Hopefully we gain immense growth and insight as a result of these wrenching and traumatic events. But in terms of a life that is infinite, we are never made to endure such experiences for very long, even though subjectively any period of suffering seems interminable at the time.

Third, if, as we have asserted, this metaphysical reality takes on an identity when this associative relationship with the body begins, then obviously the point of association defines the true beginning of a human life. The Bahá'í writings define this association as beginning at conception, and yet, as we have noted in our fable, conception itself is a process, albeit a rather rapid one.

In the final analysis, we can conclude that despite this bit of mystery, medically *conception* is more or less synonymous with *fertilization*. In this sense, the emanation of the metaphysical essence may occur before any further development in the process inasmuch as the relationship is associative, not physical. In short, identity may occur metaphysically before it becomes distinct from the precise completion of any embryological or physiological process.

Fourth, while we may recall events or impressions as early as when we were two or three years old, there is clearly no single point at which cognition occurs. We see in the newborn child all sorts of reactions to pleasure and pain that are quite beyond any learned response or mere autonomic responses. Likewise, mothers recount instances where the child in the womb moves about without outside stimulation. My youngest son James actually managed one night (which Lucia recalls) to create a "true knot" in his umbilical cord. He made a loop, somehow went through the loop, and then managed to stretch it out tight. Knowing him as I now do, I am almost positive he did this on purpose.

Therefore, if cognition and will are properties of the metaphysical self, and if, however meagerly, these powers express themselves and are receptive to sounds or other sorts of external influences, we must conclude not only that personality is an inherent property of the essential self, but also that there is much for us to learn about the complex developmental process of that personality during gestation. In a discussion of the progress of the essential self, 'Abdu'l-Bahá notes: "The personality of the rational soul is from its beginning; it is not due to the instrumentality of the body, but the state and the personality of the rational soul may be strengthened in this world; it will make progress and will attain to the degrees of perfection, or it will remain in the lowest abyss of ignorance, veiled and deprived from beholding the signs of God" ('Abdu'l-Bahá, *Some Answered Questions*, p. 240).

Fifth, since the potential for this incipient organism to become human is no greater at eight or nine months than it was at conception, we must likewise infer that it is as likely that the associative relationship—the beginning of personhood, personality, individuality, and, therefore, of humanness—is from the beginning. Certainly we know this is true with the physiological aspects of the creation, that no two creations are exactly the same, that even identical or monozygotic twins are distinct.

This is the Bahá'í theory of the essential parameters of the human reality, then, that our essential reality, our personhood or individuality, begins with its emanation from the spiritual realm when it associates with the embryo at conception. As we have noted, however, this association in no way implies that the essential self derives from or is somehow contingent on the progress of the physical temple with which it is associated. The human reality associates with the human temple, even as the human mind associates with the human brain during our physical existence. But both the understanding of and the reason for this relationship need to be understood before any of this process makes complete sense.

In short, if the essential self is fundamentally independent of the physical body, then what is the value of a process in which this associative relationship occurs? Why have we been created to endure the persuasive illusion that these two realities are one, that we are physical beings, and that our own survival and viability are dependent on a healthy physical self? Furthermore, how is divine justice rendered when some souls must associate with physical temples that do not survive or are deficient? Likewise, since no two life experiences are exactly the same, nor are the precise capacities or skills the same for any two human beings, how is equal justice meted out so that all have an equal opportunity to receive the bounties of divine bestowals?

Only by continuing our discussion of the mysteries surrounding our death can we discover the answers to these and other enigmas about the inevitable outcome of our shared journey through this brief life.

5

THE LAMB WHITE DAYS

Oh as I was young and easy in the mercy of his means,
Time held me green and dying
Though I sang in my chains like the sea.
—Dylan Thomas, "Fern Hill"

The first thing I remember about my own childhood is an image from somewhere around three years of age. It is a single image, but not at all like a snapshot because it has dimension and I can enter it as if it were a virtual reality machine. I can look at it from various angles. This must have been a scene I saw repeatedly over time.

The place is a wooden crib, and I remember the color and texture of the wood. I remember a blue blanket, and I remember a white rabbit with pink eyes, its fur so soft that it may well have come from a real rabbit. I recall that rabbit as a dear companion, and I remember the window opposite the crib brightened by the light reflecting off the white wood siding on the house next door. I remember pine fronds moving slightly in the breeze. That's all.

From that point on, childhood for me is a pastiche of vignettes whose chronology I might possibly be able to assemble by studying albums assembled by my mother. Interestingly, while my brother's album (he was five years older than I) is complete in every detail, mine stops after about five pages. Instead of carefully laid out pictures inserted into little black corners, there are envelopes stuffed with photos indicating a work in progress that never got finished, much like the incomplete album I have for my youngest son, as opposed to the very complete album for my oldest daughter.

Most of the vignettes I recall have no important connection to one another. I remember playing in the sandbox, making roads and houses. I remember getting whacked in the head by a mother brown thrasher when I attempted to peek into her nest in a dogwood tree. I remember running outside naked on a dare from my brother and realizing that I could outrun and out-maneuver my frantic father who was desperately trying to catch me before the neighbors saw. I had to pretend to get caught because I was as embarrassed as he was, however much I relished the excited cheers from Bill: "Run, Johnny, run!"

Most powerfully I remember the woods, the wonderful magical pine forests of Starmount Forest in Greensboro, North Carolina, where we lived. But I do not wish to wax nostalgic. This is not intended to be an autobiography, so let me get to the point. Among the axioms I mentioned in the previous chapter is the Bahá'í thesis that personhood—what I have been calling the "essential self"—is from the beginning. This "self" includes distinct personality and other capacities that will be expressed through those physically inherited talents, potentialities, and predispositions we may have inherited through our genes or the environment, or possibly even as some aspect of the essential self that we have yet to understand.

So it goes without saying (though it is well worth mentioning all the same) that my brother and I throughout our later years were forever trying to determine which of our more grievous flaws we could blame on our upbringing and which of our talents were inherent, as opposed to being developed by individual grit and determination.

What was clear from the beginning was that our personalities were always there and always extremely different—often quite antithetical. So were our physical appearances and our skill sets. But one thing among the many things we shared was our mutual assertion that everything we were or became had its roots in a childhood that was incomparably wonderful.

We played in the woods daily. We played house tag—a game we invented in which the person who was "it" had to tag someone as we all scampered around the various rooms and floors of the stud frame in a new house being built in the neighborhood. Naturally, this game took place in the late afternoon when the workers had left, and needless to say, it was extremely dangerous.

We played jumping off stuff—a high embankment where the leaves would pile up. I once played jumping off the garage with an umbrella as a parachute. It actually sustained me for a millisecond before it suddenly buckled back and let me experience how unforgiving the law of gravity can be. In winter, we raced our sleds down the long terraced yard at the Tanner's house or the shorter run at Janie Flynn's.

The neighborhood was filled to overflowing with children my age and older, and filled with childhood things to do. The woods, filled mostly with tall Carolina pines, had a lovely meandering creek, and all manner of trails and secret places to hide. I spent the better part of each day there, and the magic of that time and that place occupied my mind constantly, both day and night.

I remember once when it snowed, I thought about how neat it would be to go to the place where I had made a hideout by burrowing into a large clump of leafy vines. I imagined how cozy it might be to crawl in without disturbing the snow blanketing the vines and look out through the snow as if it were a crystalline skylight. So without telling Mom, off I trekked to my secret place, and it was precisely as

I had imagined it would be—clean white mounds of vines inside of which was my "Fortress of Solitude."

I remember the curving road that went to Hamilton Lake where there was a sand beach and a cement pier. There was a tall tower out from the pier where only good swimmers could go. We would challenge one another to jump, and since going down the ladder was not allowed, the climb, once begun, was tantamount to entering into a contract with your own courage.

But that's enough about my particular wonderful childhood. Many artists much more talented than I have created such potent images of the power and value of childhood that it is needless for me to attempt to do much more than point to a couple of those masterpieces by others and say, "That's what I mean!"

Of course, the childhood to which I refer is nowadays such a rarity that I feel the need to allude to those images a little, especially for those who may never have had these experiences themselves. Not that a happy childhood is confined to a particular culture or environment, but the most commanding images of childhood to me come from writers who grew up many decades ago in a less perilous age, or else those who were raised on farms, or in the country, or in small towns and villages, though Neil Simon's Brighton Beach Memoirs gives a similar sort of nostalgic recollection situated in a more urban setting.

Certainly Wordsworth is one of the English poets most acclaimed for exalting the state of childhood as a source of adult spiritual and philosophical inspiration. In his poem "Lines," he meditates on the beauty of the Lake District of Cumbria, an area just south of Hadrian's wall in northwestern England. He recalls what intimations of immortality were his in a childhood untrammeled by drudgery or the exigencies of adult life in all its myriad forms of distraction and stress. Wordsworth convincingly recreates the beauty of the Lake

District. He vivifies images of the natural serenity of place, but, more important to our theme, he shares authentically the impact of that paradisiacal setting.

Presumably drawing on the Platonic notion of preexistence, Wordsworth, like other early English Romantics, portrays childhood as a time when we are freshly emerged from the spiritual dominion. From this metaphysical realm we emerge attuned to the spirit that animates all reality. So it is that, "trailing clouds of glory," we must become gradually exposed to the realities of the material world of "experience"—a reality that in time tends to blur those sanctified recollections and to erode the intimacy we have with nature, a childhood communion in which we are capable of intuiting the symbolical and metaphorical messages that nature can impart, even if we are to express them well.

In Wordsworth's verse, however, this early relationship with nature, which is but the logical extension of the proximity to the divine as intuited by the child, need not be lost forever or abandoned. Indeed, the poet exhorts us to recall and recreate these visions for our own edification:

> Oh! yet a little while
> May I behold in thee what I was once,
> My dear, dear Sister! and this prayer I make,
> Knowing that Nature never did betray
> The heart that loved her; 'tis her privilege,
> Through all the years of this our life, to lead
> From joy to joy: for she can so inform
> The mind that is within us, so impress
> With quietness and beauty, and so feed
> With lofty thoughts, that neither evil tongues,

Rash judgments, nor the sneers of selfish men,
Nor greetings where no kindness is, nor all
The dreary intercourse of daily life,
Shall e'er prevail against us, or disturb
Our cheerful faith, that all which we behold
Is full of blessings. (Lines ll.119–134)

It is the implicit argument in Wordsworth's philosophical perspective that one can willfully, through dedicated reflection and meditation in later life, synthesize that spiritual vision intuited through the innocence of childhood with the adult awareness of the reality of a world less attuned to matters of the heart and soul—the harsher world of ordinary experience.

It is in this sense, as it was with so many of the romantic poets in England and with the transcendentalist writers in America, that nature and childhood, and childhood lived at one with nature, become symbols of a sacred state of being, a condition in which we are attuned to the divine attributes that permeate the entirety of physical reality and our experience in it:

But oft, in lonely rooms, and 'mid the din
Of towns and cities, I have owed to them
In hours of weariness, sensations sweet,
Felt in the blood, and felt along the heart;
And passing even into my purer mind,
With tranquil restoration:—feelings too
Of unremembered pleasure: such, perhaps,
As have no slight or trivial influence
On that best portion of a good man's life,
His little, nameless, unremembered, acts
Of kindness and of love. (Lines ll.26–35)

Of course, not all of those who exalt, and exult in, the innocence and sublimity of childhood arrive at the consolation that Wordsworth achieves—a conscious recollection of childhood and a willful forging together of those early childhood intimations of immortality with adult experience and retrained sensibilities. Nor did the delight in the power of individual genius, in the divinity of nature, and in the yearning to invent a just society last more than a couple of decades among these young minds in the early nineteenth century.

There were many forces that caused these writers and others to lose faith in recollections of the idyllic beauty and inherent divinity of a childhood spent in nature. Western Europe soon experienced the dehumanizing effect of the industrial revolution. Then, in 1859, Darwin's publication of *The Origin of the Species* also helped quash much of the romantic impetus to perceive human beings as divine emanations from the world of the spirit. Instead, science took another giant step away from accepting the existence of a metaphysical reality by asserting that the emergence of human life on earth was a chance mutation. We evolved from the muddy recesses of bubbling primordial muck, an origin even more inglorious than our having sinned by eating forbidden fruit in the fabled Garden of Eden.

Even many of the earliest among the romantics were not so optimistic as to think that the innocence of childhood could be recaptured and applied to the "real" world. William Blake's *Songs of Innocence and Songs of Experience,* and his later works, particularly *The Marriage of Heaven and Hell,* portray a stark contrast to his simple verses about the pure and untainted perspective of childhood. Blake instead portrays the wrenching ruination of innocence brought about by an uncaring society and a perverted religious tradition, images that decry the loss of the sacred within and without.

Where Wordsworth, Coleridge, Keats, and Shelley would later focus on the divine in nature and in the human soul, Blake strikes out vehemently at decadent social systems that obliterate that innocence. He condemns physical abuse resulting from child labor practices, as well as the spiritual perversity of religious institutions that he portrays as having utterly distorted the truth of human capacity and purpose: "As the caterpillar chooses the fairest leaves to lay her eggs on, so the priest lays his curse on the fairest joys."[2] Blake was not against religious belief per se, nor against the concept of divinity. Rather he decried what institutionalized religion had done by way of enslaving and debasing the healthy instincts of natural passion, instinctive joy, and innocent delight.

In the context of our contemporary society and the almost total alienation of children and youth from nature, we might think that Blake was indeed prophetic in his analysis. Of course, not even Wordsworth expected or intended that all should journey with him to the lake country. Like Thoreau, Wordsworth was contriving a mental experiment to examine the human heart and soul. In particular, he and other Romantic poets and philosophers, like Rousseau, appreciated the fundamental goodness latent in human nature if the human spirit be carefully guided to fulfill its inherent and nascent powers.

The latent goodness of human nature is at the heart of the Romantic doctrine about the human journey from the divine world of infancy, through a childhood at one with nature, to some practical synthesis of that childhood purity with daily life in adulthood. Whether that amalgamation be accomplished by a literal journey to a childhood setting, or, more likely, by a mental reflection about the dreams and visions that once emerged spontaneously from the realm

---

2. Quoted in *The Norton Anthology of English Literature*, 7th edition, Vol. 2A, *The Romantic Period*, eds. Abrams, et al. (New York: WW Norton & Company, 2000), p. 76, line 16.

of the spirit, this willful attainment of what Wordsworth calls "emotion recollected in tranquility" is what helps empower us to become fully human. Wordsworth thus touched on a theme that is extremely relevant to our quest to discover a consolation for the loss of childhood innocence, as well as a logical solution to the evaluation of all that succeeds the "lamb white days."

THE PROBLEM OF LEAVING PARADISE

For me, the poems of Dylan Thomas epitomize the attempt to capture the sheer rapture of childhood joy and innocence. But in his poem "Fern Hill," perhaps his most celebrated poem akin to the Wordsworthian tenor of the unleashed indulgence in childhood delight, there lurks an underlying fear. In one sense, the focus of the poem is actually on the brevity of that special interlude between birth and youth, that period of the suspended consciousness of our own mortality, a brief respite when we are old enough to relish nature, but young enough to be oblivious to our own transience.

In the last stanza of "Fern Hill," Thomas renders the irony of this paradox intensely clear when he observes how time allows each of us so brief a period to have this state of unalloyed joy and enchantment:

Nothing I cared, in the lamb white days, that time would take me
Up to the swallow thronged loft by the shadow of my hand,
In the moon that is always rising,
Nor that riding to sleep
I should hear him fly with the high fields
And wake to the farm forever fled from the childless land.
Oh as I was young and easy in the mercy of his means,
Time held me green and dying
Though I sang in my chains like the sea.

At some point, no matter how blissful, innocent, and joyous this state of wonder might be, we will awaken to discover our own mortality, that death is not merely a theory, not simply an accident that happens to others. We realize that life is not near as simple as we had assumed.

In his poem "Janet Waking," poet John Crowe Ransom, my own mentor, succinctly describes the point at which one particular child becomes aware of mortality. He portrays how little Janet marvels in her grief that her pet hen Chucky, so animated and so dear, could suddenly cease to exist. This enigmatic experience wakens Janet from the lamb white days of innocence, and we know that she will never be able to return again, not completely.

> Beautifully Janet slept
> Till it was deeply morning. She woke then
> And thought about her dainty-feathered hen,
> To see how it had kept.
>
> One kiss she gave her mother,
> Only a small one gave she to her daddy
> Who would have kissed each curl of his shining baby;
> No kiss at all for her brother.
>
> "Old Chucky, Old Chucky!" she cried,
> Running on little pink feet upon the grass
> To Chucky's house, and listening. But alas,
> Her Chucky had died.
>
> It was a transmogrifying bee
> Came droning down on Chucky's old bald head
> And sat and put the poison. It scarcely bled,
> But how exceedingly

And purply did the knot
Swell with the venom and communicate
Its rigour! Now the poor comb stood up straight
But Chucky did not.

So there was Janet
Kneeling on the wet grass, crying her brown hen
(Translated far beyond the daughters of men)
To rise and walk upon it.

And weeping fast as she had breath
Janet implored us, "Wake her from her sleep!"
And would not be instructed in how deep
Was the forgetful kingdom of death.

Obviously the key word thematically in this very accessible verse is the "sleeping" followed by the "waking" of Janet—her becoming aware of mortality and death. In spite of her present brief refusal to accept the fact that Chucky cannot be awakened, we know that she is on the verge of becoming awakened to reality, that she has now become aware of time's inescapable chains.

GREENSBORO IN THE WOODS

My brother took a trip a few years back that was quite Wordsworthian in purpose. He traveled to Greensboro a few years before his death, partly out of nostalgia, but mostly, so it seemed to me, as an experiment. In any case, what he discovered was quite revealing in terms of what may have happened to Thomas, which is certainly quite the antithesis of what Wordsworth concluded.

I have often considered such a trip myself, simply to cure myself of the recurring dreams of the place, but I returned only once to

Greensboro, almost six decades ago when I was twelve. It was eventful because I was able to defeat my childhood nemesis, Chippy Hutchenson, in a playful but highly touted wrestling match. I also impressed my former childhood companions with a one-and-a-half dive off the Hamilton Lake tower. Perhaps it was because my return was heralded as a victory of sorts that I never went back again. I knew I wouldn't be able to top my earlier success.

But in his late sixties, Bill did go back, and he went back specifically to examine whether or not the magic was still there. More important, he wanted to discover if the people in our former middle-class neighborhood, so emblematic at the time of the great American dream, were still enthralled with life as we had been so many years ago. He took with him a collection of my poetry *A Sense of History* so that at the gathering, which was held at a Holiday Inn conference room, they could use the section of poems dedicated to that time and that place to help kick off the ruminations about childhood, about Greensboro, or at least about Greensboro as it had been more than a half century before.

From what he told me upon his return, together with the few notes about the gathering in his unpublished autobiography, he concluded several verities that bear importantly on the power of youth and our experiences during that formative age to shape all that we aspire to become and all that we ultimately do become.

First, he discovered that indeed each and every one who attended recalled their early youth in that place during that time in the forties exactly as had we—as a time of idyllic enchantment, of pure joy and mostly innocent fun. But strangely, those who had stayed behind, those who had not been wrenched from this mythic land of dreams, were no less haunted than we were by the loss of that recollected spate of years.

Bill and I had been forced into exile. Dad's transfer forced us to move away. We had left Greensboro behind changeless in our minds. But for those who had stayed, this time and place had incrementally morphed into something grotesque and unfamiliar to them. Their childhood was no less vanished than was ours, but they could not escape the daily haunting by something that was there, and yet not there.

This is not to say that none did well or that none succeeded. But from Bill's observations, it seems that all successive phases of their lives could not compare with those perfect lamb white days. While we who left were forced to set aside that era as if it were an album collection of lovely visions, we could periodically take from the shelf and revisit, they could not. For us, this was a narrative with a beginning, middle, and end. If we longed to return, we were aware that it would be a fictional homecoming, a product of our conscious recollection or reverie, not something we could fashion in reality. It was the past, pure and simple.

But for those we left behind, those who stayed, there was no neat segmentation of life, no departure or exile from that time and place. The transformation for them occurred by degrees as the city evolved, as new neighborhoods sprang up and surrounded our own, as a noisy and vile super expressway cut a lethal path right through the very heart and soul of the woods behind Homewood Avenue.

Bill observed that one consistent and sad result was that a number of those left behind had become alcoholics. Others had met with some mild success, but each and every one of those who had stayed had become eerily haunted, not blessed, by that enchanted past. After all, what could compare with such grace, such innocent perfection, such simple and complete pleasure?

After that reunion, my brother told me he no longer considered our imposed departure a tragedy. He sincerely believed this fracturing of our lives had actually forced him to break free of those "chains" and put closure on his childhood. It enabled him to move ahead with his development as a useful and productive human being. In fact, he told me he was sure that had he stayed behind, he, too, would have become a lost child and would have succumbed to the endless longing to recover or recreate those lamb white days. Like Peter Pan, he, too, would have remained a *puer eternus*.

I observed the same syndrome in some of those with whom I grew up in Atlanta. I was only seven when we moved there. Atlanta during the late 1940s and on into the 1950s was little more than a somewhat overgrown southern town. It had streetcars, a handful of relatively tall buildings, but a citizenry that was explicitly segregated, and not merely racially. The white community had a lower class, a well-defined middleclass, a somewhat more affluent nouveau riche class, and a very explicit upper class aristocracy of old money and storied families whose names appeared on street signs and park monuments. It was no coincidence that Margaret Mitchell wrote *Gone with the Wind* in this environment where, prior to Sherman's "blasphemous" march to the sea after burning the town, there had been plantations and imperial colonial homes to rival the best anywhere in the south.

But the point I'm trying to make is that during my youth, Atlanta was a special place, a stable place, a peaceful place, a place marked by the eminence of noble leaders and elegant paradigms of social splendor. The African-American community was no less so, populated as it was by some of the best African-American colleges and universities in the United States, and a stratification of classes no less well defined and changeless than those of the white community. The last thing Atlanta really wanted or needed was to become what it is today—a chamber of commerce dream-come-true, the southern hub of capitalism itself, the leviathan of middle-class affluence, its every avenue bumper-to-bumper with fancy cars and every inch of viable space occupied by cubes of glass and stainless steel, though viewed from overhead gliding into town to its massive airport, there is still so much greenery that the illusion of what it once was still remains. And in the spring when the dogwood trees lining the streets bloom like snow, all the citizens most probably praise the god of mercantility for the privilege of occupying this Mecca of the American Dream.

The transformation was so quick, so utterly complete, that by the time I left for college, or shortly thereafter, nobody knew who was who. The classes blurred, and the influx of new money made the stately mansions look dated and silly, like a man in a white tie and tails at a barbeque. But as was Bill's experience in his return to Greensboro, I knew that those who stayed behind tried desperately to hold in their hearts and minds Atlanta as it had been in the fifties.

Most who saw the boom coming rose up with it as doctors, lawyers, or entrepreneurs, but it was nothing like my youth when everyone knew who were the most reputable lawyers, most competent doctors, or most prosperous business tycoons. Consequently, no matter what degree of success my friends achieved, most were forced to live in the fading shadow of the success and esteem their fathers and mothers, grandfathers and grandmothers had achieved, a primacy that no longer had currency among the exponential influx of new names and changed values that had little or nothing to do with the remnants of the Old South. The old Atlanta of Margaret Mitchell got steamrolled by the rapid onset of the machine of commerce, beside which the classical marble encrusted Candler Building or the once stately Carnegie Library seemed oddly anachronistic and cacophonous.

This was nothing new, of course. We see this same paradigm of change and loss of values in the novels of the early twentieth century by noted writers such as Dreiser in his novel *American Tragedy,* Sinclair Lewis in his novel *Arrowsmith,* or succinctly and simply in a poem like Edward Arlington Robinson's "Richard Cory":

Richard Cory went down town,
We people on the pavement looked at him:
He was a gentleman from sole to crown,
Clean favored and imperially slim.

And he was always quietly arrayed,
And he was always human when he talked,
But still he fluttered pulses when he said,
"Good-morning," and he glittered when he walked.

And he was rich—yes, richer than a king—
And admirably schooled in every grace:
In fine, we thought that he was everything
To make us wish that we were in his place.

So on we worked, and waited for the light,
And went without the meat and cursed the bread;
And Richard Cory, one calm summer night,
Went home and put a bullet through his head

Faulkner received a Nobel Prize for cataloguing the decline of traditional values that happened throughout the 1940s and 50s, a collapse that occurred not merely in the vanishing of the Old South in the United States. The gradual decline of shared values, dependable virtues, and trustworthy social systems was taking place throughout the western world, and, in the decades to come, this cancer of materialism would metastasize to afflict all corners of our increasingly small planet.

WHO WANTS TO GO HOME AGAIN?

In his classic novels *Look Homeward Angel* and *You Can't Go Home Again*, Thomas Wolfe examines this syndrome of childhood nostalgia as he speaks of his own pilgrimage back to his upbringing in quaint and picturesque Ashville, North Carolina. His childhood was as tantalizing as my own, and his autobiographically-based novel fleshes out that reality like the tapestry of a master painter.

But after college, I seldom returned to Atlanta except for the periodic visits to my parents. For whatever reason, I had no desire to do so, possibly because my parents had moved up the social ladder a bit and had purchased a house in the Buckhead neighborhood that had been enemy territory when I was growing up. It was here that lived those who played on opposing high school football teams from more ascendant classes—Northside High and North Fulton High. Even now these names can evoke in me a disdain for all that is pretentious in the world of high school athletics, a rather trivial world, I suppose, compared to our newly emerged global civilization.

My father died there on the fourth of July in the bicentennial year of America's birth, 1976, an appropriate date to end this life for a man who dearly loved America and the American Dream, and who was seriously pained to behold what he believed to be its incremental decline, its fall from grace. He was spared seeing what would be the further transmutation of American values he held so dear, and of Atlanta, whose sports teams he had followed from his college days at Emory University.

But since my mother continued to live in Atlanta until she "passed on" at age ninety-six in 2001, I had the privilege, if such it can be called, of watching the finishing touches of Atlanta's transformation into a megalopolis unlike anything we who came as emigrants in the late 1940s could have imagined in our most ghastly nightmares. The total effect of my periodic visits over time was like watching a time-lapse film of something fine, simple, and gentle morphing into ever-mounting cubes of glass and stainless steel. No piece of land bigger than a football field remained untouched or barren.

Perhaps for those who remained behind, this transmutation was not so glaring or obvious, but with each successive visit I could see expressways twisting in sinuous strands across the forest slopes like anacondas loosed upon the land. It was so complete and astounding that very little was left from what I had known and loved, except for Morningside Elementary School. I did manage one brief visit to Grady High School while it was being reconstructed—the distinctive fragrance of those aged wooden desks and window frames that were being pulled out had a more profound impact on my psyche than any pictures ever could have managed.

PARTING LOVERS

It would appear, then, that if we are not forcibly extricated from the lamb white days, awakened by our knowledge of mortality in general and of our own mortality in particular, we may have to struggle mightily and persistently to escape the myths and illusions of childhood.

It is a departure somewhat similar to what we face in a romantic relationship gone bad. After the inevitably unsuccessful attempts at remaining "friends," the lovers must in time leave each other's presence knowing that any attempt to define boundaries are doomed. The more intense and authentic the love, the more essential it is to establish literal space and visual absence between lover and beloved, or else the wounds will never heal. Real life will never be able to compare with the selective recollection of a past love. No new love can ever finally defeat these defiant apparitions.

Even when true love succeeds, we must in time set aside our intoxication with the initial bloom and glow of mindless attraction—unwary as we are of its source and chemical powers—in order to progress to a relationship whose foundation is the sound knowledge of that to which we are attracted. Bahá'u'lláh in his mystical treatise on spiritual ascent describes this transition as moving from the Valley of Love to the

Valley of Knowledge, and He does not portray this transition as easy or even as fun. But He asserts that this "escape" is absolutely necessary if we are to progress, to get on with our life and our life's purpose:

> And if, confirmed by the Creator, the lover escapes from the claws of the eagle of love, he will enter the Valley of Knowledge and come out of doubt into certitude, and turn from the darkness of illusion to the guiding light of the fear of God. His inner eyes will open and he will privily converse with his Beloved; he will set ajar the gate of truth and piety, and shut the doors of vain imaginings. (*The Seven Valleys*, p. 11)

As Bahá'u'lláh makes clear in this work, we should not infer from this excerpt that the initial stage of enthrallment is undesirable or unimportant. The capacity to be vulnerable to that attraction and to examine the nature of its power on us is vital, perhaps essential, if we are to progress. Otherwise, we will have no need or desire to attain knowledge by examining the worthiness and character of that which entices us so powerfully to draw near.

True, Bahá'u'lláh notes, love in this initial stage of its evolution may derange our perception and delude our reason: "Love setteth a world aflame at every turn, and he wasteth every land where he carrieth his banner. Being hath no existence in his kingdom; the wise wield no command within his realm. The leviathan of love swalloweth the master of reason and destroyeth the lord of knowledge" (Bahá'u'lláh, *The Seven Valleys*, 10). But the end result of allowing ourselves to become susceptible to its call, to become singed with this fire, to indulge in this insanity, to become giddy with this intoxication, is that the illusion that this enthrallment is the sum total of love itself is the best means by which we can then set ourselves on the endless path toward true love. This is a love that is not circumscribed, not a changeless passion, but an eternal process that is ever changing and constantly growing. This is a love that strives toward successive stages of sanity and sobriety.

The value of the initial stage of love, the ecstatic attraction to the beloved, is a means by which "the veils of the satanic self be burned away at the fire of love, that the spirit may be purified and cleansed and thus may know the station of the Lord of the Worlds" (Bahá'u'lláh, *The Seven Valleys*, p. 10). It is in this same context that the stages or milestones of our childhood and youth, whether idyllic or hideous and abusive, must be set aside if we are to proceed to the next milestone. It doesn't matter if we are haunted by nightmares of affliction, or taunted by romantic visions of longing and return. In time we must slay the past if we are to conquer the future. Otherwise we are doomed to a life of stasis and regret, of waiting for some miraculous return to what once was, instead of being propelled into a life of striving for the possibilities that lie in wait for each of us.

Wordsworth thought he had discovered a palliative cure for his childhood—extracting whatever inspirational verities and images it possessed and synthesizing them into an impetus for dealing with the present and shaping the future. Thomas could not, and it may have killed him. Each of us, possessing as we do a special character and our own unique blend of talents and subsequent responsibilities to employ those skills as well as we are able, must find the best solution to dealing with this stage of our life's journey. The next stage we approach is one in which we clearly possess a sufficient degree of will and personhood that we sense ourselves becoming accountable for all that follows, for pursuing all the milestones that loom before us on the horizon like the skyline of a distant village.

6

ACHILLES' CHOICE VERSUS MORAL RESOLVE

The embryo in the womb of the mother gradually grows and develops until birth, after which it continues to grow and develop until it reaches the age of discretion and maturity. Though in infancy the signs of the mind and spirit appear in man, they do not reach the degree of perfection; they are imperfect. Only when man attains maturity do the mind and the spirit appear and become evident in utmost perfection.
—'Abdu'l-Bahá, *Some Answered Questions*

Those old enough to remember the country singer Faron Young singing "Live Fast, Love Hard, and Die Young" are also old enough to remember the heroic years of the mid 1950s when Chevrolet ruled, when James Dean died in a car accident while driving his Porche, and when Buddy Holly died in a plane crash. If you were a young male teenager in America at that time, you probably also went to the neighborhood movie theater every Saturday to watch plenty of heroic exploits involving U.S. Marines fighting on island beachheads in the South Pacific.

One of my favorite movies, and probably the scariest, was *Guadalcanal Diary. Sands of Iwo Jima* wasn't bad, except that John Wayne gets shot at the end. Another favorite of mine was *Flying Leathernecks,* because I loved (and still do) the Chance Vought F4U Corsair, even though, as I recall, the patched-in footage showed chubby Hellcats shooting down Zeroes—it angered me that the movie maker thought I could not tell the difference between the sleek body of the Corsair with its inverted gull wing, and the chubby Hellcats with their straight wings.

Many were the Saturday afternoons I spent at the Army Navy Surplus store in downtown Atlanta rummaging through all sorts of gear: machetes, jungle hammocks, canteens, real army patches to sew on my jacket, and other surplus miscellany. The store smelled of waterproof canvas. There were piles of helmets, army knives, and pup tents. All of this, I presumed, had been used by somebody in battle.

At night I dreamed of beachheads and jungles with bullets zinging past my face as I aimed my Garand semiautomatic rifle or Browning automatic rifle (BAR) in the jungle palms to catch a sniper unawares. I remember making my one bedroom window into the cockpit of a fighter jet by fashioning an instrument panel out of cardboard, and nailing a steering wheel in front of a small wooden stool. I sat down and pretended to fly out over the front yard, releasing torpedoes on unsuspecting Japanese carriers or triggering spats of machinegun fire on an ascending Zeke (a Japanese Mitsubishi A6M Zero). The window peered out through a narrow gable on the second floor, so little pretense was needed.

Whether it was from those movies or from some more neurotic aspect of my indomitable romanticism, I early on, especially as I began to incorporate girls into my daydreams, had as my ultimate dénouement to every imagined heroic scenario some version of my being injured while coming to the rescue of my comrades in arms. When females began to become part of my imagined heroic exploits, then naturally they would be the ones to be rescued, or else they would play the role of a sympathetic nurse to tend my wounds.

But for some reason I have yet to figure out completely (though I'm sure any second-rate psychology student would instantly apply some polysyllabic term to befit my syndrome), the greatest joy I would derive from my reverie would be a sort of public adulation mixed with unabashed compassion for the injury I had incurred. That's why in the movies I always envied the solider who had his arm bandaged, or a trickle of blood down the side of his face, but nothing grotesque, nothing that would maim or disfigure.

He would usually have a cigarette hanging out of the corner of his mouth, his shirt off, and really neat paratrooper boots. I remember one time when I was in the first grade I put my arm in a mock sling because a guy in my class who had actually broken his arm got so much attention for it. I was unable to fathom why the teacher scolded me so harshly for doing precisely what this other kid had done. I suppose she thought I was making fun of him, but I had no understanding of what a broken bone was. How could a significant body part just break?

Not infrequently my dreams of glory involved my death, something I am sure I got from seeing Spencer Tracy or Clark Gable receive incalculable amounts of sympathy, admiration, and belated affection from Jeanette MacDonald, Gene Tierney, Carol Lombard, or some similar icons of feminine perfection. Naturally, my imagined glorified death had to be repeated in a variety of different scenarios, since it was hard to imagine myself in any sort of extended afterlife condition in which I would get the same thrill from the accolades and lamentations bestowed on me for my heroic acts.

But at the heart of this desire was the winning over of the really neat girls whom I sensed might otherwise be out of reach for me since I never considered myself to be among the really neat guys. I was convinced that I could never be with those girls until I had demonstrated my concealed heroic character by performing my daring rescue and after I had been awarded my really neat bandage for my dramatic wound.

Later on in the tenth grade when I was a teenager in the ROTC (Reserve Officer Training Corps), my army dream fell apart. I did not like being ordered around by guys who obviously relished the faux power they thought they possessed. I did not like being criticized for not having shaved close enough or for not having polished my shoes or my brass belt buckle to their standards, especially when I had done what any reasonable person would consider a fairly decent job.

So when I extrapolated in my mind spending extended periods of time under the complete control of such characters, my dream of becoming a soldier lying prone on a beach was quickly deflated. Moreover, after a few summers working as a counselor at an outpost camp in the Blue Mountains of North Georgia, I realized that I was also not that crazy about being isolated from family, friends, and my independence. But I had not yet fully suspected that my entire childhood vision of sacrificial heroism was also inherently flawed.

All that changed when I was fifteen. I was a relatively gifted athlete, always had been, and was about to become first string on the varsity football team. A week before the second game in which I was to start, I went to a doctor because I had noticed that I was bumping into things. I also noticed that when I was running with the ball, big things (such as tacklers) were running into me without my being able to see them approaching.

It turned out that when I had been poked in the eye while indulging in the pleasure of blasting into another human being, my retina had become detached and was hanging precariously at the back of my eye. The next day I found myself in the hospital where I had to stay for four weeks, flat on my back with my head braced by sandbags so that my sight in my left eye could be saved.

At last my dream had come true! Right? The doctor had examined my eye only one day before the big game, and he said to me in hushed tones (and I'm not making this up), "My Lord. Johnny Bump (they called me "Bump" because I was always falling from something or getting hit by something when I was a child), I am afraid you will never play football again!"

Who could ask for a more dramatic or more heroic sympathy line?

There was only one major catch—no one else was there to hear it. There was no cheerleader beside me with tears rolling down her cheek. I was later informed that at school they said prayers for me on the intercom during morning announcements, but I didn't learn this until months later when it no longer mattered since I had already had to go through the recovery by myself. During my stay in the hospital I could have no visitors, except for the coach, who was briefly allowed in to tell my father what great expectations he had harbored for my ascent as a star running back.

And when I eventually returned to school, twenty pounds lighter, forced to wear stupid-looking pinhole glasses, and four weeks behind in all my courses, I did not find myself basking in the glory of sympathetic sighs and tears from others. I was no longer a football player, and I was miserable. All that I had struggled for three years to achieve was irreparably and irretrievably gone. I could never play football again, or basketball either. No contact sports, the doctor had said.

I think it was then that I realized my lifelong dream of glory was not only logically flawed (pain, suffering, and permanent injuries are not fun), it was an emotional trick. It simply did not work. Dramatic injury, dramatic dying, or death itself, however emotionally evocative on screen, was not fun at all in real life, and the really popular girls were still more interested in the really popular football players who were *not* injured.

But there is one important ancillary lesson I have learned about that flawed vision of the sympathetic wound on the maimed hero lying on a bed with a grieving girl sitting beside him: It was not and is not just a product of *my* invention. I was not, and am not, the only neurotic person in the universe. I had been trained, tutored, and teased with this lie from childhood, even as had countless generations of young boys before me.

I came to realize that these dreams of glory are precisely the reason that military recruits are, by and large, so eager to go to war and become heroes, precisely because they are too young and too inexperienced to have learned the fact that pain, isolation, and subordination to mostly mindless automatons do not make for an easy or fun game from which you quickly recover and emerge as a hero—not in real life.

And yet how far back in legend and literature this image persists, whether as the dying Tristan awaits the white sails of Iseult's approaching ship (which arrives exactly too late), the cursed and comatose sleeping beauty, or the heroic Beowulf who gives his life to save his warriors. In the ROTC the sergeants who were our instructors, and who were also survivors of actual battles they fought in World War II, took great pleasure in showing us footage of the concentration camps in Europe, the emaciated Americans on the Bataan Death March, the burned out buildings and pieces of bodies from the Dresden fire bombing, or heavy earth-moving equipment shoving hundreds of skeletons into mass graves.

There was nothing noble, neat, fun, daring, or enticing about any of this, not at all. This was carnage, mindlessness, inhumanity, nothing more or less than insanity. Suddenly all my fascination for things military turned to a stark terror of my ever being drafted into the service where I might be exposed not merely to such horror, but to a mindset that could ever countenance such atrocities, let alone take part in them, and then have pride in it.

I remember many years later during the Vietnam War when I was teaching a senior seminar at the University of South Florida. We devoted a good deal of time to debating the morass of contentious issues and perspectives regarding that grotesque conflict. That same week, a young man in his late twenties came to my office. He was somber, but wanted to discuss the poetry of Wilfred Owen. The young man, whose name I have long since forgotten, had recently returned from some of the most horrific battles fought in Vietnam during the Tet Offensive.

I was amazed that an ordinary foot soldier fighting in Vietnam would know so much about a poet killed on November 4, 1918, only eight days before the armistice in the First World War. I was even more surprised that these verses would have such an impact on a soldier some fifty years later, though I guess the emotions associated with all wars are pretty much the same.

In particular he liked one passage from *"Dulce et Decorum Est,"* probably Owen's most anthologized piece. The poem describes the effects of mustard gas as soldiers march in the mud behind a cart filled with the bodies of dead soldiers.

> If you could hear, at every jolt, the blood
> Come gargling from the froth-corrupted lungs,
> Obscene as cancer, bitter as the cud
> Of vile, incurable sores on innocent tongues,—
> My friend, you would not tell with such high zest
> To children ardent for some desperate glory,
> The old Lie: *Dulce et decorum est*
> *Pro patria mori.*

"It is sweet and proper to die for one's country," went the line from Horace quoted at the end of Owen's poem, and the Vietnam veteran knew it to be a lie quite as profoundly as had Owen. In a calm, almost detached voice the young man told of his experience fighting in the jungle, seeing his twin brother "stitched" before his eyes as an automatic weapon severed the body in two at the waist.

I asked this articulate veteran to speak to my class about the war because I had inferred that the class was fairly evenly divided between those who brazenly denounced the military and any soldier who had not escaped to Canada, and those who felt we should support our armed forces regardless of whether or not we understood or agreed with the task at hand.

But there was no division among them as they sat stunned, rapt in respectful silence for three hours listening to this young veteran speak. They heard his stories, more vivid than the gory footage the evening news showed every night, more ghastly than the daily statistics of dead and wounded.

At the end of his low-key narration, they heard how, having come home from wounds physical and mental, the soldier found himself no longer afraid of death and, to their surprise, no longer moved or affected by seeing death. In fact, he was no longer able to feel emotion about much of anything at all.

He turned his thoughts to an incident he had recently experienced involving a good friend he had made at the small apartment where he lived. The soldier had gotten to know an older black man who had terminal lung cancer, Mesothelioma, from working with asbestos. He described how they had become compatriots for six months and how he had watched the disease begin to devour his friend from the inside out. The young soldier then described how one afternoon as they were talking, he heard his friend cough in a sort of exploding and resonating sound, a sound he had heard more than once in Vietnam, the same one described in Owens's poem.

He told the students how he took his friend's hand and told him matter-of-factly, "You're going to die now." Within the hour his friend had passed away. The young soldier noted that he did not weep, nor did he mourn. He seemed almost surprised himself at the recollection of his lack of feeling as he realized how inured he had become to death, to dying, to mutilation, to the smell of burning flesh, to seeing body parts, to seeing dead villagers of every age and sex and size.

I don't know if the class believed him. I'm not sure I did, but as he told the story, he was not animated in the least. The toneless and factual manner of his voice made the narration all the more wrenching.

If this were some kind of catharsis for him—as some psychologists of the day presumed such personal narratives to be—the remedial effects were certainly not apparent.

The war had not made him brave or bold. The war had bereaved him of affect, and not for dying only. He had no feeling for anything except the accuracy of Owen's poetry, Owen and anyone else who could speak to him about the truth of the dark place where he now lived, any voice that could penetrate that space and assure him that he was not insane, that he was feeling, or not feeling, exactly what any normal human being should.

WARS AND WARRIORS

Our history—our "human" history—seems to be spliced together with wars. Our heroes for the most part were warriors: Alexander conquered the world. Caesar conquered it again. So did Napoleon. All of these "great heroes" were serial killers, except they did it openly with bravado. They did it for a living.

Our mythic heroes are the same. Achilles was given a choice: to live a long and happy life but be quickly forgotten, not having achieved any fame in his life, or to become a renowned hero, but die young. While Homer is hardly simplistic in his depiction of Achilles' choice in the *Iliad*, nor is Greek mythology for that matter, the fact is that according to tradition Achilles chose the latter. He would die young, but by golly he would be remembered through the ages as a magnificent soldier and hero. So he died heroically and young, and here we are thousands of years later still talking about him. It worked! It worked for Beowulf, a somewhat more shadowy figure from fifth century Anglo-Saxon culture. We now know he actually lived and may have accomplished heroic exploits for the sake of his people. Of course, we are right to question the veracity of his encounter with a sort of Scandinavian Sasquatch (Grendel), or the fire-breathing dragon. Nevertheless, we remember his name and study a poem about him because, according to legend, he made the heroic choice—to give his life to save his people, but mostly to retain his good name that he might be remembered and his story recounted around the hearth at night, after the virtuous meal and flasks of mead had mellowed the soldiers and readied them to become inspired by the most common theme for motivating soldiers: *Dulce et decorsum est pro patri mori* ("It is sweet and proper to die for one's country").

History and historical places are also haunted by another equally persuasive theme regarding death, the familiar *ubi sunt* refrain, a Latin phrase that began many medieval lyrics about the transience of life: *Ubi sunt qui ante nos ferunt* — "Where are those who existed before us?"

This is the persistent rhetorical question to which the answer is ever the same—they are dead, buried, and all traces of them are fading from our memories. It is the cynical question arising out of the memorials erected to the heroes who attained what they thought to be immortality, the retold legends residing in the hearts and minds of the generations who recount wondrous acts of selfless sacrifice.

The *ubi sunt* phrase expresses brusquely the verity that no matter how strong, how powerful, or how influential you might be or might ever be capable of becoming, your ultimate destiny is death and the loss of all you have accomplished or accumulated. In time, everything you become or create will be lost. It is this stark and simple sameness of all our lives that causes the most mighty and heroic to gawk in terror at the great equalizer among us, that peaceful and implacable passage into the next world.

Death impels the mightiest among those who have peered into the dark and pitiless abyss of nothingness to do anything in their power to forestall it or undo its fatal logic. Somehow they will accomplish something so unimaginable that it will endure to remind the world of who they were, be it as inconsequential as a plaque on a park bench or as impressive as a pyramid. To some it matters not whether their enduring fame be as saints or as tyrants, so long as something of them remains.

One of the more well-known *ubi sunt* poems is Shelley's "Ozymandias," a poem about a crumbling monument to Ramses the Great. This brief ironic paean is aimed right at the heart of this rhetorical question. The speaker notes that in the desert "Two vast and trunkless legs of stone" stand atop a pedestal on which is inscribed the following epitaph:

> "My name is Ozymandias, king of kings:
> Look on my works, ye Mighty, and despair!"
> Nothing beside remains: round the decay
> Of that colossal wreck, boundless and bare,
> The lone and level sands stretch far away.

As we have noted, the irony of the rhetorical question is that the answer never changes—whether they were prince or pauper, all are dead and gone. But not only are they gone; so are the armies they assembled, the empires they built, and all but the remnants of the monuments they had constructed as everlasting tributes to themselves. Their one chance at a sort of immortality comprehensible to their materialist minds—something that everlastingly could be seen, touched, or admired—even that has decayed, crumbled to dust, and vanished.

Perhaps the vanity of attaining the immortality of the hero can be appreciated by posing to ourselves a simple but reasonable query: How many among us would at this very moment trade our life for the life of any single one of these heroes? Would we trade our present circumstance for all the fame, the power, and the riches the greatest figures in history acquired, if simultaneously we had to accept one hitch in this Faustian pact? Like them, we would suddenly be dead. What is more, this covenant would require that we would be presently experiencing whatever afterlife was due them.

Doubtless there are some who, like Achilles, would accede to the bargain because their present lives are so miserable that the future bodes little possibility for alteration in their circumstances. But that's the price of glory, isn't it? "Paths of glory lead but to the grave," observed English poet Thomas Gray in his haunting poem "Elegy Written in a Country Church-yard." He also observed that many a genius passes through this life unnoticed and unnoted because they were not at the right place at the right time:

> Full many a gem of purest ray serene
> The dark unfathom'd caves of ocean bear:
> Full many a flower is born to blush unseen,
> And waste its sweetness on the desert air.

DEHUMANIZING HEROISM AND THE HERO

I suppose that heroes have always been a breed apart, whether as solitary leaders, as special agents, or as part of some elite band of similarly desensitized warriors. And I believe that in the final chapters of my own life's journey, I have finally come to figure out why these figures have such an appeal to us, whether we are male or female.

First of all, they are impervious to pain. Second, as regards death, they can take it or leave it. They are completely and utterly fearless, which means, if we are honest about it, they are effectively nonhuman. They are more like automatons than human beings. They may look human. They may be quite charismatic and charming in their own way. But the complete disregard and fearlessness they display in the face of death is something most sane human beings cannot imitate. Third, they can carry out super-human accomplishments precisely because they are intrepid and pitiless. Fourth, they are totally socially and emotionally autonomous. They can be tortured and make love, but ultimately they will endure the pain and never become oppressed or possessed by love. They will certainly never be *in* love, because they will never make the necessary concessions or become sufficiently pliant to make the compromises that love requires of us.

In sum, heroes, at least our modern versions of heroes, are emotionally lobotomized and asocial. With some, we are given clues as to how they got this way. Like the Vietnam vet who visited my class, they have seen too much, done too much, have had too much done to them. Most have some psychic scar that will never fully heal. And because they are spiritually maimed, they will never again invest themselves or their emotions in anything perdurable, whether it is a love interest or a pet dog. They will never fully trust anyone or any ideal again, not without a lot of time and possibly some capable professional assistance. Yet we extol them, admire them, and, on some level of pure inanity, want to be like them.

These Ramboesque androids appeal to us because we know they will ultimately break the spirit of all who oppose them, and in fiction, those who oppose them are worse than they. But if we are willing to detach ourselves, even for a moment, from the initial infatuation we feel for these ostensibly indomitable spirits, if for a few minutes we were to consider the everyday lives of these characters, we would also quickly confess that we would not like them as a father, or as a lover, or even as a friend.

On some level we know that they are incapable of being any of these things, because a good person, a noble and deeply human being, has human relationships, depends on others, and is sincerely moved by the plight of others and by his or her own losses—characteristics that none of these heroic figures seem to posses. This is the enigma of these contemporary heroes—that the same lack of vulnerability and affect that makes them so stoic and resolved, that very same wall that protects them from frailty and failure, is also the wall that keeps us out, that shields them from humans and prevents them from being human themselves.

There was a time, of course, and not that long ago, when we admired the well-rounded hero or heroine. The "Renaissance man" we call such figures, who supposedly existed along with the chivalric code as exemplars of knighthood. This sensitive soldier could dash off a sonnet while fighting a duel, very much like Cyrano de Bergerac (1619–1655), whose autobiographical fiction portrayed precisely such a figure. Him I admired as far back as my first viewing of the movie in 1950, especially José Ferrer's brilliant portrayal of this ostensibly unlovely duelist-poet. He had it all—the heroism, self-sacrifice, the fatal wound, and dying in the arms of fair Roxanne whom, unknown to her, he had loved dearly all along, even as she would have loved him in spite of his long nose, had he only dared to reveal his true romantic nature to her.

During my own period of hero-worship, I chose Gene Autry as my paradigm of virtue. Like his primary cowboy competition, Roy Rogers, Gene could sing beautifully as he rode his horse Champion among the rocky terrain of West Texas until, as the final phrase of the song still hung in the air, gunshots would echo through the canyons, signaling the beginning of plot and adventure. Like Cervantes' parody of the picaresque hero with his wonderful character Don Quixote, both Gene and Roy had their clumsy and comical Sancho Panza companion—Gene had Smiley Burnette and Roy had Gabby Hayes—but Gene was less gaudy, less flamboyant than Roy.

Also like the prototypical Quixote, Gene lived out a code as threadbare and fictional as the archaic chivalry to which the impossible dreamer, Don Quixote, devoted his life. The "cowboy code" was created by Autry as a tribute to those of us who listened to his adventures on the radio, because he really felt a moral obligation to us. It went something like this:

1. The cowboy must never shoot first, hit a smaller man, or take unfair advantage.
2. He must never go back on his word, or a trust confided in him.
3. He must always tell the truth.
4. He must be gentle with children, the elderly, and animals.
5. He must not advocate or possess racially or religiously intolerant ideas.
6. He must help people in distress.
7. He must be a good worker.
8. He must keep himself clean in thought, speech, action, and personal habits.
9. He must respect women, parents, and his nation's laws.
10. The cowboy is a patriot.

The hero depicted here is not eager for death. He is sensible, and, most important of all, he has none of the antiestablishment rage and antiheroic, antisocial unruliness of contemporary heroes such as Dirty Harry, James Bond, Rambo, or Robocop.

Another important but unwritten part of the code, at least insofar as film was concerned, was the dictum that no bullet should ever leave much of a hole in the human body. There should never be much blood, even though the forty-four caliber Colts would, in reality, have blown to bits any body part they struck. Even more ironic, I suppose, is that the heyday of the "Wild West" actually lasted only a decade or so during the period immediately after the end of the American Civil War, from about 1865–1875.

Nevertheless, these two periods—the chivalric knight of the medieval era and the cowboy-gunfighter of the American West—even though totally fictive as they are portrayed, are for our purposes useful to consider because they are quite revealing in a couple of ways. For one thing, the myth of the knight served to encourage young men to set out on the crusades to defeat the Muslim "infidels" who had taken over the Holy Land. And the fanciful and fictional Wild West heroes of the dime novels inspired young Americans to strike out with glee for Europe to participate in World War I, the "War to End All Wars."

THE MINDSET OF THE HERO

I do not wish to characterize the period of youth and maturation as totally consumed by heroic urges, but this does seem to be the time when most young men go off to war and end up as nameless statistics on the spreadsheets of generals who view fighting in terms of tactics and strategies instead of human lives with names and families. They still promulgate the same old lies to entice young men to give their all for their country so that parents may salve their eternal grief with the consolation that their son (or daughter) gave his or her life doing what he or she loved most, or so they sometimes say in the tasteless and unfeeling interviews for local television programs: "How do you feel about your young son being blown up by an improvised explosive device, Mr. and Mrs. Jones?"

But before we proceed to the next part of our study of death according to the successive stages in our life, I think it well worthwhile to examine two distinct mindsets that typify two entirely different sorts of heroes and heroines, each of which embodies distinct attitudes about this rite of passage from childhood into the real world of hard choices.

In light of the axioms, ironies, and absurdities associated with heroism as we have thus far discussed it, especially the common fate of all heroes and heroic endeavors, we might well ponder exactly what motivates one to cast aside all care and apparent self-interest to make the ultimate sacrifice. This theme is especially curious when we study those who do not have some certitude about any sort of continuity of self after death nor any explicit expectations that, if there is an afterlife, they will be rewarded for their sacrifice.

The obvious response is that the Aristotelian Golden Mean (discovering the path of moderation between the extremes of possible responses) still holds true today. For example, true courage is a path of action somewhere between the extremes of cowardice and foolhardiness. From this point of view, a canon of law or a handbook of rules cannot suffice us. We are constantly involved in discerning the point of balance. Courage is thus always a matter of judgment in any given situation, not a reflex, not a simple response. Even so, the heroic choice often requires instantaneous or reflexive responses of us.

This dilemma brings us to yet another question regarding heroism in relation to death: Is true heroism or courage being unafraid as we undertake some perilous course of action, or is true heroism or courage deciding to act in spite of being afraid? We have already cited a passage in which Bahá'u'lláh says that "whatever decreaseth fear increaseth courage" (*Epistle to the Son of the Wolf*, p. 32).

And yet, implicit in that passage is that various forms of knowledge decrease fear. In particular, we might infer that Bahá'u'lláh is alluding to the knowledge of the continuity of our lives in the spiritual realm beyond this life. Consequently, we might well endanger our lives for a worthy cause, knowing that our objective in this life is to prepare ourselves for further development beyond our physical experience.

This is a worthy question with which to probe our mental images of heroes and heroism. Do those heroic figures in legend and popular culture act against self-interest because they have a vision of something more encompassing and more important than their individual existence? Or are these heroic figures simply uncaring and antisocial misfits who have nothing to lose? There is a significant difference between the two motives.

While we cannot go back in history to interview these figures about what motivated them to perform their sacrificial actions, we can make logical inferences about most. Achilles may have wanted fame, but Joan of Arc had a mission that went beyond whatever personal attention and acclaim she received or anticipated receiving after being burned at the stake. Certainly we presume the same sense of purpose motivates many who die in battle to protect the rights of others, if preceding the battle the soldier had given careful consideration to the reasons for going to war.

But there is a mindset that can be acquired or induced that works mostly along the lines of foolhardiness, a sort of addiction to the adrenaline rush that comes with pitting our will against the will of another, a sense of strength and power derived from mob mentality. The collective will of onlookers or of fellow participants in an action can have immense power over our own will and can imbue us with the capacity to perform amazing acts of prowess, for good or for ill.

Like so many, I have personally experienced this contagious sort of mindset primarily through participation in sports, both as a participant and as a spectator. I first encountered the remarkable effects of this phenomenon in football training, then later in martial arts, and even later in life vicariously through watching sports and also as a professor of literature.

My first epiphany about the internal effects of the external collective mentality occurred at high school football practice. We used to have a drill for us running backs, who usually also played the defensive position of linebacker. Consequently, the drill was designed to make us proficient in running "through" someone on the offense, and capable of stopping someone trying to run "through" us on defense.

The drill was simple enough. Two blocking bags were placed about five feet apart. These were set up as the boundaries. We would then line up two at a time facing each other about seven feet apart. The coach would blow his whistle as he pitched the ball to the runner, and the two players would explode forward and crash together.

The running back would try to power through the tackler, while the tackler was determined to stop the runner in his tracks. Any gain was a slight victory for the runner and a bit of defeat for the defender. If the defender could drive the runner backward, he could feel heroic for the rest of the day. Likewise, if the runner could break free and stay on his feet, he could replay that sensation for days to come.

Because the bags as boundaries were so close together, it was impossible for the runner to go around the tackler, so there was very little finesse required. There were some important laws of physics involved. Whoever plunged ahead harder using his head as a weapon usually won. And whoever hit lower also usually won, because the runner would knock the legs out from under the defender, or the defender would submarine the forward progress of the runner.

To a disinterested observer, this exercise would have seemed pretty mindless and pointless. But it wasn't. In one short afternoon I still can recall, this exercise marked a turning point in my life, as a runner, as a defender, and as a human being.

I was facing a young man who was everything a running back should be—large, muscular, and fast. But for some reason, I sensed in his body language that he did not like this drill, that he actually did not want to lower his body and run headlong into something that was not going to move or that might even do him harm. I realized that it was not a matter of statistics or even of strategy in any refined sense. It was my will versus his will, and I knew I could muster more determination than he could because I could detect some increment of fear emanating from his manner.

I don't recall whether it was in his facial expression, or the way he ran when he encountered an opposing player, but I suddenly knew I could run into him as hard as I wanted. I realized that whatever the laws of physics might dictate should happen in this encounter (that he should probably win because he was larger or stronger than I) could be quickly undone by the sheer power of will on my part.

From that afternoon forward, I never flinched. From then on, it didn't matter whether or not I sensed fear from the opposing player. I actually looked forward to these drills. I relished the challenge. I took joy in the crash, knowing that the worst that could possibly happen to me was a stalemate. And when I encountered someone else who had acquired this same mindset, the challenge was all the more joyful, because in my own mind I had become convinced that no one could muster more willpower than I could.

This same attitude, or "zone" as I sometimes thought of it, worked equally well when at age thirty-five I began the practice of martial arts, eventually becoming a fifth degree black belt master. I found that what I loved most was sparring (free fighting) because I could once again draw on the resources from this secret storehouse of will.

I think that's why you see these athletes hug each other after a difficult match. They are members of this clan, the society of willful ones who can tap into the resources of sheer willpower. If by chance we would come up against someone who also knew this secret, then that was best of all because after every encounter, you would smile at each other and pat each other on the back knowing that neither one would win but neither one would ever give up. Stalemate was a mutual victory, a sense of belonging to a clandestine society.

This lesson, this realization that I could overpower almost any opponent by force of will, remains with me today, even though it has almost gotten me killed on occasion. It is a principle that goes something like this: "I am willing to accept and respond to anything you can do to me."

HEROIC WILL IN FICTION

I am not at all sure that this "zone," or determination to outdo an opponent, has one iota to do with true courage—it may not. In sports or other activities that can also create this highly competitive mindset, such as high finance, it can ruin you. But the principle can be seen in two extremely well-known works of American fiction that help us gain some insight into this phenomenon. One is a novel by Stephen Crane and the other is a short story by Ernest Hemingway. In fact, Hemingway acknowledged his indebtedness to Crane for both this point of view about heroism and Crane's sparse style. This theme of heroism and fear in relation to death was also stated succinctly by William Faulkner in his acceptance speech for the Nobel Prize for literature when he said that "the basest thing of all is to be afraid" and that every poet needs to express this, or else his words are hollow.

Crane uses the knowledge of this internal awakening as the theme and turning point in his brief and powerful novel *The Red Badge of Courage*. The setting is the Civil War in mid-nineteenth-century America. A nineteen-year-old private named Henry Fleming first flees when his battalion of Union soldiers is attacked by a screaming line of charging Confederate soldiers who, to Fleming, seem unstoppable because they fling themselves forward apparently totally oblivious to fear.

Fleming's first wound, or "badge" of courage, occurs accidently when he is butted on the head by a fleeing soldier. Fleming is carried to the rear with the other "wounded" soldiers because it is assumed he has been grazed by a bullet. But as he sits among these truly brave men who discuss the battle and who are worthy of their "badge," Fleming becomes transformed by their camaraderie and feels honored to be considered one among them. Their heroism, their attitude, is infectious and addictive to the impressionable young soldier.

From this point on, Fleming determines to be deserving of the distinction of belonging to those who have earned their badge of courage. His newfound grit and determination, amplified by the adrenalin rush of battle, help impel him to cast aside all self-interest and plunge headlong into the fray as heroic leader of the battalion. He has become fearless, impervious to injury, or even to death itself. He leads the charge while holding the colors as he runs toward the Confederate lines.

Hemingway employs this exact same theme so often that his "code heroes" are somewhat predictable, but not the variety of his artful telling of their stories. In perhaps his simplest and most straightforward portrayal of this transformation from coward (or "normal" person) to hero (or "foolhardy" one), Hemingway describes the ironic conversion of an upper-class sports hunter on an African safari.

Francis MacComber has come to Africa with his domineering and condescending wife who, aware of her husband's cowardice, has no respect for him whatsoever. After having fled in fear when the hunting party is charged by a wounded lion, the humiliated husband, Francis MacComber (notice the feminine name) talks one evening with the professional hunter and guide, Robert Wilson, who, MacComber is aware, has already had an affair with Margot, MacComber's wife.

Unashamedly, MacComber inquires about courage, hunting, and life in general. He is so candid about his fear that Wilson is at first taken aback and embarrassed. But quickly the savvy hunter finds himself attracted to MacComber's simple honesty about his fears. In particular Wilson is won over by MacComber's sincere desire to change, to overcome his fear and become courageous. Once he has helped MacComber realize that he can face down his fear, Wilson states axiomatically what is the essential verity of the story insofar as heroism is concerned: "Worst one can do is kill you."

This is the ultimate axiom about heroism and life that Hemingway seems to offer—that true heroism can be acquired only after we have come to terms with our own mortality, only after we have conquered the fear of death. Or stated somewhat more philosophically, once a person is willing to accept the worst possible outcome of any given situation, then he or she has the potential to overcome all fear.

It is precisely in this sense that courage and heroism, when it is something other than fanaticism fueled by ignorance and cheering companions (mob mentality), is not the absence of fear, but rather the willful suppression of fear with a larger dose of resolve and acquiescence to the moment. It is only in this sense, Hemingway might argue, that heroism can become a virtue and not foolhardiness—the extent to which the determination, whether carefully considered or as instant reflex, prevails. What is not always apparent with the Hemingway hero is whether or not there lurks as motive force behind the machismo something worth defending, a cause or integrating principle that supersedes the value of being considered heroic.

Nevertheless, it is in this sense that the title takes its full meaning, that between this conversation with Wilson and the moment when MacComber is accidentally killed by his wife (or possibly on purpose, according to Wilson), that MacComber is truly happy. For the first time in his life, we are to infer, MacComber is his own man because he has become fearless.

Unfortunately, like most Hemingway heroes, this special perspective is portrayed as mostly understood by men, though Hemingway does have some heroic women in his works. But rarely do men and women share this existential delight together, except for a moment or so in *For Whom the Bell Tolls*. Possibly, aside from Hemingway's avoidance of any enduring consolation to life, this rejection of some ultimately felicitous or enduring love of another is itself "unmanly," but allowing one's self to be held captive by love of another suddenly nullifies the ability to plunge fearlessly headlong into the fray. When there is hope or something tangible to live for, the code of heroism is no longer so mathematic, or so simple.

UNSUNG HEROIC CHOICES

I suppose the point I am getting at with regard to fear in relation to death is that heroism, when considered in the light of reason rather than in the darkness of passion and machismo, is not becoming impervious to fear, at least, not that alone. Heroism in truth implies acting in spite of fear precisely because there is a cause, a set of values, an integrating principle that we consider more abiding and important than our lives as individuals. For even as Socrates notes that the unexamined life is not worth living, so we might say that mindless heroism is not worth having.

The concept of heroism as the willingness to risk one's life to advance the well-being of another or for the attainment of some lofty objective is perhaps the definition most profoundly and commonly paraded before us on a daily basis by every mother (or father) who is dedicated to advancing human progress. Without such personal sacrifice or willingness to devote ourselves to something greater than ourselves, we are mostly lost, and the progress of the human body politic as a whole will cease.

This choice, the choice to devote ourselves to the advancement of civilization, while not as public or as heralded as Achilles' choice, is certainly more heroic over time, requiring as it does not a single grandiose gesture or one blinding flash of bravado, but a daily reassertion of the noblest of routines that poet Robert Hayden aptly characterized as "love's austere and lonely offices," where there is no obvious resolution to problems, no single decision that suffices, but a daily rededication to unconditional love expressed in almost imperceptible increments of self-sacrifice.

120

Of course the term "unsung" implies a hero whose choices are made in private, whose sacrifice is not celebrated or "sung about" as are the exploits of tribal heroes that are celebrated in verse and song around the hearth. Such a "private" hero is wonderfully depicted by Faulkner in his most often anthologized short story "Barn Burning." In this fictional work, Faulkner implicitly "sings" the praises of a young boy whose courage is demonstrated by private choice to defy all he has been taught solely because he has within a sense of justice that outweighs the bonds of familial loyalty.

The boy is Sarty, the son of a vicious, vengeful, and depraved barn burner, Abner Snopes. For years, the story implies, Sarty has had to endure moving with his family (the nameless brother is a crucial figure in this) from town to town as tenant farmers. But unlike his brother, who has inherited or chosen to become complicit in Abner's obsession, Sarty has an inner sense of justice coupled with a dream of a life characterized by dignity and nobility.

While Sarty's concept of nobility is confirmed by his glimpse into the life of the family landlord, Major de Spain who is a refined gentleman living in an elegant home, it is clear from the way Faulkner has created this microcosm that the vision of virtue in Sarty is a thing of the spirit, not something he has acquired from "outside" influence. Clearly Faulkner intends to debunk the notion that we are merely the sum total of all those influences that have forged us.

Consequently, when Sarty realizes that once again his father is going to strike out without motive at a world he cannot have—or chooses not to strive to attain—by burning the barn of the aristocratic de Spain, Sarty determines he will no longer remain passive and silent. Even though he knows on some level that what he is about to do will effectively sever his relationship with his father and his family, Sarty runs ahead in the night and warns de Spain of Abner's intentions. Afterward, he flees frantically down a dirt road into the darkness until he hears the distant shots from a rifle. He knows immediately what has happened:

> He went on down the hill, toward the dark woods within which the liquid silver voices of the birds, called unceasing—the rapid and urgent beating of the urgent and quiring heart of the late spring night. He did not look back.[3]

As we mentioned, Faulkner said succinctly in his Nobel Prize acceptance speech that "the basest thing of all is to be afraid," but out of context, this phrase might seem to imply that the corollary of this axiom is the Hemingway code—that heroism is simply a state of being fearless. However, Faulkner's heroism as portrayed in this story is something quite different from the mere willingness to risk life and limb. Sarty's happiness, if it ever comes, will not be so short-lived as that of MacComber, and his heroism has been undertaken for the sake of a principle, not as an end in itself. And in this distinction we infer as well the difference between a heroism that is a sort of existential rush, like that of the athletic fearlessness I depicted as characteristic of my own experience, and heroism that is based on devotion to an abstract principle, to the belief in virtue as a viable force in the universe and not merely a social construct fabricated to uphold equally artificial norms.

It is precisely in this context that Faulkner has implied that true heroism involves a decision to risk life and limb for a cause that has inherent value, and further, that this value must derive from time-tested ideals, human virtues without which art itself is mere ornamentation:

---

3. William Faulkner, "Barn Burning," *The Norton Anthology of American Literature,* 6th edition, Volume D (New York: W. W. Norton, 2003), p. 1803.

Our tragedy today is a general and universal physical fear so long sustained by now that we can even bear it. There are no longer problems of the spirit. There is only the question: When will I be blown up? Because of this, the young man or woman writing today has forgotten the problems of the human heart in conflict with itself which alone can make good writing because only that is worth writing about, worth the agony and the sweat.

He must learn them again. He must teach himself that the basest of all things is to be afraid; and, teaching himself that, forget it forever, leaving no room in his workshop for anything but the old verities and truths of the heart, the old universal truths lacking which any story is ephemeral and doomed—love and honor and pity and pride and compassion and sacrifice. Until he does so, he labors under a curse. He writes not of love but of lust, of defeats in which nobody loses anything of value, of victories without hope and, worst of all, without pity or compassion. His griefs grieve on no universal bones, leaving no scars. He writes not of the heart but of the glands.[4]

---

4. William Faulkner, "Nobel Prize Award Speech," *The Literature of the South*, eds. Beatty, et al (New York: Scott, Foresman & Company, 1952), p. 1060.

7

JUMPING TRAIN
IN NASHVILLE

Two roads diverged in a wood, and I—
I took the one less traveled by,
And that has made all the difference.
> —Robert Frost, "The Road Not Taken"

Perhaps it's different now, but when I was ending my days in high school, I knew I would then go to college, after which I would get a job, marry, have children, get a house (with an appropriate mortgage), a car, eventually a nicer house and better car, in time have grandchildren, retire, and die. There might be some minor variations in the sequence, but this was basically life as it had been designed by someone I had neither met nor questioned.

The sense of this paradigm was not that I had alternatives, other than the choices I made about which college, what sort of job, which wife, how many children, what city I would live in, how nice of a house I could afford, and so on. This was the "good life" for middle-class white America. Those of us privileged enough to participate in it did not dare to think we might question its validity. Our parents modeled it, the media hyped it, and President Eisenhower played golf to reassure us that this was the way things should be and that there was really nothing to worry about.

The Cold War was a theoretical game played out by people we did not know, and the frenzy to build bomb shelters soon faded over time as we all were able to set aside (or store away inside) the fear of imminent nuclear holocaust—we kept that secret snugly tucked away in some segment of our brain we rarely visited.

BOARDING THE WHITE MIDDLE-CLASS TRAIN

The entire scenario for all our lives was preplanned as if we had boarded this sleek train early in life, before we were able to make a decision about whether or not we wanted to get on. No one remembered getting on it, and certainly none of us (male or female) remembered deciding to buy a ticket. And though this train rumbled by a multitude of important mile-markers along the track (the senior prom, graduation, college, another senior prom, another graduation), it never stopped or even slowed down much, except for life-threatening emergencies and group photographs.

If we jumped off the train, or did not get back on at one of the rest stops or photo ops, we suddenly found ourselves among strangers. It seems that one of the ideas of riding this train was that we would all be the same age and pass all the milestones together, even to the "end of the line" (a wonderfully appropriate song by the Traveling Wilburys). For example, my parents ended up in Atlanta with several of their best friends from Greensboro. It seems that in the world of business, Atlanta was the next stop (or mile-marker) after Greensboro. Two couples that were Greensboro friends ended up on the same street.

It's not that there weren't *any* choices. There were. At the station where we boarded the train after high school, we could pick our destination and climb aboard the train heading for the college we had chosen, a choice that would be determined by how well we had done in school, how well we did on our SATs, how much money our parents had, and where our friends were going.

Once in college for a year or so, we would divide up into groups according to our chosen "major"—implicitly a vocation we would follow the rest of our lives—and get on that train. We were required to make this second choice at eighteen or nineteen, even though few of us had enough life experience to make a meaningful decision, certainly not one that would determine what we would like to be doing every day for the rest of our lives.

After this college train reached the end of the line at graduation, we were then expected to get on the marriage train by choosing the best available husband or wife, and so we did. It mattered little whether or not we were ready to choose someone with whom we wished to spend the rest of our lives. The choice was not whether or not to get on board. All the signs seem to say that's what we should do, so we did it.

And thus did our lives rumble along, choice by choice, train by train. We boarded the job choice train, the city choice train, the house choice train, the children choice train. In due course we found ourselves quite a distance from where we had boarded and among only a handful of those friends who had made the same choices. In fact, when we disembarked, many of us found ourselves among strangers in a strange land, suddenly not really sure how we had managed to get so far away from home so quickly and, once we paused to scan the countryside, not totally sure we wanted to be there at all.

But certainly we had invested too much time and energy to get to this destination to even consider going back, even if we could figure out how to retrace all the various lines we had taken to get where we were. It would be like getting plopped down in a metro station and beholding a spaghetti-like map with a red dot saying "You are here!" and then trying to find amid the maze of stations and lines where home really was, where you had gotten on board. It would just be too much trouble, and besides, as Lady Macbeth says, "What's done cannot be undone."[5]

Or could it? Here we were, having accomplished by age thirty or so what had taken our parents a lifetime to achieve because we knew exactly what choices were available to us, when to get on board, and what subsequent choices would then be required of us. What was more, we did not have to worry about the Great Depression or a world war. Chronologically, the very best of our lives lay before us, and yet there were no more signs, no more trains to board. We had reached the end of the line.

So what did we do? What could we do? We had no governing principle, no shared philosophy except the American Dream. Most of us divided up the children, the furniture, the pots and pans, the cars, and climbed onboard another train heading back in the general direction from which we had come. We would try a do-over. We would make the whole trip again, only this time we would make more careful choices. This time we would do it all correctly because, after some group therapy, we had determined that the whole problem had been our failure to find a good fit for us in our choice of vocation or spouse. This time we would choose what we really wanted to do instead of what had seemed like a neat idea when we were still teenagers.

It never occurred to us that there could be something wrong with the white-American middle-class dream itself. After all, it was time-tested! It was touted by the best minds of the century! We had just not done it properly, that was all!

JUMPING TRAIN IN NASHVILLE

My train went by way of a small university, Vanderbilt University in Nashville, Tennessee. It was a very fine small college my brother had

---

5. Act V, scene i, line 68.

attended. I chose that train partly because my brother had attended, partly because many of my fellow high school friends were going there, and partly because it was near Franklin, Tennessee, where my father had grown up and where my uncle, aunt, and cousins lived.

My roots there, in fact, went back more than a century. My grandfather had been in the first graduating class at Vanderbilt Medical School in 1875. My great-grandfather had fought in the most vicious battles of the Civil War at Chickamauga, Kennesaw Mountain, Atlanta, Franklin, and finally Nashville. Actually, the very road on which I drove back and forth from Atlanta to Nashville in my 1950 Ford, U.S. Highway 41 (in the days before expressways), was the same path my great-grandfather had walked as his company fought retreating battles against Sherman's army.

Sometimes along the way I would stop at the battlefield memorials and try to imagine what he had experienced, because he had not been a youth going off to defend the honor of the Confederacy. He was a thirty-six-year-old farmer with a wife and three children. He was sensitive to death and carnage, and he described in graphic detail in eloquent letters sent home to his wife Mary Jane what he was going through.

I read those letters. In time I would write a series of poems about what I imagined he might have felt at the end of his tour of duty, which ended up in what was statistically one of the bloodiest battles of the war, and was fought near his own homestead close to Franklin. But my poems underestimated the man. Ironically, one poem is called "Choosing," and it assumes that he finally could take no more. It assumes (as had my relatives, his heirs) that being but miles from his farm and having experienced with his fellow soldiers heinous decisions made by the obdurate, proud, and deluded General Hood (who ended up virtually demolishing the entire army he commanded), that he would have done the sensible thing and deserted to go protect his "little family," as he called them.

It was decades later with the benefit of computer research about his company that I discovered he was discharged two battles later at Murfreesboro along with most of the remnants of Hood's mutilated army. General Hood himself had been conveniently "retired" to his home in Louisiana to write his memoirs. My great-grandfather had been more courageous and more dutiful than any of us had imagined.

I guess my point is that part of my education at Vanderbilt was realizing the fundamental nobility of the ancestry from which I had descended. Not that one's preferences or character are predetermined by such forces, but we can be inspired and sustained by them if we wish to be, and I have always chosen to be affected by them because I was blessed to have extremely fine forebears to portray for me what real nobility looks like, sounds like, and lives like. Their actions helped set the bar for me, and I did not want to betray their standards or besmirch the good name they had established, even if it were a repute known only by kinfolk.

It was while becoming educated to this inheritance that I realized how the same courage to choose, which was diffused through my grandfather John William Hatcher— a doctor, farmer, and lay Methodist minister—and then through my dad with his lifelong loyalty to a corporate entity, was now mine to carry on. Only, like Sarty in Faulkner's story, my vision of the noble choice might not be to follow the "correct" thing as defined for me by inheritance, not in Godless and guideless times, which I had long since determined my age to be.

I remember vividly going with my mom to pick up my dad at work—we would never have considered having two cars. And I watched him finishing up some paperwork, his glass-encased cubical of an office as clean and orderly as an operating room. It was the end of an eight-hour work day, and he looked as well-kempt in his suit and tie, as refined and respectable as when he had left the house at seven that morning. As manager of the Atlanta Branch office of the

Retail Credit Company (now Equifax), he commanded appropriate respect from "his men," as he called the investigators who worked for him.

He slipped into his overcoat, put on his hat, picked up his leather briefcase, and strode easily toward the door like a general reviewing his troops. "Hold 'em in the road, men," he would say. And every one of them would immediately look up from what they were doing as if they were taking a snapshot of that handsome, tall, well-dressed emblem of fairness and caring, and respond in kind: "Same to you, Mr. Hatcher!"

"Dad," I said as we walked the marbled hall to the car one afternoon, "I could never do that."

"Do what, son?"

"Work in an office all day like that. I don't think I could stand it."

Ultimately, as upper management reduced his funds to hire capable investigators and as succeeding decades of investigators, no longer war veterans happy to be working for such a man, were increasingly illiterate, he would end up spending more and more of his Saturdays and then his Sundays rewriting what they were supposed to have done. With the help and insistence of Mom, Bill, and me, he jumped from the career train at sixty-three.

He took early retirement rather than suffer the indignities that were incrementally being heaped upon him. He salvaged what was left of his life after thirty-six years with "the company." He received a beautiful pen set, a pair of binoculars, and his old office desk—actually more than I received upon my own retirement after thirty-nine years at the university.

My point is that he had originally made a choice based on one context, an environment of loyalty and fellowship. But even as Arthur Miller implies about the changed values of America in *Death of a Salesman*, the environment that my father had first entered had mutated so gradually that it took the three of us to wake him up to the reality of what had become of his "good life."

But he was the one who finally had the courage to make another choice, to get off the train and spend his remaining years, his "golden" years, taking walks and trips with my mom, visiting the grandchildren, going to Europe. This was the happiest period of his life so far as I had known. He read, watched sports, played bridge, and mowed the lawn. He had earned this respite, this time of reflection and ease. This, too, was part of the paradigm of the "good life."

And so it was that during my sophomore year at Vanderbilt I found within myself a sudden desire to jump from the train even as it sped its way toward the next milestone. I do not wish to catalog the details of my leap of faith from that train speeding toward the American dream of the "good life"—this is not about me, nor do I consider what I did any remarkable sign of heroism or valor. As I recall it, I simply could not tolerate any other course of action. The train ride had frankly become all too predictable, the passengers all too much alike, and the destination too certain and unsatisfying. At the time I called it "tunnel vision," not knowing that this was a medical condition in which peripheral vision is lost. For me it represented the ability to see all the way to the end of a sequence of events—namely, my life—and not being in the least excited by what I saw. Indeed, what I saw was more terrifying than death itself.

Of course, the destination of anyone's life is always death, but the stuff in between now and then has always been for me most exciting and fruitful when I am not aware of what's coming next. It's especially nice to think that there are no limitations on what we can achieve or become. Whereas the journey and destination I saw at the end of my "tunnel" portended a stagnant and wrenchingly pitiful decline, like the beaming light of the engine disappearing into the dark. As a young man in my early twenties, I could predict—no, I could actually envision very precisely—the rest of my life.

I still find it fascinating that thinkers and writers of the late nineteenth century—James, Ibsen, Tolstoy—had already anticipated the very syndrome I was just beginning to grasp, the dreaded plague of middleclass materialist mentality. Part of what inspired me to take the leap was a 1903 novella by Henry James called *The Beast in the Jungle*.

The plot of the story is fundamentally a parable about our tendency to want fate to shape our lives for us rather than make hard choices. The central character, John Marcher, withholds himself from making any important decisions, the most obvious of which is not responding to the love of May, a woman who respects John and even becomes enmeshed in his expectation of some impending transformative event that he is certain will determine his destiny. The resolution of the story is hardly consoling, nor is it meant to be. As with any parable, the analogy is everything.

The great "beast in the jungle" that John is sure lies in wait to alter his life, the spectacular distinction that will mark his life as a journey unlike that of any ordinary soul, is that he throws away his entire life, including the love of May, based on his egoistic conviction that fate has in store for him some special role to play, even though, as it turns out, destiny couldn't care less about him. Indeed, the defining attribute of his life is that it has no defining attribute! Obviously the implication of the parable is that only by assuming responsibility for forging something out of his life could Marcher have become a truly remarkable individual.

As I noted, James's observation about this characteristic passivity on the part of the "modern" American middleclass mentality is replicated by many other fine authors of the time, but their observations, which might have served as forewarnings, did not connect with that many people at the time. The pathology of this syndrome is not solely, or even most significantly, the requirement that one set aside or forestall existential delight to nurture future fulfillment. At the heart of the perilous American dream is the very idea that material comfort, order, decorum, and stability are sufficient goals for our brief lives. But while John Marcher realizes his mistake too late to change anything, Nora, the heroine in Ibsen's *A Doll's House*, seems to discover her mistake in time to salvage herself. This play set in Norway, also a sort of morality play about middleclass life, ends with her abandoning what her husband Torvald, an officer at a bank, believes to be their perfect life.

While it could be argued the play is less a parable and more a story of carefully fashioned individual characters, the various occasions in the play for dialogue about women's rights and their roles in middleclass Norway clearly indicate that as shallow and flawed as Torvald might be, his dream of the "good life" represents a social norm, not merely his private take on the imperatives essential for success and happiness.

Of course, many have difficulty seeing Nora as being altruistic in her motives or actions to "get off the train" of expectations. She leaves behind her children and determines that before she can be a real mother, she must first become a complete person in her own right. In other words, the logic of her conclusion and subsequent action is somewhat undermined by what we might consider an overreaction to her former submissive and compliant role as the model wife in an artificial society.

Behind the scenes she has been the source of stability that has enabled Torvald's illusion to subsist. She has been an "enabler." Furthermore, as audience we are never privy to his full recognition of how inauthentic and fragile his dream of life actually has been, assuming he ever achieves such an epiphany. Still, Ibsen's main theme, it would seem, is perfectly clear—that to accept and even to facilitate social expectations of what is correct, proper, and fulfilling is to incur the punishment of being a slave to decisions that are not our own and of receiving as our only reward the public perception of having been proper and compliant.

Ibsen's alternative, one infers, would be to live a life of considered judgments, of freely chosen paths, all coordinated by some meaningful integrating principle, a principle that is sadly lacking in the lives of these characters as well as in the middleclass dream of material comfort and leisure.

I suppose for me the most powerful portrayal of this illusion of a materialist system of values is Tolstoy's disturbingly powerful novella *The Death of Ivan Ilych*. The work begins as a very pointed disdain of bourgeois mentality. Ivan's greatest aspiration, like that of Torvald, is to have a life that is mildly successful but uneventful.

The phrase from the work that captures succinctly Tolstoy's version of the "good life" occurs after Ivan has attained a sufficient level of success so that "on the whole his life ran its course as he believed life should do: easily, pleasantly, and decorously." There is no passion, no love, no authentic bond between Ivan and his wife. There is no intimacy or expressions of affection between him and his children. But into the path of this uneventful train ride, Tolstoy flips a switch that derails the entire journey.

Ivan injures himself when he falls while hanging curtains in his new middleclass home. Over time, the injury becomes gradually more painful and debilitating. The rest of the novella is Tolstoy's masterful and terrifying depiction of dying. For no reason he can discern, Ivan becomes cursed to die a slow, agonizingly painful, and lonely death that the reader must also endure. As the rest of his family indulges itself in the life Ivan has wrought for them, he deteriorates behind the scenes, more a nuisance than a source of grief to his desensitized family. Only a lowly servant, Gerasim, seems to care or to be capable of providing some degree of comfort and companionship for Ivan.

It is in his dying and his evolving relationship with Gerasim that Ivan comes to discern the artificiality of all he had held most dear— the middleclass family living a middleclass life with no values other than social status and material comfort.

THE SHORT-LIVED AMERICAN DREAM

I can say with a certain degree of conviction and certitude that a good percentage of the post-Depression "baby boomers" met with the same fate I did. We realized about halfway through completing the death-defying train ride that what our parents epitomized as the apex of the American dream was not a dream we had chosen for ourselves, nor was it as complete or sufficient for us as it had been for them.

Not everyone reared in the atmosphere of that frail dream realized the vacuity of this ride. Not all had the sufficiency of material well-being to have the luxury of such reflection. But a good many came early to the conclusion that something was seriously amiss, something that made them leap off the train and try again, or else turn to alcohol or other diversions rather than face the truth that they must start over, must blaze some new trail less traveled by if they were to find some special path of their own, some place where they could explore what special gifts they might possess, and some innovative way to develop those capacities.

For my father there were no goals beyond his American Dream because no one in his family had ever achieved this much. They had lived on a farm and barely survived. He was the trailblazer for this new dream. For him the "good life" was sufficient because he had grown up amid want, difficulty, instability, and uncertainty. He had grown up during the Great Depression, and for him the most daunting threat to society was that someone or some group or ideology might disturb or undo this way of life that he had fought for, had won, and was finally enjoying. He had paid his dues, and he was reaping his appropriate reward.

Like a plot that had reached its climax, the rest was a winding down, like the falling action on the Freytag pyramid, an act of his play that would, in time, end in death, but a death that would come in its own gradualness as it should. And as one by one his Emory classmates, fellow businessmen, members of the church, or his Sigma Chi fraternity brothers met their final destiny, each life was recognized, celebrated, and revered, even as Dad's was when he passed in 1980 at age seventy-six. He died early enough that at his funeral were hundreds of friends, former employees, and colleagues. Devising a eulogy for this fine man was an effortless task, and we all grieved our loss accordingly.

Certainly I grieved and grieved. I melted into a pool of pure anguish, even though I was convinced of the eternality of his existence. But he was so entirely kind and gentle that I did not want him gone, neither him nor his simple dream of life because on some level I also realized that Dad's dream and the dream of his generation was dying with him.

AWAKENING TO AN ALTERNATIVE DREAM

During the summer of my junior year in high school, I was introduced to the notion that there might be a world vision that challenged the one I presently had, which was not one I had spent much time examining. The worldview I had been given while growing up was certainly not hard wired in my brain, since it gradually began to shift as I explored new theories and ideas.

I had been raised in the Methodist church, but the Methodist church, or at least the one I attended, did not insist that I accept or advocate some mindless dogma, at least none that bowled me over with its fanaticism or absurdity. I had since childhood felt closeness to the world of the spirit, to God, and especially to Christ, Who for me was an approachable spiritual presence with Whom I could converse freely. I felt a sense of comfort and companionship with Him as I mulled over His sane and simple advice and examples of right conduct, and at night I would think about His life in the New Testament and commune with His spirit.

After my puerile and needless rebellion against parents, society, and sanity around age fourteen, I made a conscious effort to reform my behavior. The stupidity of my conduct and those with whom I associated was laid bare before me in such a way that I never felt tempted to behave in that way again. Within a few years, I began to conduct myself accordingly, wearing decent clothes, following the rules, and studying.

At sixteen I was elected president of the youth department at St. Mark Methodist Church where we arranged to have philosophical discussions on any number of complex questions, such as whether or not a Nazi might be forgiven if he sincerely believed he was doing the right thing. We also got into more complex theological and doctrinal matters about the station of Christ—whether the Nicene Creed was to be taken literally or not. Was Christ indeed God—were They one and the same essence?

It was about this same time I discovered that my brother, then a pre-ministerial student at Vanderbilt who had been planning to attend Yale Divinity School, was studying the Bahá'í Faith, a religion that, he informed me, asserts that everything Christ said is true and accurate, that Christ was indeed the Messiah, but that there was a more encompassing plan of God that included everything before Christ and everything since.

This "plan" he described as the Bahá'í core belief in progressive revelation, the idea that all the world religions throughout human history are really one religion revealed in progressive and successive stages. I discovered that this religion also confirmed the beliefs I already held—that the essential reality of the human being is the human soul, a spiritual or metaphysical reality, and that the soul continues to exist perpetually after the body's demise.

There was much more, and bit by bit, little by little, I extracted from him the various parts of this belief that I wished to know. He was careful not to explain more than I asked and, still in the process of investigating it for himself, he was likewise vigilant about not imposing these concepts on me. But the logical foundation of this belief system so attracted me that it quickly became my Ockham's razor, my touchstone, my *mizán* or balance with which I weighed all other theories of God, religion, and human history, which, according to Bahá'í belief, is organized by the advent of the successive Prophets or Manifestations of God.

This seed of an idea that had been planted in my brain began gradually to germinate. At first I was barely aware of it, but over time it seemed to appear at every turn. Gradually, I became more seriously challenged by answers it offered to the questions I had long since given up trying to resolve, questions that my Methodist ministers would allude to as "mysteries" of Christ and Christian belief. They would portray these mysterious facets of belief as something to be cherished and marveled at, but not to be understood logically, not to be resolved. In contrast, I considered mysteries to be puzzles that demanded to be solved.

Indeed, I had already arrived at the inescapable conclusion that God was certainly more logical and intelligent than the professional clergy whose very income depended on perpetrating this veil of inscrutability about religious belief. For me nothing transcended logic. This capacity to discover how things work—whether it was my bicycle or the gas engine on my model airplane—was among God's most precious gifts to me.

Not that I had been terribly dissatisfied with what I had been taught until this point. I had accepted the best and discarded all that seemed patently inane, and I had done so without fear of damnation or retribution. Furthermore, prior to the implantation of this new theory of reality in my mind, I had not been frantically searching for answers. I was, for the most part, happily submerged in and tantalized by the joys of youthful passions and material delights, though I had long been aware that the group thing—social clubs, fraternities, "belonging"—was not attractive to me, that I was a "loner," but not in the sense of being a rebel or a hero. I simply enjoyed my own company.

I certainly did not consider myself an intellectual or a recluse. Actually, I was not aware that I was a "loner." I was only aware that I did not much enjoy having others tell me what to do or call the shots in my daily life, and I had always thoroughly enjoyed doing stuff by myself, whether in the woods or in my workshop making model airplanes.

My point is that in no way was I perturbed by or inhibited by the prospect of pursuing something that was not "mainstream" thinking. I found it a joy, not a challenge, to jump off the choice train from time to time, however socially awkward it might have been to some. Possessing this "new theory of everything" that the Bahá'í teachings offered was for me like putting on a new pair of glasses with which I could see reality as it really was instead of "through a glass darkly."[6]

Perhaps a better analogy would be to compare my newfound delight in this theory of the universe and human purpose to the joy and sense of freedom early astronomers experienced when they first encountered the Copernican theory. Imagine what energy was unleashed when these curious minds suddenly found themselves able to set aside the convoluted description of reality that the once useful Ptolemaic theory had become. In its stead they could now set before

6. St. Paul, 1 Corinthians 13:12.

them a theory that resolved all consternation, a lens through which the kaleidoscopic heavens suddenly became logically structured. But even more exciting for them was the fact that this theory became not a conclusion but a platform from which they could ascend to the heights of speculation and study.

Perhaps Copernicus's gift of this new *mizán* (balance) was like giving an eager child a bright light with which to enter a formerly darkened room filled to overflowing with a wonderful array of toys. The scientists who accepted this new perspective felt liberated, empowered, and stimulated. They no longer needed to fear the oppression of traditional perspectives.

This was the gift that learning about the Bahá'í theory of religion and history had on me. At the time I first learned the fundamental tenets of the religion from Bill, I was a member of a discrete group of students selected by the one really good teacher I had in high school. His name was Grady Randolph, and he culled us out of his advanced classes and would periodically invite us to his elegant house for a sit-down dinner and a lengthy dialogue. The young men wore suits and ties, and the ladies wore their best dresses. He was not only educating our minds but also trying to impress upon us social skills and a sense of decency in every respect.

Most of the students who were part of this group were among the brightest in our class, the acknowledged "intellectuals"—I presumed he chose me because I persistently asked challenging questions in class. I certainly did not consider myself an intellectual, but I was eager to present questions to the group, and the very first theory with which I challenged the little discussion group—we called ourselves the "Inquirers"—was the Bahá'í theory of progressive revelation as an explanation for religious and secular history.

I wanted the Bahá'í Faith discussed not to promulgate the religion, but to test it on students who might take an equal delight in examining the Bahá'í theory of history and reality. At this point in my investigation of the Bahá'í theory of everything, I had no vested interest in whether the theories were right or wrong. In fact, after my brother became a member of the Bahá'í Faith and declined his fellowship to Yale, I felt obliged to challenge the Bahá'í viewpoint because I knew my brother would be the last one to act on impulse or to follow some mindless or trendy philosophy. Like me, Bill was not a joiner.

Anyhow, at one of the meetings of the Inquirers, we learned that a group advocating world peace and world unity was coming to town, a group called "Moral Rearmament." They were giving open invitations to see a musical play they were putting on, which had great production value and fine singers and actors. One of the members would then team up with each of us after the performance. We would then go to a restaurant for a conversation in which they would try to convince us to join their movement.

It was by no means a subversive group, nor was their invitation to join particularly obnoxious or overbearing. It was not menacing, not a cult, and not really political. MRA, as it was then known, had its beginning as a spinoff from the religiously oriented Oxford Group begun in 1938. Another spinoff from the same Oxford Group was Alcoholics Anonymous. But at the heart of the MRA movement, its integrating principle, was the advocacy of global peace through moral reformation one individual at a time. And at the heart of this reformation of character were what it called the Four Absolutes. These four principles consisted of practicing absolute honesty, absolute purity, absolute unselfishness, and absolute love.

The group has since changed its name to Initiatives of Change and now funnels its funds and energies into supporting the UN and other global agencies working for international peace and cooperation. But at the time I saw the play and spoke to one of its members (1957), their objective was to go from city to city throughout the world performing this very moving play, a sort of modern morality play, and then to invite those who attended to join their group by having members separate the individual attendees, pair them with an MRA spokesperson, and give them the MRA pitch.

My "teacher" was a very amicable English gentleman with whom I had a lengthy and valuable dialogue, valuable to me primarily because the group shared the Bahá'í goals of world peace and world cooperation through moral transformation of the citizens of the world. It also was similar in openly advocating abolition of prejudice and the establishment of racial unity and accord. Here was yet another opportunity for me to test the Bahá'í theory of reality and its proposed solutions to world problems.

At first, I admittedly toyed with my MRA representative with his theory of "absolutes" as a kitten might bat around a ball of yarn. "Would you tell your best friend if his wife were cheating on him? Would you be absolutely honest?"

"No," he responded. "Being absolutely honest does not mean you are mandated to say everything you know, but what you say should always be the truth."

"Even if the truth is devastating to someone else, even if the truth may cause great pain and anguish?"

"Well . . ."

And so it went for a half hour or so until I asked him how MRA proposed resolving world crises and bringing about unity and accord, besides exhorting people to be good. His response was that they were going about trying to get as many people as they could to join, and that, so far as I understood it, was all they had.

I questioned the logistics of this, especially because I, for example, at age seventeen could hardly be expected to give up my schooling, nor did I have the funds to travel around watching the same play every night and talking to strangers about doing the same thing.

But it was his desire to be "absolutely honest" that I wanted to draw on. So for the next hour or I asked him to honestly respond to the Bahá'í solution to the same problems MRA was addressing. I proceeded to set forth for him the Bahá'í theory of reality and the Bahá'í blueprint for establishing a world commonwealth of nations. I articulated as best I could the essential components of this process: the establishment of universal compulsory education, the establishment of a universal auxiliary language, the establishment of a universal currency and system of weights and measures, the establishment of a system of universal suffrage based on an election process in which there were no parties, no nominations, no electioneering, but secret ballot and election by plurality vote. I went on to describe the underlying principles of unity of the races and religions, the abolition of all prejudice, the recognition of the essential equality of men and women, the unity of science and religion, the theory that all religions proceed from God with a single mission—the progressive education and transformation of the human body politic into a single global community.

Since he knew I was not a Bahá'í and was merely pitting one theory against another, he did not question my motives. I was asking him as a clearly intelligent and upright individual attempting to be "absolutely honest" if he would tell me in all honesty which theory or which approach to accomplishing the same fundamental goal would likely be the most efficacious in accomplishing this objective. In particular, I asked him which path would be most propitious for someone like myself wanting to pursue ancillary goals—getting a job, having a family, having children.

His "absolutely" honest answer was that the Bahá'í Faith seemed to him to have a better chance of succeeding in this objective. But more important to me personally was that he acknowledged that he could find no logical flaw in the fundamental beliefs and principles that the Bahá'í Faith professed.

THE TRAIN BACK TO NASHVILLE

I have no clue what course this very fine man's life took after our encounter. I may have unintentionally planted in his brain the same seed that was beginning to sprout in mine. Over the next two years, the heart of my intellectual and spiritual life was focused on this experiment.

If proselytes from a religion came to the door, I invited them in to see if they could refute this concept or offer something better. I did the same with the various ministers associated with St. Mark Methodist Church.

When I got to Vanderbilt the following year, I did the same. In my history seminar my semester report was on the Bahá'í theory of history. In my literature class, I wrote a paper comparing the cynical and frightening image in Yeats' "The Second Coming" with the Bahá'í notion of the Second Coming and the End Days as something propitious, as a coming of age of humankind as opposed to any concept of the end of time. With my friends and companions I would do the same, not to teach or preach or vindicate, but to probe, to test, to challenge this theory of reality.

The more I pursued this goal, the more I became personally invested in the answer for one very obvious reason. If this theory of reality was correct, I could hardly reject it. I could not simply acknowledge its validity without becoming involved in the course of action it offered as a means for bringing about the divine intentions God had devised for the age in which I lived. There was no logical alternative. However, if there were some logical flaw or some misrepresentation in the Bahá'í religion in either its theories or in its practices, I would naturally be obliged to help my brother discover the error in this path he had chosen.

Halfway through my sophomore year at Vanderbilt, I jumped the train. Effectively I had already made the leap, but I was simply holding in abeyance my total disembarkation until I received some sign, some crucial point when the train was sufficiently noisome, its passengers sufficiently obnoxious, or my discomfiture finally too intolerable to endure.

During the fall of my sophomore year, I began to feel the weight of my own status as a nonentity. Without realizing it, I really was no longer on the train. I had dissociated myself from those who had signed up for the entire trip, who seemed to find great solace and fellowship in having parties, wearing expensive insignias with Greek symbols that had for them astounding social connotative value. They would dress up nattily, only to end up the next morning with variously colored fluids splashed across their clothes, beds, and floors, and unable to recall any part of the soiree that had perpetrated this malodorous disarray.

All this confusion on my part came to a head one afternoon when I was hitchhiking back to campus, and a very nice Baptist minister was kind enough to stop and give me a ride. We chatted. He found out I was a student. As a minister, he quite naturally asked me the loaded question about my religious affiliation. I paused, because I realized I really had none, none I could say was truly mine anymore. I was still officially a Methodist, but I had now been studying the Bahá'í Faith for almost three years. Yet, I was not a Bahá'í, but neither had I been to church once since coming to college.

It was an important moment. I would not be rehearsing it now some fifty years later had it not been. "I am a Methodist, but I am presently studying the Bahá'í Faith," I finally answered.

His head snapped as he turned to look at me with a stern scowl. "Son, son, you get yourself over to the First Methodist Church and you talk to reverend Withers. You talk to him. He'll help set you straight."

I nodded approvingly with a smile. I thanked him for the sugges-
tion, and we said nothing more about religion. Either he did not know
enough about the Bahá'í Faith to respond with any explicit concerns
or refutations, or as a Baptist minister, he did not want to usurp the
job of being a pastor to a member of Reverend Withers' Methodist
flock. But the most important part of the story, besides my realizing
that I was no longer on the train in the middle of nowhere thumbing
a ride to no place in particular, was that I decided to follow his advice.

Perhaps I was nondescript and a bit directionless, but I still needed
and desired some infusion of spirit, and for me a beautiful sanctuary
with stain glass windows, a heavy-duty pipe organ, some hymns and
prayers and scripture might provide a boost. Certainly as a nominal "sheep" in the Methodist "flock," I owed it to myself to give my
"shepherd" one more chance at pulling me out of the bramble.

The following Sunday I went to the First Methodist Church. It was
larger and grander than St. Mark Methodist Church. It was packed to
the rafters with parishioners. Withers was smiling and spritely in his
doctoral robes, all ready to give us the Word. The organ pumped out
in vibrating rapture some of Charles Wesley's best stuff, the same familiar chords and melodies I knew by heart. Then came the "apostles'
creed," the recitation of my creedal ascent to the trinity and what I
had now come to consider its convoluted assertion that Christ and
God were literally the same.

I could not do it, not anymore, not in "absolute honesty," not even
with mild hypocrisy. Then the polished brass collection plates were
passed from row to row—in the Bahá'í Faith, all are admonished to
contribute to various funds, but it is entirely a private matter with
no one having the right to know how much anyone else contributes.
I knew this, and now I found I did not wish to place my portion
into that plate as it arrived in my hands stacked to overflowing with
greenbacks of various denominations. I watched others watching how

much each person deposited, though I tried not to watch who saw me put in nothing.

Finally came the coup de grâce, Reverend Withers' sermon. I did not catch his theme, nor do I recall the verse of scripture that served as the starting point for his exemplum in the formulaic structure that all sermons must take. "My sermon today comes from the second word of the third verse of chapter twenty of St. Paul's letter to...." And so it goes. But I do recall that where in the past I had mostly put my mind in neutral and simply enjoyed the atmosphere, I found myself actually listening to what he said, listening and evaluating it, as an academic might assess the validity of a scholarly paper being presented at a conference.

As I listened, I found myself periodically wanting to stand up and ask a question or make a comment, something I had never felt before. I wanted to ask how his observation could possibly be true based on some other verse of St. Paul or based on Christ's own teachings. I remember in particular his citing a verse in which Paul said that nothing we can do will win us salvation, or so Reverend Withers interpreted it. This, of course, is the foundation of Protestantism, that only faith can get you "saved" or "justified." Works or deeds have no currency, except as signs of your inner condition.

Ironically, only days before, I had read the seventh chapter of Matthew where Christ admonished his followers that simply listening and verbally affirming belief was not sufficient to be a follower. In order to be "saved," one must demonstrate belief with obedience and actions. Christ even goes so far as to map out that course of action in the previous two chapters, the Christian life as codified by a list of laws and exhortations.

But it was not that contradiction alone that transformed my condition of relative serenity to a state of wanton rage and insurgence. The whole sermon came down on me like that. Had I followed my inclination, I would have abandoned all propriety, would have gotten up and walked out, or else seized the pulpit and noted all the logical inconsistencies in Reverend Withers's explication of scripture.

But on another level, I felt free and totally energized by this experience. I sensed a mounting fire in my heart and mind: "I disagree with that point, and that one, and that one," I felt myself saying. "I can disprove that assertion, and that one, and that one." So when I left the church to walk across the street to the campus that bright fall morning as the trees were beginning to shed their rainbow harvest, I decided to go down toward Centennial Park where the replica of the Parthenon stood in all its faux Grecian glory in this "Athens of the South."

When I reached the stately edifice, there were signs cautioning about the concrete freezes. Seems the acrid atmosphere of Nashville had caused parts to decay and fall onto the heads of visitors. It seems that for some reason I still don't understand, with all our modern technology, we could not match the skills of those ancient craftsmen who worked the real marble with hammers and chisels and bandaged hands.

Apparently we also could not match their logical discourse, I thought to myself, having only recently studied Socrates' allegory of reality in *The Republic*. But was religion meant to be a thing of logic, a product of the mind? I wondered. Could faith and belief somehow be cleverly dissevered from our persistent need for logical relationships in our other daily pursuits? Could we indeed segregate our Sunday self from our work-a-day practical self without fragmenting our souls, without disintegrating our humanity? Down what path would such a journey take us, I wondered, and where could it possibly end except with ourselves at war with ourselves?

I recalled Frost's "The Road Not Taken" and realized that once again he had tricked me with the guise of his simplicity. Sure, he had chosen "the road less traveled by," but the title of his poem was about the other road, the road he had refused to follow. He had jumped the train at the station where the two roads diverged. But it was that road he did not choose that was the tempting one, the popular one, the one where all my friends were going. Did I really dare reject it?

8

A NEW MIZÁN FOR A
BROKEN BUMP

*Say: O leaders of religion! Weigh not the Book of God with such
standards and sciences as are current amongst you, for the Book itself
is the unerring Balance established amongst men. In this most perfect
Balance whatsoever the peoples and kindreds of the earth possess
must be weighed, while the measure of its weight should be tested
according to its own standard, did ye but know it.*
—Bahá'u'lláh, the Kitáb-i-Aqdas

Whether one jumps from the train or falls accidentally, the results are
bound to be pretty messy. Of course, when one chooses to jump, as
I did, then one has already become aware that the unity of the unrelated parts of life was fragile to begin with, that the shell of wholeness
was mostly an illusion. That awareness is what motivates us to jump
in the first place.

PICKING UP PIECES
After I went to that church service, I awoke from my dream life, from
the illusion that my life was whole and organized when it was not.
I also awoke to the fact that the life I had been living was not really

mine, not something I had consciously chosen. I had basically been told what to believe, and was merely along for the ride. But after studying the Bahá'í Faith in some depth, I realized that I had, in fact, already taken the leap of faith from the train. I simply had not yet let myself or anyone else know about it.

Part of the reason for my negligence or reticence was the law of inertia—it was easier to lie there in pieces watching the train rumble off than to muster the energy to look around and survey where I had landed, let alone take the first steps toward cleaning up the mess. Another deterrent was a promise I had made to my father before I left for college. I had pledged to him I would not make any drastic change in my itinerary until I had finished college, at least insofar as religion was concerned.

My parents were aware that I was studying the Bahá'í Faith, and while they did not object, they did not want me to take any precipitous action based on the fact that my big brother had redirected his own life's course by becoming a Bahá'í—since there is no clergy in the Bahá'í Faith, he was now going to be a professor of theoretical math instead of becoming a Methodist minister.

I don't recall my parents being particularly disturbed by this decision. My brother had always been an enigma to them and a little beyond their complete understanding and quite beyond their control as regards emotional or intellectual inclinations. He had attended a church of his own choosing, and they had respected that. During about a six-month period in high school, he had toyed with the idealism of communist political theory, and they were not shaken by that. He played chess by mail, listened to classical music, did not do sports, and was sometimes moody, if not erratic in his affective relationships with all three of us.

But everyone in our nuclear clan of four loved everyone else quite unconditionally and openly, so nothing that was done by anyone had any lasting impact on the tangle of relationships. Yet now that Bill had become a Bahá'í and had settled on a more "reasonable" career, they found it hard to argue with the calming effects his own "jump" had wrought in this young man they had fostered but had imprecisely understood.

It was in this sense that I was their last chance at having spawned a "normal" southern gentleman who, like both of my grandfathers before me, might go on to become a doctor, or, like my own father, a respected businessman. And thus far I had more than fulfilled their hopes and expectations. Before getting injured, I had been a successful athlete. In high school, I was among the "popular" kids, or seemed to be. As I have mentioned, I had been a little rowdy for a while, but by graduation time I had settled down to be "respectable" and socially acceptable, or so it seemed.

Now at college, it must have seemed to them that I had begun to go astray again, like the kind of sheep a shepherd must constantly pull from crevices because it always tends to be wandering off somewhere.

The first sign of this tendency to stray from the prescribed path, which they had presumed ended with my early high school escapades, was my sudden choice to extricate myself from the fraternity system, and thus from any important social connection with the university itself. I would be *in* the university but not *of* the university.

They were aware that I had chosen not to become a member of the Sigma Chi fraternity to which my father had belonged at Emory. But at least I had decided to join the fraternity to which my brother had belonged. At least I would be in some socially acceptable organization, because they, too, knew that there was no social life outside the milieu of "Greek" life on the Vanderbilt campus.

But as I began studying the Bahá'í Faith more intensely during my freshman year, I began to feel less comfortable with a system that was specifically geared to reinforce stereotypical classifications of people. It was considered a fun game to guess the fraternity or sorority someone belonged to by his or her appearance, demeanor, dress, or some other relatively peripheral characteristic, charm and humor being examples of these. The problem was, it was not hard to win this game because this classicism and stratification was obviously based on values that were prejudicial and divisive, the very antithesis of what my new perspective gained from the Bahá'í Faith had set forth as appropriate standards for the advancement of human society.

Of course, there were no blacks in fraternities because in that southern milieu, there were only a handful of black students on campus. There were no Jews in non-Jewish fraternities. There were no ugly people or deformed people or physically challenged people in any fraternity. The so-called "black ball" system ensured that any applicant or potential member found unpleasing to any member of a fraternity was arbitrarily disinvited. This "election" system consisted of each member placing a ball into a box to express acceptance or rejection of the proposed applicant. A white ball meant acceptance, but even one black ball dropped anonymously into the voting box meant social rejection by this group.

In all fairness, however, I should confess that my most overpowering motive for wishing to remove myself from this systemization of social life was that I liked being on my own. I was not a group person, not in the ordinary sense. I am not able to be in a group based on a source of authority that I do not think worthy of respect and obeisance. So after having been accepted into my brother's former fraternity, I quit.

I went before my fellow pledges and active members of the fraternity, and I told them that I had nothing against them and that if I desired to belong to such a group it would certainly be theirs. This was true. I concluded by telling them that I had decided not to be a part of the fraternity system itself, that it simply didn't appeal to me because it took up too much of my time and too much of my freedom. This was also true. I didn't feel that it was the time or place to elucidate for them the deeper moral principles guiding my decision.

Coming as it did the second semester of my freshman year, this decision and public proclamation condemned me to an undergraduate life of being a nonperson. Being an "independent" at Vanderbilt was tantamount to being an outcast, or, worse, an untouchable, a nerd, a geek, a loser. Indeed, only one other person in the fraternity ever said another word to me, and he did so indirectly, through his girlfriend.

I was at a dance where even geeks could go, a freshman prom of some sort, and as I danced with the young lady he was dating, she told me he thought my stand and my action quite noble. "Robert admires what you did," she said.

I presumed this meant he admired the way I had jumped off the train, not the jumping itself, or else I imagine he would likewise have taken the same leap of faith. One could possibly slink off the train barely noticed. One could fall from the train by perpetrating some abominable act so that the other passengers would assemble and push off the negligent one. But I had asked for the attention of all the fellow travelers, had told them, "I don't like this train or where it's going and so I'm about to jump! Here I go!"

From this one individual I was privately awarded a "10" for style points, as if I had done a perfect one-and-a-half with a full twist off the tower at Hamilton Lake and slipped in with no splash whatsoever. Indeed, after my feet disappeared into those dark waters, none of them ever saw me again. I was invisible.

Now in terms of heroism as we have discussed it thus far, and in terms of any really important and demanding act of fortitude, this action of mine was downright minuscule and meaningless. And to be totally honest, I don't remember it being all that painful, awkward, or even really hard. It actually felt quite liberating. I had certainly not taken this action to make a statement about a flawed social system. What is more, these young men had been immensely friendly and kind to me, and I felt I owed them an explanation, and I did. So I gave them one.

In any case, no longer did I have to report to the frat house every afternoon after track practice. Furthermore, the Bahá'í Faith forbids drinking, and while I was not yet a Bahá'í, I had developed a serious abhorrence to seeing people, especially friends I otherwise respected, drunk at social gatherings.

It was not a religious repugnance, not moral disdain. I simply found it strange and disquieting to observe people assume a distinctly different personality than the one they normally manifested, a transformation based not on achieving a new perspective, but one derived entirely from strange chemicals coursing through their brains.

I remember extremely retiring individuals who, after consuming a predictable quantity of alcohol, would become quite clever, charming, outgoing, and vivacious. I remember one who affected an English accent. I remember another in my dorm who was normally kind, funny, and friendly. But once inebriated, he would vehemently denounce Christianity. What was worse, he would physically attack anyone who laughed at his ranting, something I experienced firsthand.

Perhaps worst of all were occasions when I would attend some soiree and have a really heartfelt conversation with someone who seemed only a bit tipsy, but still coherent. We might chat for an hour about some weighty philosophical matter. But I discovered to my dismay that a day or so later, the conversation no longer existed. All intellectual and emotional intimacy we had shared had been totally eradicated from their memory.

ONCE A BUMP, ALWAYS A BUMP

As I noted in the previous chapter, in the fall of the following year, my jump from the train was still a work in progress. After leaving the fraternity system, I continued my study of the Bahá'í Faith, and such was my interim status when I hitchhiked with the Baptist minister. But the final parts of my slow-motion dive came a few months after my venture to Reverend Withers' church and my subsequent stroll to the faux Parthenon to watch chunks of faux antiquity fall amid the autumn leaves. It was there, standing amid orange and gold foliage (and pieces of a Greek frieze) that I reflected on my status as a nonentity on campus in relation to my promise to my father. I realized that to complete my dive from the train, I would have to incur another "bump."

As I mentioned earlier, "Bump" was my nickname as a child growing up—Johnny Bump. I acquired this dubious epithet by literally striving beyond my reach, usually in trees or on playground equipment. I was foolhardy. I would execute, or attempt to execute, almost any physical feat, whether from a dare or from my own curiosity. If I could imagine it, I would attempt it. For though the term "foolhardy" was more accurate, I gloried in the appellation "daredevil"!

I remember realizing that I could walk across the single bar of the twelve-foot high swings at elementary school by simply concentrating on the bar and blanking out the rest of reality from my mind. The teachers naturally went nuts and stopped me after the second time I accomplished this high bar act, threatening me with untold hours in the principal's office should I repeat such reckless disregard for my safety, and their sanity.

But I was not always so successful. I had fallen from ladders, trees, the garage, once from the second story of a new house being built across the street when I attempted to inch my way atop a course of freshly laid brick. I still remember that sense of falling headfirst, the quick gashing of my forehead on a scaffold plank, and landing in the soft red mud below. I still have a crease over my right eye from that one.

I had been hit in the head by a baseball when my brother asked me to pitch a hardball to him from about ten feet away. I had been hit in the head by a baseball bat when I was asked to be catcher for a kid who really did not know how to swing a bat properly. I had been hit in the head with a rock in (get this) an unsanctioned "rock and stick battle"—we weren't totally nuts; we used trashcan lids as our shields against errant missiles.

Only a few of these bumps were life-threatening, but most of them did end up with me in the emergency room of various hospitals throughout my life. I could probably write a decent book surveying the quality of various emergency rooms in North Carolina, Georgia, Tennessee, and Florida. Later, in organized sports, it was no different. I guess I was fearless to a degree, but I would certainly be in better shape now had I been more restrained and less undaunted by the possibility of permanent injury. I have, so far in my life, had twenty surgeries, all but three of which derive from my participation in some organized sports activity at some point in my life: football, track, basketball, martial arts, and "adult" soccer, the meanest of them all.

I now see that part of this daring was the desire for attention, the realization that when I performed these remarkable acts of derring-do, I could hear audible gasps from my compatriots, who would then rally me on with shouts of encouragement. Possibly their motives were some perverse desire to observe human carnage firsthand, but I did not care. For example, when I was six years old, hearing my friends' calls from the pier at Hamilton Lake as I stood on the tower was all I needed to overcome any reticence I might otherwise have had.

"Jump, Johnny! Jump!" they'd call, and off I'd go sailing out into space, basking in their awe as I tumbled through that clean summer air. Eventually there would be the crash into the cold water below, but for those few milliseconds I was someone to be admired. Only afterward would I worry about the consequences, most often as I was on the way to the nearest emergency room.

As I grew older and continued my journey on the train, praise only seemed to come through besting others at the milestones—those points of conclusion to some phase of our collective ride through the grades, those commemorations of how far we had come or how close we were to our next destination.

But here I was once again about to incur a rather large bump should I finish my dive from the train by becoming a Bahá'í. Besides, this self-inflicted plunge into these unfathomed waters would not evoke the "oh's" and "ah's" of awe from the "peanut-crunching crowd," as Sylvia Plath so aptly describes them in her poem "Lady Lazarus."[7] I would be a hero to no one.

THE *MIZÁN* AND ME

In the Bahá'í writings, many of which are originally written in Persian, there is a word I've found that is used quite frequently. I most often associate it with a talk by 'Abdu'l-Bahá, the son and appointed successor of Bahá'u'lláh, in his reference to the standard or measure against which we can gauge our own character and progress. It is the word *mizán*, and it refers to a "balance," as in a balance between scales or weights, the sort of scales where one puts an amount of something on one side and offsets that with precise weights on the other. Once the scales are even, once balance is attained, we merely add up the weights to see how much stuff we have, be it gold or goulash.

The point is that metaphorically the term "balance" or *mizán* alludes to the standard by which we weigh or evaluate ourselves or our

---

7. Sylvia Plath, "Lady Lazarus," *The Norton Anthology of Modern and Contemporary Poetry*, 3rd edition, Vol. 2 (New York: W. W. Norton, 2003), p. 613, l. 26.

performance. Prior to Copernicus, all observations of the movement of heavenly spheres were weighed against the accepted standard established by Ptolemy. This was the *mizán*. Quite obviously the accuracy of a "balance" or "standard" is predicated on the extent to which the *mizán* itself complies with reality. In time we discovered that Ptolemy's geocentric standard was flawed, and most calculations based on that *mizán* were likewise inaccurate.

On the train, no such question arose about the accuracy of the *mizán* we were all using to measure the success of our lives. We did not weigh the decision about where we were being taken or whether or not it was wise to go there because we were never made aware that we could or should pose such questions. This normative train was particularly impervious to questions of religion.

Religion was more or less a name we bore, an organization to which we belonged, very much like a fraternity of similarly inclined individuals. Our religious affiliation might come up in conversations, but for most people on the train, it was not the organizing principle of their daily lives, nor was it intended to be. Religion ministered to our private self, our "Sunday" self. Rules of commerce and high finance governed the real world.

Increasingly, after leaving the prescribed social order of the fraternity system, I began weighing the rest of my reality using the *mizán* of the Bahá'í teachings as my standard. I did so because what it proposed to me was the possibility of a fully integrated way of life in which everything I aspired to or did could be coordinated and evaluated by a single inclusive and coherent perspective, a worldview that was at once personal and yet entirely pervasive. It was like a unified field theory of metaphysics.

As a liberal arts student at an excellent university, I was exposed to what was then considered to be the best that human beings had thought and wrought, whether in art, architecture, literature, philosophy, history, religion, or science. But while the courses were generally taught as discrete arenas of learning, the Bahá'í Faith increasingly enabled me to see in every one of these fields an encompassing and logical relationship.

While it would be impossible and, for the present purposes, entirely unnecessary to catalog the critical links and vistas of insights this *mizán* unveiled before me, I should mention a few that most immediately transformed the drudgery of classes into a personal adventure in which everything in creation had some relevance to everything else in creation.

Perhaps the most exciting way in which my study of the Bahá'í Faith enhanced and coordinated my understanding of all that I was being taught in these diverse courses in these ostensibly unrelated fields was my progressively more acute appreciation of the theory that underlying the evolution of all human advancement and knowledge was a single motive force—the advent of Divine Emissaries from the realm of the spirit—the Prophets of God, what the Bahá'í writings allude to as "Manifestations" of God.

According to the Bahá'í theory of human history, all advancement of society and learning proceeds or emanates from the successive periodic appearances of divinely ordained teachers. They appear approximately every five hundred to a thousand years at various places on the planet, and as I attempted to apply this theoretical paradigm to world history, as well as to what had occurred in literature, philosophy, and social and political movements throughout history, I began to discern this organizing force at work.

Suddenly, all my studies began to make sense in terms of this larger expression of human purpose. I came to theorize that the emergence of classical Greek philosophy may have had its beginning in the influence of Jewish thinkers. I came to examine how the Roman Empire rode the crest of the wave of emerging Christianity. I came to perceive how the Renaissance in Western Christendom may have actually emanated from the influence of the Islamic dispensation. I came to see in particular how the advent of the Bahá'í Era was the primal motive force behind the Industrial Revolution and behind all the astounding transformation in global society that has taken place in the short span of little more than one and a half centuries since the Bahá'í Faith began in 1844.

My understanding of this integrative force in human advancement was hardly confined to the more recent influence of the Abrahamic religions. I could discern the same process at work under Hinduism in the Indian subcontinent, with Buddhism in the great Chinese dynasties, with Zoroastrianism and the eminence of the Persian Empire, with someone like Akhenaton and the Egyptian Empire, as well as the influence of the belief in Quetzalcoatl in Central and South America, and even more ancient Manifestations whose names are forever lost to our collective memory, though remnants of their influence linger in Africa, the Australian Continent, and among the peoples of the South Pacific Islands. Clearly, no place on earth was left without the influence of this divine guidance.

I don't mean to imply that I had researched every aspect of this theory or that I had achieved some breakthrough in anthropology in conjunction with the Bahá'í concept of progressive revelation. I simply mean that I luxuriated in experiencing subjectively the logical foundation of my personal worldview of an infinite number of possibilities for the applicability of this theory to all my studies. And this vista about learning, this integrating principle, excited me as nothing had before, because it demonstrated to me that nothing I studied was isolated from anything else I studied, that every field of learning was really but a vector of insight that, when assembled with other such vectors, could implicate an image about the whole of reality itself.

Before this, I had proceeded in all these discrete areas of learning like the blindfolded men in the proverbial story who examine various parts of an elephant and argue about the validity of their individual perceptions: it is skinny like a whip, says the one touching the tail; it is thick, round, and straight like a tree trunk, says the one touching the leg; it is flat and thick like a blanket, says the one touching the ear.

It is possible that over time these experts in their separate fields of study might cease contending, might consult, collaborate, and assemble their findings to emerge with some consensus about the reality of the elephant. But how much more rapid their progress would be were one to appear among them who had already seen the elephant, who knew that all of the pieces of the elephant fit together, and, most important of all, who would gladly share this integrated vision of reality.

This was precisely what I began to believe Bahá'u'lláh and all the Manifestations before Him had done. They had appeared among us to remove our blindfolds so that all who sincerely desired to know the truth about reality could see the "wholeness" of it for themselves.

THIEVES IN THE NIGHT

This understanding that the divine purpose of the Manifestations related to all forms of human knowledge and understanding led me to a second weighty insight into the appearance of these Emissaries from the divine realm. They come in disguise, like a "thief in the night," as Christ explained. They appear among us as kind and erudite, but in the guise of ordinary men. Yet from these extraordinary Figures emanates a transformative force that alters the course of human history, even if we are not always conscious of the source of that change.

'Abdu'l-Bahá states the axiom succinctly, affirming that without the appearance of these Manifestations, human civilization would not progress or even exist in the first place:

> Without the bounty of the splendor and the instructions of these
> Holy Beings the world of souls and thoughts would be opaque

darkness. Without the irrefutable teachings of those sources of mysteries the human world would become the pasture of animal appetites and qualities, the existence of everything would be unreal, and there would be no true life. That is why it is said in the Gospel: "In the beginning was the Word," meaning that it became the cause of all life. (*Some Answered Questions,* pp. 162–63)

These Manifestations of God possess such power, the Bahá'í writings go on to explain, precisely because They are not ordinary human beings, but preexist in the spiritual world. They voluntarily agree to appear among us, even though They must veil from us the complete nature of Their station and powers and withhold from us all that They could reveal. Were we capable of understanding and applying a more complete outpouring of insight, They would reveal more than They do, even as Christ remarks to His disciples, "I have yet many things to say unto you, but ye cannot bear them now" (John 16:12).

This is not to say they withhold from us Their divine origin or divinely ordained purpose or mission, but They do not seek to accomplish this task by sensational displays of their powers (through miracles, for example), nor by insinuating Themselves into positions of social or political power. Neither do They seek to acquire material wealth or status, but instead bring guidance and allow Themselves to be subjected to the whims of those in power. They willingly submit to those around them, even though in reality They could at any point overcome imprisonment or humiliation and unleash a sufficient demonstration of Their power to dumbfound the most recalcitrant and devious souls among Them. This indirect teaching method forces us to recognize Them according to our perception of Their spiritual attributes, and not because we are exposed to any mundane displays of Their lofty station.

There was also a third jewel among the many insights that confirmed for me the validity of this *mizán*—that the Manifestations are not only perfect or immaculate expressions of Godliness in human form; they are also perfect educators. And as I was rapidly discovering at the university, the best educators were not those who goaded the lethargic sheep into rote memorization of what they had learned from their own mentors. Masterful teachers are inevitably masters of indirection, of subtlety, and empowerment.

The Manifestations are keenly aware of what any great teacher or capable parent knows, that authentic enlightenment—true education—cannot be imposed. It can be made available. It can be encouraged and lovingly exhorted, but, like authentic love, authentic learning must ultimately depend on the free choice or desire on the part of the student, coupled with a willingness to give this choice priority in life.

A fourth and, for me as a nominal Christian, most enlightening discovery I came upon as I applied this new Bahá'í lens to reality in this Copernican-like epiphany was how it unleashed for me the real power and significance of what Christ had done and said. Instead of distancing me from what I believed as a Christian, this *mizán* gave an entirely renovated and more expansive meaning to so much of what Christ said and suffered. I could sense His frustration when the very people for whom He especially came, the Pharisaic Jews, simply didn't "get it"—that He was indeed their Messiah who had come, not to destroy their Jewish law, but to fulfill it.

But even more important for me was how this concept of the Manifestation as being more than a man but infinitely beneath the Creator made clear all of Christ's statements about His station and purpose. In academic terms, this insight resolved for me all the questions related to the scholarly arena of Christology and the theories about the nature or station of Christ. He acknowledges the sublime station of Abraham and Moses and clearly asserts that He is indeed the Messiah, that He is fulfilling all They had promised. But He also clearly proclaims that another Manifestation will appear after Him to explain all that He would tell them had they the capacity to understand and utilize such knowledge and insight.

As a perfect manifestation of all the spiritual attributes of God, Christ could thus respond to Philip's desire to see God the Father by observing that by seeing Christ, they were effectively experiencing as much of the Father as they could comprehend: "Jesus saith unto him, Have I been so long time with you, and yet hast thou not known me, Philip? He that hath seen me hath seen the Father; and how sayest thou then, Shew us the Father? Believest thou not that I am in the Father, and the Father in me? The words that I speak unto you I speak not of myself: but the Father that dwelleth in me, He doeth the works" (John 14:9–10).

And yet, while forthrightly proclaiming His perfection and godliness, Christ likewise cautions His hearers not to be tempted to equate His station with that of the Father: "Jesus cried and said, He that believeth on me, believeth not on me, but on him that sent me. And he that seeth me seeth him that sent me. . . . For I have not spoken of myself; but the Father which sent me, He gave me a commandment, what I should say, and what I should speak" (John 12:44–49).

So it was that I began to reread all the scriptural statements of Christ and all the allusions to Christ and to His purpose and station. And in so doing, I suddenly understood with precise clarity how the Trinitarian doctrine had come about and what it really meant in terms of reality as described by this *mízán*. While the literal Trinitarian doctrine was logically untenable—that Christ and God and the Holy Spirit were one essence, as Muḥammad Himself would later confirm—there are portrayed in Bahá'í theology three parts to the process of revelation that roughly parallel what the early Christian patriarchs were so desperately trying to explain.

There is God the Creator from Whom emanates all creation. There is the Holy Spirit, that spiritual force that emanates from God and animates all creation and all created beings, including the Manifestations. And there are the Manifestations Themselves Who, though functioning as conduits for that creative and energizing force of the Holy Spirit, do not manifest the essence of God. They are not pieces of God, though they are able to dramatize perfectly in human character and actions all the divine names or attributes of God. Ergo, there is God the Father/Creator, the Holy Spirit emanating from God, and the Manifestations who are charged with translating the will or wish of God into increments of information, education, and transformation.

Still another essential jewel or gift that this perspective offered me was demonstrable evidence of the unity of the world religions, clear proof that all the religions throughout human history are really a single religion, the religion of God, but revealed in successive and progressive stages according to the needs and capacities of a given age and place. Part of my delight in this realization derived from my studying the frequency with which Christ alludes to His relationship to the Manifestations who precede Him, particularly to Abraham and to Moses. I further noticed that in virtually every passage spoken by Christ, He employs explicit allusions to the Old Testament scripture, particularly those passages that refer to His own appearance.

For example, I saw in a footnote to Mark 15:34 a rather important explanation as to why in His dying utterances Christ "cried with a loud voice, saying, *Eloi, Eloi, lama sabachthani?*" This is translated as, "My God, my God, why hast thou forsaken me?" And it had always bothered me that Christ, an exemplar of Godliness, would sink into despair, even so briefly and under such dire circumstance. Now I came to realized that He was not despairing—for those Jews who looked on, He was reciting a memorable verse from their own texts—the first verse from Psalm twenty-two, a psalm that foretells the crucifixion in exacting detail.

Perhaps the most relevant discovery that the application of this *mizán* provided for me was a matter that had been a substantial issue or mystery in my many discussions of Methodist and Protestant theology—the relationship between faith and action, between salvation and deeds. Could one who had been officially saved (which in my church was a mystery in itself) become unsaved by becoming an unsavory character or by committing reprehensible acts against individuals or society?

According to the Bahá'í standard, each Manifestation brings two categories of teachings or guidance. The first is a renewed and incrementally more advanced understanding of reality. They provide a new outpouring of knowledge about all aspects of truth. The second aspect of the teachings of the Manifestations consists of specific instructions in the form of a daily regimen and a social order. Most often, this aspect of their revelation contains laws, ordinances, exhortations, a paradigm for personal behavior, and, in most cases, a design for how to construct communal life structured on spiritual principles.

This concept of a vital interplay between knowledge and action, between faith and deeds, was totally at odds with all I had been taught at Sunday school, though not at home. At the end of the first paragraph of the Kitáb-i-Aqdas, the Most Holy book, the repository of Bahá'u'lláh's laws and plan for social reformation, is a very powerful pronouncement that these two processes (knowing and doing) are inseparable, reciprocal, and interdependent. Recognizing the personal Savior or Manifestation for the age in which we live is indeed the first step, but it is not sufficient by itself. The signal of our recognition is a willful reformation of our character: "These twin duties are inseparable. Neither is acceptable without the other" (¶19).

The power of this one concept was such that in my mind it effectively disentangled the basis for the age-old warfare within Christianity that had begun with the argument between James and Paul, and had finally resulted in the Protestant Reformation, the schism between science and religion, and ultimately the splintering of a single revelation into a thousand pieces. For where Paul asserts that faith alone suffices, James affirms that faith without action is dead, even as Christ Himself had affirmed that "every one that heareth these sayings of mine, and doeth them not, shall be likened unto a foolish man, which built his house upon the sand: And the rain descended, and the floods came, and the winds blew, and beat upon that house; and it fell: and great was the fall of it" (Matt 7:26–27).

Logical? Purposeful? Coordinated? Could it be that the Creator actually knew what He was doing, was actually as smart and logical, as kind and loving as we are? What an incredible idea! After all I had experienced in the guise of religion, I began to realize bit by bit how much doubt and confusion I had set aside in some private place unknown even to my own conscious mind. Now it all came pouring out.

I had been confronted by my church Sunday school teachers with a vision of God as jealous, wrathful, vengeful, capricious, and unpredictable. This was the case especially with the God of the Old Testament—no telling what sort of intervention He would perpetrate because of some trivial miscue on the part of a people or the foible of a leader. Let Moses tap that rock twice and *ziiipp!* There goes His one chance to enter the Promised Land. Let Lot's wife look back just once and *ziiipp!* She's a pillar of salt.

Even as a youngster I sensed that I could do a better job of being God than that! After all that Moses had been through, I would have made some young followers carry him on soft cushions to the Promised Land if I thought it would have been a good idea. After all, had not this Manifestation of God endured capricious rejection on the part of his own people after He had saved them from slavery? Did He not train them for forty years moving from place to place to teach them about how to construct a just tribal community by practicing it over and over?

Then, of course, I had been confronted with a God who had come to earth in the guise of an ordinary man and who, on the eve of His own execution, according to the church's teaching on the trinity that Jesus was in fact God, prayed to Himself to be relieved of this onerous sacrifice—a sacrifice He must have foreknown He was about to make because of His own will to save humankind from the wrath of Himself for what two people (Adam and Eve) had done four thousand years before in the Garden of Eden. When looked at in this way, it becomes a convoluted story that's impossible to accept as a sequence of events overseen by an omnipotent God of love and forgiveness.

Even more perplexing was that this same God had in the course of His ministry said authoritatively: "I say nothing on my own authority but by the authority of Him who sent me," a statement that, when we substitute the antecedents for the pronouns reads: "I have said nothing on my own Authority but by the Authority of myself." Or, in an even more perplexing formulation of the same statement, "God says nothing on His Own Authority, but by the Authority of God."

Probably the most critical confirmation for me on a purely cerebral level of assessing the accuracy of the *mizán* of the Bahá'í perspective was exploring its capacity to elucidate and untangle the strands of contention that my university studies had showed world history to be, particularly religious history and philosophical discourse. Finally I had an answer for the biggest question I had about God in history—if God exists, why doesn't He express Himself by intervening in human history?

The answer seems that through His Manifestations, God has done precisely that, but perhaps not in ways we might wish, not in time to stop us from doing all the stupid stuff we had as a body politic perpetrated over the course of our relatively brief existence on planet Earth. This answer, even in its most succinct and axiomatic form, worked completely for me. I could figure out the particulars of this theory on my own, and began to do so. I knew it worked and was sufficient to explain the wisdom of the manner in which the Creator intervened without literally taking charge of things. Over time, we had to do that ourselves. The coming to earth of the Kingdom of God would be guided by the Manifestations but performed by human hearts and hands as a collective spiritual exercise.

Suffice it to say that I had accepted this theory of human history wholeheartedly, because it made sense. I had only one abiding question, the answer to which I approached with no small degree of trepidation.

THE FINAL TEST OF THE *MIZÁN*

The final test for me, both intellectually and emotionally, had to do with a principal axiom that Bahá'u'lláh makes about the entire system of progressive revelation. He states point blank that all the Prophets are equal in capacity, power, and station. They are unified in Their purpose and differ only in the need to fashion Their Revelation to befit the exigencies of the age in which They appear. To deny any one of These Divine Teachers, therefore, is to deny all of Them.

While I could accept the notion that Bahá'u'lláh might indeed be the One Promised from time immemorial to usher in the Most Great Peace at the end times, this theory also meant that I had to accept the fact that Muḥammad succeeded Christ. And if I accepted Muḥammad as the successor to Christ, then it followed that Christianity had effectively become supplanted by Islam in the year 622 CE. Furthermore, since a new Manifestation does not appear, Bahá'í theology affirms, until the religion of the previous revelation has experienced discord, decline, and corruption, I had to accept that by the year 622 CE, Christianity must have become mangled beyond repair.

My study seemed to support such a thesis. I realized that final coup to the Christianity that Christ had brought may have ended effectively at the Council of Nicaea in 325 CE when the Trinitarian Doctrine was finally devised and approved by vote. Christ and God were now doctrinally the same, which effectively severed Christianity from being on an equal footing with all other religions, whose founders had been Prophets of God, but clearly not God Himself. The fact that Christ never claims to be God and that He makes it logically obvious that He is but an Emissary from God made little difference to those followers of Athanasius gathered at the Nicaean synod.

Nevertheless, it was one thing to accept this on a theoretical basis, and quite another to accept it on a personal subjective level that Muḥammad was Christ's equal and successor, and that Christ's allusion to the Paraclete or Comforter (John 14:16) was a clear reference to Muḥammad and Islam. After all, I was approaching this theory fifty years ago when Westerners were hardly aware of Islam in any sense. It was not perceived as any sort of a threat, even though the Muslim defenders had defeated the Crusaders some seventeen centuries earlier, and still occupied the Holy Land.

But neither was Islam considered seriously as an important religion or religious movement by most of us in the middle-class white West. The Nation of Islam had been founded in Detroit in 1930, but was yet unknown because this was prior to Casius Clay's conversion and prior to Malcolm X's milestone pilgrimage to Mecca. All we students of Western Civilization knew of Islam was the influence it had in Cordoba with the invasion of the Moors. In all the medieval literature I studied, they were always referred to as the "pagans," the enemy, the "other."

It was in this context that I sensed one final test would be to confront Muḥammad, to see if He bore figs or thistles, and the only way to do that in any unbiased form was to read the Qur'án itself. And yet, even this was a bit of a problem. Shoghi Effendi, the Guardian of the Bahá'í Faith, had praised the translation of the Qur'án by Rodwell, a Christian scholar who in 1861 had done a remarkably poetic and accurate rendering of the work, but who had also attached footnotes from an incredibly biased Christian perspective, comments that thoroughly disdain any possibility that Muḥammad might be anything but a dissimulator. Certainly he could not be considered a true Prophet of God, and from Rodwell's point of view, it would the grossest sort of blasphemy to countenance the possibility of Muḥammad being a divinely empowered Emissary on par with Christ.

Yet the Bahá'í writings were totally unambiguous about the station and status of Muḥammad in world and in religious history. He is to be considered the successor to Christ, the final Prophet before the Day of Resurrection—which was fulfilled with the advent of the twin revelations of the Báb and Bahá'u'lláh. Furthermore, since Bahá'í beliefs regarding theology and ontology depict all the Manifestations as equal in station, even if some religions excel others in their impact on the advancement of civilization, then Muḥammad is equal to Christ in status or station. Accordingly His revelation, which is considerably more lengthy and detailed than the sum total of Christ's personal statements in the New Testament, would logically be consistent with all that Christ says regarding spirituality, and even more advanced in setting forth these principles and in establishing a social order and laws of personal and collective conduct.

I remember to this day where I was when I first began to read the Qu'rán. I remember the time of day and the degree of apprehension with which I first dared open Rodwell's translation and began to read. What if something Muḥammad said was totally at odds with anything I could accept? And if I found Muḥammad unacceptable, what would become of the love and logic I had discovered in the Bahá'í Faith?

On an intellectual level, I knew that it was I who was really being judged, even as are all the people of previous dispensations who must discern the advent of the new Manifestation. But I had to do this a little differently. I had pretty well accepted the station of Bahá'u'lláh, so I was being judged in reverse. I had one piece missing from this vast jigsaw puzzle of theology, history, and philosophy. I held in my hand the missing piece—the Qur'án, and my acceptance of Muḥammad as a Manifestation of God. I could look at the gap in the puzzle and I could look at the piece individually, but now I had to pray that the piece would fit flawlessly into place, even if I had to turn it around a bit to configure it just right.

So there I was in my small attic apartment sipping some tea and bracing myself for the possibility that all I had studied for almost three years was about to be undone. If I found in this work something at odds with what Bahá'u'lláh had said or what Christ had said, or if the words did not comply with my own critical standards of what constitutes holy scripture, then the *mizán* with which I had experimented would suddenly be endangered and I would be in a state of critical doubt. I would have to look elsewhere for some integrating principle for my understanding of reality, or I might become so discouraged and disheartened as to abandon the search altogether.

After glancing through a few passages, even as some Muslims do—poking my finger among the pages to see where Providence pointed me—I decided it would be most important to see specifically what Muḥammad had to say about Christ.

First I encountered Muḥammad's explicit confirmation of the concept of progressive revelation in the following passage in Sura 2:81:

Moreover, to Moses gave we "the Book," and we raised up apostles after him; and to Jesus, son of Mary, gave we clear proofs of his mission, and strengthened him by the Holy Spirit. So oft

then as an apostle cometh to you with that which your souls
desire not, swell ye with pride, and treat some as imposters, and
slay others?

My muscles began to relax a bit, and my heart beat faster. I looked
in the index and began reading those verses in the several suras where
Muḥammad comments about Christ. Immediately I was drawn to
those passages that the index said were explicitly discussing the doctrine of the trinity.

As I read, I was overjoyed to discover that so far He agreed with
me, with everything I had concluded! (Obviously on a deeper level I
was aware that, inasmuch as He had said this some twelve centuries
earlier, I was actually agreeing with Him):

O ye people of the Book! Overstep not bounds in your religion;
and of God, speak only truth. The Messiah, Jesus, son of Mary,
is only an apostle of God, and his Word which he conveyed
into Mary, and a Spirit proceeding from himself. Believe therefore in God and his apostles, and say not, "Three:" (there is a
Trinity)—Forebear—it will be better for you. God is only one
God! Far be it from His glory that He should have a son! His,
whatever is in the Heavens, and whatever is in the Earth! And
God is a sufficient Guardian.

The Messiah disdaineth not to be a servant of God, nor do
the angels who are nigh unto Him. (4:169–170)

Of course, I was well aware that to most Christians coming upon
this verse, the word *only* would jump out of context and ruin the true
purpose of Muḥammad's observation, that there is only one God,
and that the Manifestations, though lofty in rank and far beyond the
understanding of ordinary human beings, are *not* God Himself, but

"only" servants of God, the son of God, or an apostle of God. Furthermore, as Muḥammad also points out, the Manifestations hardly "disdain" this position or deem it lowly or servile. The Manifestations one and all humble Themselves before God and praise God for having ordained Them to render this important service to the advancement of God's prize creation, humankind.

I now felt myself literally warmed with delight and mounting conviction. I found another passage where Muḥammad cites the statement of Christ regarding this same issue—that God is Christ's Lord, that while being the true Messiah, Christ is still a servant of God and not synonymous with Him nor His coequal: "Infidels now are they who say, 'God is the Messiah, Son of Mary'; for the Messiah said, 'O children of Israel! worship God, my Lord and your Lord'" (5:76).

Muḥammad thus acknowledges that Christ is precisely who He claimed to be, the promised Messiah, the Anointed One! Muḥammad even acknowledges the virgin birth of Christ, something many Christians have difficulty accepting. But most confirming of all for me was the entire Sura of Houd (sura 11), which discusses at length how each of the Prophets of God, including Noah, Abraham, Moses, and Christ, were all denied by the very people they were sent to teach.

The power of this brief sura for me derived in part from its vindication of Old Testament prophets and history. But in addition, the Sura of Houd also sets forth the very same discussion about the persistent rejection of the Manifestations that Bahá'u'lláh Himself discusses at the outset of His principal doctrinal work, the Kitáb-i-Íqán (*the Book of Certitude*) where He refers to those same passages.

The more I read, the more I wanted to read, because instead of reading with hesitancy or trepidation lest I discover aught that might undermine what I now realized was becoming my own personal *mizán,* I now read with the eagerness of a miner who has come upon those bits of gold that portend near access to a major vein.

How had all this been left unsaid by so many for so long? How was it that Muḥammad, in spite of what unjust deeds might later have been perpetrated in his name, had so clearly confirmed Christ's teachings (even as Christ had foretold He would) and had provided a historical perspective on progressive revelation that clarified all that had become so entangled and distorted by the patristic authorities in early Christianity?

Among the ancillary jewels I discovered that night were that the Council of Nicaea, at which a close vote in 325 CE determined that Christ was God, was, in fact, a politically motivated synod convoked by Emperor Constantine to unify what had become a divided and discordant Christian religion. He knew that before he could use its energy to reunify the fragmented spirit of the Roman Empire, he would first need to ensure that Christianity itself was unified.

I also came to appreciate that contemporary Islam, more than twelve centuries after its beginning with Muḥammad's Hegira in 622 CE, now bears no more resemblance to authentic Islam than does contemporary Christianity with its thousand sects and denominations bear any resemblance to the simple but profound verities and laws that Christ taught two thousand years ago.

In addition, since I was now beginning to accept and appreciate the Bahá'í belief that a new Manifestation appears only after the "Day" (the dispensation or duration of that Manifestation's teachings) of the previous Prophet has ended, I realized that by the time Muḥammad appeared and revealed the Qur'án, Christianity was so mutilated, both doctrinally and institutionally, that it was indeed damaged beyond repair, and that a new religion was necessary to convey the teachings of God to the faithful.

Intellectually, I was now at peace. I had but one last task to complete, and that was a personal obligation I felt. I was convinced I had the new knowledge. It now remained for me to lay out for myself the new course of action, a new path—one unknown to most, tread by only a few. I had leapt from that perilous train of the American Dream, bounced around a bit upon hitting the ground, but I had finally stood up, and I was smiling.

9

ON THE ROAD AGAIN

The Road goes ever on and on
Down from the door where it began.
Now far ahead the Road has gone,
And I must follow, if I can,
Pursuing it with eager feet,
Until it joins some larger way,
Where many paths and errand meet.
— JRR Tolkien, "Roads Go Ever On"

By midway through my sophomore year at Vanderbilt, I had finished testing alternative theories of religion. The more I applied the Bahá'í concepts of creation, of physical reality, and of the divine plan by which God is gradually educating humankind on planet Earth, the more I began to appreciate the logical coherence of all my studies.

What was more exciting still was that I began to appreciate how everything I studied was somehow related to everything else I studied, even as Bahá'u'lláh states in the Hidden Words: "Out of the wastes of nothingness, with the clay of My command I made thee to appear, and have ordained for thy training every atom in existence and the essence of all created things" (Persian, no. 29).

Suddenly Emerson's poem "Each and All," and the tumult of the Industrial Revolution, the onset of New Physics, and the lasting importance of Plato's *Republic* all took on a new and coordinated meaning for me. Every branch of learning was but a window into the Bahá'í portrait of reality as an organic and integrated expression of divine purpose.

The one remaining question concerned my personal commitment to this vision. Was I now truly ready to make the Bahá'í Faith my personal path on a permanent basis? I loved my solitude, cherished my own contemplation and inner dialogues. As I have noted earlier, I did not do well with figures of authority or with the idea of authority itself, at least no authority I had thus far in my life encountered. Most of the rules set by the authority figures in my life until this point had all seemed too arbitrary.

Even Dad's admonitions and restrictions had often seemed to derive more from his fear of something "going wrong." He was best off when the Oldsmobile was running well, the house was clean and orderly, and everyone was doing what he considered the proper thing, though gradually my brother and I would accustom Dad to accepting decisions that his own Christian farmer father back in Franklin, Tennessee, would have thought quite bizarre and inappropriate.

Consequently, I think it providential that it was at my parents' house over Christmas break in 1959 that I chose as the setting for my final examination of the new *mizán* before accepting it as my own. For while I had by this time employed the Bahá'í Faith to assay other theories of everything, it was now time to use my last resort, my last Ace-in-the-hole, to appraise the Bahá'í Faith as the standard I personally would apply, as a name I would acquire, as a new label for Johnny Bump.

AN EVENING AT THE FIGHTS

I remember so clearly in the early 1950s watching Gillette Friday Night Fights on TV with Dad. We loved it because we really cared about these guys—Jake LaMotta, Kid Gavilan, Rocky Graziano, Carmen Basilio, Archie Moore, Rocky Marciano, and the best, the very best, Sugar Ray Robinson. So it was my intention on a winter's eve at the end of 1959 to set up a match equal to the best I had seen on any of the Friday Night Fights.

My brother, like me, was home from school. He knew about my increasing interest in the Bahá'í Faith because any question I could not answer, I would ask him for the answer and a source in the Bahá'í writings to back up his response. Likewise, my former high school teacher Mr. Randolph, who had now become a respected personality on educational television in Atlanta, in addition to being a lawyer with a master's degree in history, was more than happy to oblige my request. He, too, had known of my interest in the Bahá'í Faith since our discussions in our Inquirer soirées.

I invited Mr. Randolph to come to our house for dinner, after which there would ensue what I hoped would be a battle of wits between these two intellectual icons of mine. It must be understood that Mr. Randolph was not conceited or bombastic. He was restrained, a true gentleman and a scholar. More than anything else, he respected logical discourse as the best method for getting at truth, whether it was examining a solution to what was then global polarization stemming from the cold war, or some more esoteric matter of physics or philosophy.

I knew that if there were some flaw in Bahá'í theology that I had overlooked, he, more than anyone else I could think of, would discover it, and he would do so unflinchingly. I also knew that above all else Bill likewise cherished logic, that without the rational basis for his belief in God, in the Bahá'í theory of reality, or in the logical proofs of the station of Bahá'u'lláh, he would have in no way considered becoming a Bahá'í. Where logic led, Bill's mind would follow, and where his mind went, his faith would soon follow, and not mechanically, not with mild affection, but with his whole heart.

I had also established in my mind that should the Bahá'í teachings survive this final test ("final" in my mind at the time), I would have no alternative but to become a Bahá'í. For I, no less than they, cherished logic. I could no longer pretend that I would allow my future choices to be dictated by any other sort of guidance. The entire decision could be summed up in a simple but inescapable syllogism. If there is a God, and if God has sent a sequence of Messengers, each with specific guidance for a particular period of time, and if Bahá'u'lláh is the Manifestation for this age, then how could I do aught else but accept His station and follow His guidance. Logically, to do otherwise would be to act against my own best interest.

COUNTDOWN TO THE FIGHT

Thus far I had established to my satisfaction that the Bahá'í theory of history seemed accurate. I had also proven to my satisfaction that the concept of successive Prophets enabled me to understand most of the troublesome or enigmatic passages in scripture, whether in the Old Testament, the New Testament, or even in the Qur'án, the Vedas, or the Bhagavad-Gita.

The first premise or proposition in this deductive reasoning is that there is a God Who has chosen to create human beings so that He might bestow upon us unconditional love. Implicit in this premise is that these beings (us) are fashioned with sufficient intelligence to obtain knowledge about the Creator and with sufficient free will to pursue attaining that knowledge of the Creator.

Another premise is that since we cannot instinctively know how to go about comprehending an essentially metaphysical being (God), especially one possessing properties or attributes to a degree beyond anything we ourselves can achieve, we require an educator who can translate that essentially unknowable reality into terms and images we can more easily comprehend, a being who inherently possesses this knowledge, who does not need to be taught by others, because who among ordinary human beings could possibly know what is beyond human ken?

Furthermore, this educator would have to be willing and able not only to convey this information to us in terms that we can comprehend, but willing also to undergo humiliation and suffering to accomplish this task in a gentle and subtle method so as not to impose his will on us.

Still another proposition is that because education must take place over time in sequential increments of learning, no single educator during one segment of time could possibly provide all the guidance required for the totality of human advancement. Consequently, there have always been and will always be periodic updating of the collective advancement of the human body politic through the successive appearances of Manifestations. Like teachers of various grade levels in a school, They continue this progressive enlightenment from where the previous Manifestation left off.

The final step in this logical sequence was the clincher. If everything in these first three propositions is true, and if Bahá'u'lláh is the Manifestation appointed by the Creator to provide the needed information to guide humankind at this critical stage of transition in our collective history, then by what possible rationale could anyone not do what Bahá'u'lláh proposes? How could anyone who has studied these propositions and accepted them not become a follower of Bahá'u'lláh by joining the religion that He Himself had designed or not abide by His guidance regarding how to pursue life's journey?

Naturally I was fully aware that simply knowing the best course of action does not ensure that we human beings will follow it. Socrates long ago posited the theory that no one does evil in full knowledge, that all recalcitrance is the result of not appreciating the full impact or outcome of our wrongdoing. He theorized that, since by committing injustice, we injure ourselves and our own souls more than we injure anyone else, any perpetration of injustice on our part implies that we simply do not understand or fully appreciate the end result of our actions on our own well-being. This notion may at first seem so abstract as to be pointless, but I have discovered over time that it really isn't. For instance, one who smokes cigarettes may be aware that he or she is risking future calamity, but the distance in time between cause and effect is so great that one is able to take the long-term risk to enjoy what is perceived to be some more immediate palliative. Therefore, from Socrates' point of view, the smoker cannot be truly said to possess full or complete knowledge. The smoker possesses only a vague awareness of the theory. The possession of *full* or *complete* knowledge in this example would be the subjective experience of the throes of a dire illness—such as lung cancer—that may well be the end result of this chosen course of action.

In short, at this point in the progress of my assessment of the Bahá'í path, certainly a path "less travelled by," if I could complete the syllogism successfully, I would no longer need to question which path would be best for me. The right choice would be clear. The remainder of my choices, challenges, and milestones on this path would consist of acquiring bit by painful bit the discipline and courage sufficient to stay the course by willfully transforming my character, a process portrayed by Bahá'u'lláh as habituating by degrees the appropriate responses to life as delineated in the authoritative Bahá'í texts.

Religion would no longer be a matter of using myself or my own "comfort" level as the standard or the *mizán* for choosing what was a "good fit" for me. Having been an athlete, I knew that discomfort and persistent stress against my own inertia was the only sure method for advancing my physical condition. I likewise realized from reading Bahá'í scripture, that this same sort of persistence would be required of me were I to accept this path in pursuit of my spiritual advancement.

I always seem to return to the sports analogy when I still struggle to advance, I suppose because I still remember so clearly the strength of will required to get into condition, especially running track. While training, I soon realized that if I never ran harder or longer than what was not particularly stressful, I would never improve beyond my present state of readiness. To become a first-class hurdler, I had to run a full flight of hurdles not once or twice, but over and over. Pushing myself beyond the limits of comfort and accustoming myself over time to increasingly more strenuous exercise has remained for me a useful personal analogy as I continue to pursue intellectual and spiritual objectives.

Also related to this analogy in my own mind as I was considering the Bahá'í theory of human enlightenment and spiritual advancement was the fact that no matter how disciplined I tried to be in pushing myself, there was no substitute for a good coach. I never outgrew the need for someone who knew my capacity and knew how to stretch me a bit more than I might have been willing to push myself. Obviously in this somewhat trite analogy, the Bahá'í "coach" is the voice of the Manifestation Whose writings, when perused on a daily basis as prescribed by Bahá'u'lláh, constantly exhort us to increasingly higher levels of performance in every aspect of our daily lives.

THE FRIDAY NIGHT CONTEST

I was not anxious or concerned about the outcome of the contest between the Bahá'í theory of everything and Mr. Randolph's logical queries. I was more interested in discovering the truth rather than trying to pick a winner. I had never known my brother to be defeated in intellectual combat, but neither had I ever known Mr. Randolph to back down. Since I was still not yet officially a Bahá'í and had sincerely withheld some final commitment until I was completely certain that the syllogism was complete, I decided I would be a gadfly or moderator and judge and not a participant in this encounter.

If the dialogue became placid, I could trouble the waters a bit by tossing out some of the more abstruse questions I had tackled: Since historically the majority of people do not recognize the new Manifestations of God, how does Bahá'u'lláh account for this apparent failure of progressive revelation to succeed? What happens to those who die without having a chance to recognize the Manifestation? How does Bahá'u'lláh explain the suffering of the innocent? If all previous religions ultimately deviate from the principles revealed by the Prophet and Founder of the religion, why will that same process of disintegration not impede the goals of the Bahá'í Faith?

As always, my mother was delighted to have company over, and as usual she prepared a meal that contemporary families can enjoy only in fables—southern cooking was no myth. But afterward, she and Dad absented themselves from the living room so that the great debate might ensue unencumbered by other presences or points of view. They both knew, I now realize, exactly what was afoot and what was at stake—the future of their "little" boy, their "Johnny Bump."

After dinner we all sat down in the living room sipping Mother's coffee from her Buttercup Wedgewood china, her very best for the occasion. The conversation started off civil enough with the first rounds quite benign. Mr. Randolph already knew the fundamental premise of the Faith, so to start things off, Bill rehearsed a bit of progressive revelation and the relationship between Christ's teachings and those of Bahá'u'lláh. But there was no edge to his tone, no fire, none of the tension I had expected (and secretly hoped for).

Bill was, or could be, a fierce debater. I could ask the simplest of questions, and he would bombard me with a forty-five minute discourse. I might say, "Hey Bill, I forgot the formula for the area of a circle." The answer would not be, "Sure, John, it's πr^2." No, Bill would first be sure I understood the importance of Euclid's *Elements* as the most important math text in history, "even though it was written almost three centuries before Christ." He would then give me the history of "π" and its progress through the years, especially as modern mathematicians tried to see how far they could take this "irrational" constant that represents the ratio of circumference to diameter in any given circle.

He was still doing this in the last conversations we had on the day before he passed on to the next realm, where I feel certain he is still doing the same thing with the angelic hosts. Of note is the fact that this habit of his did not stem from a desire to demonstrate how much he knew, nor from a need to communicate with any captive audience. It was, I realized even back then, from his awareness as a teacher that simply knowing a fact means nothing if one does not understand what that fact means in relationship to the rest of reality. Otherwise you are simply enabling someone to parrot the knowledge someone else has acquired. True education must provide the basis for the answer and the tools to find answers for yourself.

The problem was, of course, that ultimately all knowledge relates to all other knowledge and Bill, if not stopped at some point, would, I sometimes felt, proceed to demonstrate the entirety of that relationship. I recall only a few occasions when the answer to a simple question ceased of its own accord without my having to say, "Bill, hold on. I really need to know the answer. Just give me the answer."

So how was it that now, when I needed this sort of overpowering perspective, he was suddenly possessed of restraint, respect, kindness, and succinct answers? Was this a trick? I knew he was not intimidated by Mr. Randolph. I knew each question posed by Mr. Randolph could precipitate an hour-long discourse under ordinary circumstances, and yet the evening proceeded apace without any hint of abrasiveness or contentiousness on the part of either of these two fine people.

Within less than two hours, the "great debate" wound down to a pleasant conversation about absolutely tangential matters of no consequence or importance to me. They had become kind, friendly, amicable. All of Mr. Randolph's questions had been answered to his satisfaction, and, having himself no vested interest in the outcome, he and Bill began to talk of politics and history, neither of which was on point as far as I was concerned.

That was it? That was the great debate? I could have done as well on my own, I thought to myself. I could have answered every one of Mr. Randolph's questions even more completely than had my big brother. Why had I bothered to arrange this confrontation that ultimately degenerated into a "meeting of the minds" more than the clash I had anticipated.

While I sat there off to the side watching and listening to this polite repartee, something rather significant occurred to me. I had my answer after all. If the brightest mentor I had come to meet thus far in my education could discover no great contradictions in or problems with this theory of everything, even when he was pitted against the brightest mentor I had been fortunate to have outside my formal schooling, then why should I be disturbed?

Why should I not feel encouraged by the fact that I could have answered these questions myself? This realization should not cause me dismay. The reverse should be true! I had become sufficiently well versed in the teachings of Bahá'u'lláh that I could attempt to explain them and possibly to defend them, even to some of the brightest minds I would encounter!

GETTING ON BOARD

Before the Christmas vacation was over, I had three more dramatic moves to make, only one of which turned out to be very dramatic at all. First, I had to inform my brother and his wife Judith that I had decided to become a Bahá'í. This occurred unexpectedly when Judith and I were returning from a talk Bill was to have given in Gainesville, Georgia.

Bill had felt ill, so Judith and I had gone in his stead. Judith gave the main presentation, a basic introduction to the Bahá'í Faith, but during the question and answer period following this presentation on the Bahá'í Faith, I found myself offering answers to those who had come to investigate this religion, or else I would amplify answers other Bahá'ís would give. I certainly was not trying to demonstrate the depth of my knowledge or my capacity to field difficult or complex questions. I simply felt that I could offer lucid answers, because the questions these seekers were asking were the precise questions I had pursued for three years, and the answers they sought were the very answers I had spent an incalculable amount of time discovering, and corroborating to my satisfaction.

On the way home in the car, I remember saying to Judith that this was ludicrous. Here I was having established to my satisfaction that the Bahá'í description of religion and religious history was true, that Bahá'u'lláh was indeed the Manifestation of God for this Day, that I was sufficiently capable of teaching others about this good news and that I could easily do so and take joy in doing it, and yet I was denying myself the bounty and support of assuming this new name on the basis of a promise I had made more than two years earlier to my father.

After all, the purpose of Dad's covenant with me was to protect me from following Bill blindly or from following a path without thoroughly investigating it for myself. But I was doing neither of these. For more than three years I had studied it, tested it, and was now advocating it to others. What sense did it make to deny myself this privilege?

So when we returned home that same evening, I approached my father with tears in my eyes as he embraced me, having no idea what was wrong. "Dad," I murmured in a broken voice, "I'm sorry, but I'm afraid I can no longer keep my promise to you. I must become a Bahá'í!" I sobbed on his chest as he embraced me firmer, patted my back and said, "Son, son, there's no need to cry about it." I backed away, and quickly my tears turned into laughter, and we all celebrated my decision.

GIVING THE PREACHER THE "WORD"

The final dramatic encounter that holiday season was to meet with my minister at St. Mark's church. This was an unnecessary move on my part. Officially Bahá'ís are not supposed to belong to other religions, though they can attend services and are even exhorted by Bahá'u'lláh to "Consort with the followers of all religions in a spirit of friendliness and fellowship" (*Gleanings*, no. 43.6). My lack of attendance would surely signal my withdrawal from the church. But I was still receiving in the mail the weekly bulletin from the church, which meant that according to their rolls, I was still officially a Methodist, and I did not want that. Furthermore, this was my first opportunity to test my mettle in defending my newfound beliefs, my new personal *mizán*.

Dow Kirkpatrick was a fine man, a daring minister, a capable theologian, and a respected friend to my family and all their friends at St. Mark Methodist Church. He continued to be so until he passed away when my mother was in her nineties. Consequently, I was certain that his response to me would be unlike that of my philosophy professor at Vanderbilt who had smiled benignly (and condescendingly) when I gave him a copy of 'Abdu'l-Bahá's *Some Answered Questions*, a virtual encyclopedia of Bahá'í answers to all major philosophical and theological concerns.

While the philosopher professor could respond with largesse without feeling any implicit obligation to refute the assertions contained in the Bahá'í teachings, surely Dr. Kirkpatrick would discern in this theory of religion a moral imperative, indeed, a sacred duty on his part to test the thesis at the heart of these teachings, especially that the advent of Bahá'u'lláh represented the Second Coming of Christ as foretold in scripture.

Was this indeed an accurate account of God's plan? Was Bahá'u'lláh actually who He claimed to be? Was He indeed the return of Christ promised to occur in the Time of the End? And if these assertions were accurate, should he himself not give up his ministry and become a Bahá'í? And if these claims were bogus, should he not protect one of his "flock" from such spurious assertions?

As one of the stalwart members of the church and former president of the youth department elected by other students, some of whom were pre-ministerial majors, I would surely present him with some sense of challenge, some sense of duty. Surely he would feel the need either to save me from this wayward and perverse notion, or to point out some subtle flaws in its thesis, or, failing either of these, he would agree to investigate its assertions for himself. How could he, or any person in such a station and with such a fine mind, find an alternative response? I was prepared for action!

I dressed in my best suit. I selected a Bahá'í text or two to take with me with particularly powerful passages marked. I also brought the Bible my parents had given me as I went off to college. I made an "official" appointment to meet with him. I said a few prayers and drove to the church with grim determination to hold my own against whichever of the three responses would ensue.

I was cordially invited into his office, and I seated myself opposite his executive desk. "So, how can I help you, Johnny?" He had a lovely, knowing smile, and an incredibly warm and comforting voice. He had always been most kind to me. I remember he had gone to the trouble to send me a newspaper clipping of my picture when I had won some award in high school.

"Dr. Kirkpatrick, I wish to have my name officially withdrawn from the rolls of St. Mark Church." I had planned out the first sentence or two, and what I said next would depend on his response, like the opening gambit of a chess match.

"Oh? Why is that?" He was serious now, but not in the least disturbed, it seemed, and that unnerved me—this was nothing at all like the Baptist minister who had given me the ride and cautioned me about the road to hell should I continue down the path of studying the Bahá'í Faith.

"I have decided to become a Bahá'í."

"Is that so?" He knew about the Bahá'í Faith because he was well aware that Bill had become a Bahá'í. Even though Bill had not belonged to St. Mark Church, Bill was still Albert and Helen Hatcher's son, and the Hatchers were close friends. Mom was head of the junior youth department, and was a firm pillar of the St. Mark community of believers. Dad was treasurer and kept watch over the Sunday contributions.

"Yes, I have come to believe that Bahá'u'lláh is the most recent Manifestation of God, that He is . . . [pregnant pause for dramatic effect] . . . the return of Christ!" He sat back away from his desk a little. There were a few seconds of silence.

"And you want your name removed from the rolls, then?"

"Uh, why, yes. That's right."

"OK," he said. "That's no problem." He smiled, leaned over across the large desk to shake my hand. "I wish you the very best in your religious journey, and I will certainly keep you in my prayers and take care of this for you."

What sort of gambit was this? This was none of the three responses I had anticipated. The non-answer answer? I would much later encounter this technique when I read Melville's wonderful short story "Bartleby the Scribner," a remarkable work about a character who successfully befuddles and manipulates his employer (the first-person narrator) simply by responding to every request that he do something with, "I would prefer not."

That's what Dow had done to me, the "I prefer not" to any possible debate or discussion. "Should you not be afraid that you are committing the same negligence as did the Sanhedrin with Christ?" I could have told him. "Are you not being challenged to recognize the Messiah even as were the Pharisaic clerics in their day?" I could have remarked in a rhetorical flourish. But, no, he would have none of that!

Of course, I now know he was wiser than that, certainly more experienced than I, who would through my lifelong journey as a Bahá'í encounter this very same non-response response from some of the best minds I met. And in time I came to respect that response as not being a denial of reality or religion or the desire to discover the truth. I came to receive it as a matter of timing, of circumstance, and, most of all, the mysterious spiritual journey that each soul must take. Even as Christ Himself had taught in the parable of the vineyard, it matters not when you discover the truth in your journey; your reward will be the same—eternal reunion with the same God.

Even though my mother through the years would send Dow copies of books on the Bahá'í Faith penned by Bill and me, and even though she herself would become a Bahá'í at the age of ninety-three, Dow never expressed too much interest that I became aware of, though he was always kind and cordial whenever we met and talked in the years to come. He was a good man, a sincere and devout lover of humankind.

In a bit of celestial irony, however, a few years after my meeting with him, Dow was transferred to one of the highest ranking jewels among Methodist church assignments, the Methodist Church in Evanston, Illinois. The great irony in this was that the entrancing and astoundingly beautiful Bahá'í House of Worship in Wilmette, Illinois, is but a few blocks up Sheridan Road from the Methodist Church. Consequently, during his entire tenure there, he was forever having students from across the street at Northwestern University besiege him with questions about the Bahá'í Faith.

A NEW METHOD FOR TEACHING ABOUT GOD?

Bahá'u'lláh abolished the clergy and prohibits proselytizing. Therefore the spread of the Bahá'í Faith to its present status of being the second most diffuse religion in the world (second only to Christianity) is the result of individual Bahá'ís acceding to Bahá'u'lláh's exhortation that all Bahá'ís teach the Cause to whoever expresses interest.

At the same time, this effort has specific constraints imposed by Bahá'u'lláh. Bahá'ís should proffer the Faith only when they have encountered a listening ear, someone who sincerely wants this information so that if "your hearer respond, he will have responded to his own behoof" and not through coercion or enticements. Therefore, the Bahá'í teacher should be careful not to "contend with anyone, nay, strive to make him aware of the truth, with kindly manner and most convincing exhortation" (*Gleanings*, no. 128.10).

Of course, this guidance means that it is entirely appropriate to ask someone if they would like to know about it—they can hardly ask about something if they don't know it exists. Nevertheless, as we teach others about what we believe to be a rather important bit of news, we must ever be aware, and impress upon the listener—whether they be seekers or simply curious—that Bahá'ís do not consider themselves better or more virtuous than people in other faiths simply because we have taken on a new name or have chosen to follow the Bahá'í path. We are well aware that people in many other faith traditions are also striving to be spiritual, to be "good" people, and on a personal level may be doing a better job than we are. As Bahá'ís we simply feel we have been privileged to be made aware of information devised to guide humanity to the remarkable confluence of all past knowledge that the revelation of Bahá'u'lláh assembles and explains.

In short, early on I became aware that taking on a new name would not make me a new person. Becoming a Bahá'í is a path and a process, the designation of the intention to pursue a lifelong goal, a *Do* or *Dao* as we call it in the Taoist tradition of the martial arts. One has accepted a new perspective, a new *mizán*. Putting that knowledge into action, that second inextricably related part of the two-part response to the teachings of the Manifestation so critical to personal spiritual ascent, would be for me another matter altogether. The next five decades would be no less an adventure for my having chosen this path, a realization I rediscover almost on a daily basis.

COMMITTING TO THE "BAHÁ'Í LIFE"

Bahá'u'lláh notes that the laws He reveals are not intended to be constraints or restrictions on personal freedom: "True liberty consisteth in man's submission unto My commandments, little as ye know it. Were men to observe that which We have sent down unto them from the Heaven of Revelation, they would, of a certainty, attain unto perfect liberty" (*Gleanings*, no. 159.4).

In my own simple way of explaining this principle through the years, I have often compared the laws of Bahá'u'lláh to those we impose on our children. Some rules are established to keep them healthy—brush teeth, bathe, eat good food. Other rules are devised to protect them from harm—don't play in the street; don't run with scissors; always wear a helmet when you're in a rock and stick battle.

The point is that experience may be the most profound teacher, but it isn't always the wisest or kindest teacher. Ask any alcoholic or drug addict whose life has become imprisoned by this physiological and psychological craving whether or not they wish they had learned this lesson vicariously rather than through personal experience.

But as I understood from the beginning of my investigation into the Bahá'í Faith, at the heart of the Bahá'í life is the attempt to become spiritual, and this process involves thousands of personal choices and judgments applied on a daily basis. For however much the laws of Bahá'u'lláh might help us establish the boundaries of the path that is the Bahá'í life, the really big decisions are left entirely to the individual: What vocation should I pursue? Whom should I marry? How do I raise my children in an environment that has so much potential to harm them? How do I prioritize my daily life according to the exigencies of spiritual aspirations?

At the heart of aspiring to spiritual development is not the avoidance of those activities that might prove destructive, nor is it a mindless adherence to those exercises that help induce a spiritual attitude, but rather the thoughtful examination of those patterns of daily action that infuse within us spiritual impetus, daily guidance, and short-term and long-term goals. Because within the context of almost every course of action recommended by Bahá'u'lláh is a breadth of possibilities insofar as personal action is concerned.

Free will and individual judgment are always at the forefront of how any individual chooses to implement his or her own expression of the overall objective of being a Bahá'í, because being a Bahá'í has no limitations, no uniform objective, no point of salvation. The individual Bahá'í, whether in this world or the world to come, is always a work in progress.

Keenly aware of this reality, I officially joined the Bahá'í Faith in the Nashville Bahá'í community immediately upon my return to school in 1960. That was where I had done my most serious study of the Bahá'í Faith, and this was the Bahá'í community in which I would now participate in all Bahá'í activities.

Fortunately for me, this community enabled me to begin my path in the bosom of a body of believers who would forever establish in my mind the essential tenor and virtues of what a Bahá'í community should be. It is especially interesting to recall that community from my present perspective of knowing what would eventually happen to each individual that constituted that remarkable group with whom I was so fortunate to be associated.

A "STRAIGHT-THINKING BAHÁ'Í"

The Bahá'í Center in Nashville was in the 1950s a well-kept white frame house just off the Vanderbilt campus. The Bahá'í community itself was about half white and half African American. Most Bahá'ís in the community were lower middle-class economically, but the majority were extremely well-educated, erudite, and knowledgeable about the Faith, and many would go on to render great service to the Bahá'í Faith in a variety of capacities.

But among the many meaningful and lasting encounters between me and the members of that community over the next several years, one had possibly the greatest impact on me. I recall one statement made to me by Winston Evans early in my association with him. He had once been a Wall Street tycoon, only to have lost his entire fortune in the stock market crash of 1929. In addition to being refined and experienced about life, he had memorized vast passages from the Bahá'í writings that he would draw on randomly during the course of any conversation.

We had been talking about the difficulties of overcoming what the Bahá'í writings allude to as the "insistent self," a phrase employed by 'Abdu'l-Bahá as an allusion to the ego, the relentless pull of selfishness and vanity. It also clearly referred to the lust for power, as well as our persistent vulnerability to vain imaginings of every sort.

Winston had just finished reading to me a short story he had written, "Midnight with Dr. X." It was a true account of his conversation with a prominent theologian to whom he had explained the teachings of the Bahá'í Faith—because of his previous status, he was often called upon to speak with people of rank and status who wanted to know about the Bahá'í teachings. And like my experience with my minister, my philosophy professor, and so many more I would in later years encounter, the non-response response of Dr. X was, in the context of this individual's training and background and professed anticipation of the fulfillment of the "End Days," so ironic as to be both shocking and terribly sad.

We both looked at each other when he finished reading "Midnight with Dr. X" and instantly knew what the other was thinking, that our sadness was not for the loss humanity would suffer because of this individual's inability to recognize Bahá'u'lláh, accept the truth of the Bahá'í Faith, and contribute to promulgating these teachings. Our sadness was for the needless loss he himself would endure for not having chosen to follow what he had already indicated he was eagerly anticipating.

Winston looked at me, reached over and with his gnarled hands took my own. "John," he said with a look I still recall, "always be a straight-thinking Bahá'í."

He did not explain what he meant by the phrase. I'm not even sure if those were his exact words. But I knew precisely what he meant, and I have never forgotten it, especially when tests have come, as inevitably they must come. How else can we grow unless we are stretched beyond what is comfortable?

What I sense Winston meant by this exhortation was that so long as I made the Bahá'í Faith my *mizán*—the standard, the balance against which I weighed my character, my decisions, and the efficacy of those ideas and decisions proffered me by others—I would never get too lost.

I have not always kept the scales balanced, but I have always known when they were out of kilter. And I would no more abandon that *mizán* than I would take my own life. Bahá'u'lláh exhorts us, "Bring thyself to account each day ere thou art summoned to a reckoning; for death, unheralded, shall come upon thee and thou shalt be called to give account for thy deeds" (Hidden Words, Arabic, no. 31).

As I understand this guidance, this daily "accounting" is a period of reflection, meditation, and review of our deeds weighed against the standard set forth by the authoritative Bahá'í texts about what constitutes the Bahá'í life. And the Bahá'í life is characterized by both inner and outer demonstrations of virtue, even as Bahá'u'lláh asserts succinctly, "Know thou of a truth: He that biddeth men be just and himself committeth iniquity is not of Me, even though he bear My name" (Hidden Words, Arabic, no. 28).

Shoghi Effendi, the great-grandson of Bahá'u'lláh and the appointed Guardian of the Bahá'í Faith, echoes the same theme with the following exhortation regarding the worldwide spread of the Bahá'í religion: "One thing and only one thing will unfailingly and alone secure the undoubted triumph of this sacred Cause, namely, the extent to which our own inner life and private character mirror forth in their manifold aspects the splendor of those eternal principles proclaimed by Bahá'u'lláh" (*Bahá'í Administration*, p. 66).

10

THE FEAR OF DEATH
IN MADRID

Thou art My dominion and My dominion perisheth not;
wherefore fearest thou thy perishing? Thou art My light and
My light shall never be extinguished; why dost thou dread
extinction? Thou art My glory and My glory fadeth not; thou
art My robe and My robe shall never be outworn. Abide then
in thy love for Me, that thou mayest find Me in the realm
of glory.
——Bahá'u'lláh, The Hidden Words, Arabic, no. 14

So is this the end of my personal story? I took the Bahá'í path, the one less traveled by, and lived more or less successfully, decorously, easily. Did I do what I was told without wandering from the prescribed twists and turns of that path? Did I pass by all the appropriate milestones so that I now eagerly await my final big milestone, the termination of the physical phase of my existence and the "transition" to the metaphysical realm?

BEING BAHÁ'Í
Well, first of all, it seems that becoming a Bahá'í is not the end of anybody's story. It's only a beginning. And while Milton may have been

correct that "they also serve who only stand and wait,"[8] the service out-
lined in the Bahá'í paradigm is not a passive process, but rather quite
an active and participatory strategy for achieving spiritual development.

There are several strategically important features of this path, this
Bahá'í life, that I feel must be understood before any allusion to my
own wild ride can be appreciated. These features, what we might
categorize as the "art of living," are likewise essential if we are to comprehend, let alone embrace, the Bahá'í concepts about the even more
demanding "art of dying."

GUIDELINES AND SIGNPOSTS

Some twists and turns in the Bahá'í life are heralded by cautionary
signs, like those we might come upon while trekking along a mountain path or a precipice or a waterfall, signs that tell us we might get
injured if we aren't really careful. In the authoritative Bahá'í texts[9] that
outline the daily regimen that Bahá'ís should follow, this guidance is
sometimes expressed in terms of various laws. There are instructions
about chastity, about abstention from drugs and alcohol, about the
daily need to pray and reflect, the obligation to have a vocation, the
caution about not wishing for others what we would not wish for
ourselves, and the constant reminder for us to avoid getting seduced
by the material trappings of this spiritual journey, even though we are
encouraged to appreciate the landscape as we go.

The point is that the art of living the Bahá'í life is not a process
of mindlessly doing what we are told, of following some vast canon
of law. Bahá'u'lláh has abolished the confession of sins and has com-

---

8. From Milton's sonnet "On His Blindness," line 14.
9. The authoritative texts of the Bahá'í Faith are the revealed or scriptural
works of Bahá'u'lláh, the writings and verified statements of 'Abdu'l-Bahá, the
writings of Shoghi Effendi, and the decisions and guidance of the Universal House
of Justice.

manded that each of us assess our own progress every day. In fact, Bahá'u'lláh abolished clergy, establishing in its stead various levels of elected administrative institutions.

Furthermore, this Bahá'í path includes a virtually endless number of valuable side excursions. In fact, it is accurate to say that each Bahá'í must design his or her own individual journey according to a panoply of personal choices. Or stated another way, there are an infinite number of equally valuable paths to arrive at the same lofty destination of learning to know and to worship the Creator, a process that is accomplished first by recognizing God's Manifestation for the age in which we live, and second by following His ample guidance for our personal pursuit of life's varied and endless objectives—what the character Ulysses in Tennyson's poem by the same name calls that "untraveled world, whose margin fades / For ever and for ever when I move":

> I am a part of all that I have met;
> Yet all experience is an arch wherethrough
> Gleams that untravelled world, whose margin fades
> For ever and for ever when I move.
> How dull it is to pause, to make an end,
> To rust unburnished, not to shine in use!
> As though to breathe were life. Life piled on life
> Were all too little, and of one to me
> Little remains . . .

SALVATION AS FORWARD MOTION

It would be helpful, perhaps, if we sum up the Bahá'í concept of life's journey and objective in somewhat less poetic terms. As with any religion of worth, the goal of being a Bahá'í is to become a better person. But unlike many religions, the Bahá'í teachings do not portray our spiritual progress as having some final point of attainment, some ultimate state or stage of "salvation."

Inasmuch as any given virtue is endlessly perfectible, so too the assemblage of these virtues for any given individual is likewise infinitely perfectible. In addition, because no two people have ever been the same or ever will be, no two life experiences, no two Bahá'í paths, are going to be exactly the same, and we do ourselves a great disservice to compare our own progress to that of another, whether to feel good about how we've done or to become discouraged at our seeming lack of development by comparison to someone else.

This does not imply that we never achieve a state of felicity or spiritual certitude or comfort. The very act of making progress at any stage is enjoyable and instantly rewarding. The point is that there is no end to this joyful journey, no point at which there is no more progress to make or nothing more to learn, whether in this life or in the continuation of life in the realm of the spirit. Thus, being in motion is existentially rewarding in and of itself.

Of course, we must constantly monitor our progress to be sure we do not rest in one place too long and thereby become stagnant or even regressive in our trek. To nudge us along this trail, therefore, we soon discover that whatever path we choose for ourselves, we will encounter a virtually endless array of tests, trials, choices, and celebrations. We will endure the astounding joy of discovery, the sadness of loss, the love of the beloved, the guilt at failures, quickly supplanted by our determination to do better.

CAUTION: FAILURE IS POSSIBLE!

It is imperative that we pay close attention to the path because it is entirely possible to make a blunder and plummet, thereby incurring a serious injury or two, most especially when we fail to recognize what misstep caused us to slip in the first place. Without reflection and assessment, we could well end up repeating the same mistake over and over again.

If such inattention to warning signs, or to the reason for our repeated failure, does indeed become habitual, we can develop another well-recognized symptom or syndrome that Aristotle characterized as *hamartia*. Known in classical theater as the "tragic flaw," *harmartia* is most often indicated by a pattern of consistent failure to make good moral choices. But because we have the capacity to recognize and overcome this flaw by making better choices, we are accountable for our own tragic fall.

WATCH FOR FALLING ROCKS!

Among the signs that caution us about the "rules of the road," are pithy aphorisms by Bahá'u'lláh in one of His first works, the Hidden Words. This summary and synthesis of all the spiritual teachings of previous Manifestations provides a succinct collection of spiritual guidance, and, for our added enjoyment and benefit, they are framed in jewel-like poetic utterances.

While there are many different Hidden Words, each one containing complete guidance unto itself, there are several major themes that are punctuated throughout this collection. Among them are the familiar advice we have received about morality and spirituality throughout the ages: materiality should be used for spiritual development, not as an end in itself; avoid speaking ill about your fellow pilgrims; try your best to help those who are having trouble along the way; do not despair when the road gets rough because change is soon to follow; use your many talents and gifts to assist all who wish to join you on this path; and, above all else, stay focused at all times on the destination so that when this physical stage of your life's journey ends, you will be ready and eager to continue the trek in the world to come.

Some of these jewels of guidance we may tend to ignore because we may think they are the obvious sort of spiritual advice we have heard so often that we can become inured to the power of the truth they portray. "Sure, sure, the Golden Rule again. I get it, already!" Over time, we may neglect to pay that much attention, the way we do when we encounter actual signs along winding mountainous roads that alert us, "Watch Out for Falling Rocks!"

But of course, few of us have ever seen these rocks falling. We may have seen some rocks on the shoulder of the road after they have fallen, or we may spot some boulders that look like a good rain might loosen them from their precarious attachment to the rock face. On some level we are probably thinking that if there really were such an immediate danger, we would have encountered a sign that was more blatant, something like, "Stay Off This Road! Falling Rocks Will Crash onto Your Car!"

Perhaps we could just wait until the rocks have already fallen, and then drive around the debris. But the clear implication of these signs is that the rocks fall intermittently, unpredictably, sometimes catastrophically. That being the case, how will keeping an eye out do much good?

For example, let us imagine that a father and son are driving along a treacherous stretch of road. "Hey Dad!" calls the observant kid in the back seat, "We're about to get hit by some falling rocks!"

The father, keeping his eyes peeled on the road ahead to avoid any debris from rocks that have already fallen, responds, "It's OK, son! All the signs along the way told us this could happen. It's just part of traveling on this road!"

The point is that we want to get somewhere, and the only road available to us has some perilous obstacles. We cannot avoid them if we are to get where we are going, but we can proceed cautiously, and we can have a plan of response should such misfortunes occur. And what the

Bahá'í guidance about navigating this path of life advises is that only by encountering such trials and coming through them successfully can we become more adept and successful wayfarers. Like an experienced hunter or hiker who knows the perils of the woods, we will become wary of the signs of poisonous plants, venomous snakes, and slippery slopes. We may not always be able to forgo the accidents, the unexpected fall or the moment of thoughtlessness, but we will know how to recover, how to heal, and how to resume our journey.

The Bahá'í life, like any other way of life, does not make us secure from tests and trials, from disease and affliction, from remorse and sorrow. Bahá'u'lláh provides all manner of guidance about how to acquire safe driving skills, as well as how to choose the safest routes, the ones without quite so many falling rocks. But He has also provided a driver's manual about what to do when an accident occurs, because we all know that accidents will occur. At some point, we are going to get hit by falling rocks, and not necessarily because we did something wrong.

In fact, the Bahá'í writings state time and time again that suffering the changes and chances of this life is an important exercise by which we learn to traverse the path successfully. And why is this? Struggle requires study, effort, perseverance, inventiveness, and courage. Struggle tests our mettle and tempers our resolve. Were this life all there is, we might not agree that this is a worthy instructional methodology. But if we factor in a knowledge that our sole purpose in this journey is to prepare us for a reality in which physical prowess and material well-being will not exist, then we can better appreciate how physical misfortune, even disease itself, can be effective training tools for every one of us. It is in this same context that Bahá'í guidance improves our capacities to endure, to navigate the path intelligently and safely, and to respond appropriately to those tests we do encounter. For example, one instructional Bahá'í prayer begins with the following invocation:

O Thou Whose tests are a healing medicine to such as are nigh unto Thee, Whose sword is the ardent desire of all them that love Thee, Whose dart is the dearest wish of those hearts that yearn after Thee, Whose decree is the sole hope of them that have recognized Thy truth! (Bahá'u'lláh, *Bahá'í Prayers,* p. 220)

Another begins in a similar vein:

Glory to Thee, O my God! But for the tribulations which are sustained in Thy path, how could Thy true lovers be recognized; and were it not for the trials which are borne for love of Thee, how could the station of such as yearn for Thee be revealed? Thy might beareth me witness! The companions of all who adore Thee are the tears they shed, and the comforters of such as seek Thee are the groans they utter, and the food of them who haste to meet Thee is the fragments of their broken hearts. (Bahá'u'lláh, *Bahá'í Prayers,* pp. 220–21)

Of course, these and other writings, such as prayers asking for tests, come under the broad aegis of the axiom stated in the Hidden Words: "If adversity befall thee not in My path, how canst thou walk in the ways of them that are content with My pleasure? If trials afflict thee not in thy longing to meet Me, how wilt thou attain the light in thy love for My beauty?" (Arabic, no. 50).

It is well worth noting that these trials and tribulations have value in our spiritual progress primarily when they result from our attempting to follow the Bahá'í path and when we recognize in these tests an opportunity to advance ourselves spiritually. It is likewise important to realize at all times that one of the bounties in following this path when the rocks tumble is the omnipresence of roadside assistance, so long as we think to ask for it.

In addition, Bahá'u'lláh has provided a comprehensive driver's manual for any and all misfortunes, whether physical or metaphysical. There are also intervals along the path that can serve as rest stops. These might come in the form of gathering with fellow Bahá'ís for prayers and fellowship, or, more special still, a pilgrimage to the Bahá'í Shrines at the Bahá'í World Center in Haifa and its environs. Finally, and most important of all, the guide for the path endorses a series of daily preventative measures to avoid external or internal damage—daily prayers, spiritual study, and teaching others.

Of course we might logically inquire about how we are to recognize the falling rocks that are divinely sent for our advancement versus those falling rocks that are simply some of the accidents and misfortunes, the changes and chances that occur intermittently in life. The simplest and most effective response to this concern is that we can never know for sure, not in this stage of our life. Therefore, we might as well proceed as if all tests are specifically designed to sharpen our driving skills because if we respond in this manner, then all tests will benefit us, whether they are the result of explicit divine intervention in our lives, or simply the luck of the road.

As far as my own journey has gone, I have greatly benefitted from certain interludes where I could complete a sequence of developmental exercises. But before I rehearse what have been for me some of the more memorable of these, let me first explain why I feel that rehearsing these exploits might assist me in the art of dying. After all, as I have already noted, if this life is but a preparation for the continuation of our life that ensues after our departure from the physical stage of our existence, then the art of dying is an inseparable aspect of the art of living the Bahá'í life. The two endeavors are integral parts of a single process. A natural and logical result of trying to "live the Bahá'í life" is that we become ever more detached from the bonds and ties of attachment to our insistent self and physical reality, a process that in turn trains us for transition to the next stage of existence.

THE VALUE OF AN EXEMPLAR

In order to follow any path without wandering off in the wrong direction, it is most essential to have, in addition to ample written instructions, an experienced guide, someone capable of leading the way and demonstrating how to plot the best course over difficult terrain.

As a Christian I was taught that the exemplar for my path was Christ. And while, as I have noted, I had always found in Christ a comforting confidant and sensed His presence in my life, I never thought of Him as an appropriate exemplar for me because whenever I attempted to pit myself against that perfection, I would inevitably feel defeated from the start.

I remember one Sunday school class at St. Mark Church, for example, when as youth we were being taught by a young woman whose parents were missionaries. She was not unattractive nor overly pious, but we her students sensed—correctly or not—that for whatever reason this young lady was somehow immune to the hormonal chaos that was then occurring in most of our young bodies. It was hard to believe she was really tempted by the same stuff that was racing through our minds.

But then she started talking about "necking," "heavy petting," "making out," or whatever term is *au currant*. Suddenly we were paying attention. This was the sort of religious discussion we could get into with fervor. What was initially entrancing was that she was even aware that such things went on in our parked cars.

"So what do you do when you find yourselves in this situation?" she asked point blank. Naturally our prurient minds immediately presumed she was referring to different ways of going about embracing, kissing, and so forth. But no one said a word.

"Well, I'll tell you," she said after a moment or two of silence. "You think to yourself, 'What would Jesus do in this situation?'"

What began with a slight snicker from one student, then two giggles from another, quickly erupted into knee-slapping gales of laughter from the entire class. Yes, imagining Jesus in the back seat of a 1950 Ford coupe was a bit more than we could withstand, and a bit more than the rational mind could tolerate.

Obviously we understood her point—that to be Christian is to attempt as best we can to assume Christ's perspective about all that we do and think. But if we were to do that, we would not have allowed ourselves to get in the back seat of a Ford with a member of the opposite sex in the first place. And that was always the problem with trying to apply Christ as my guide in contemporary situations. He had lived two thousand years ago, and we had absolutely no idea how He would have responded to our world and our lives and our problems.

In addition to Bahá'u'lláh, 'Abdu'l-Bahá, the son of Bahá'u'lláh, serves as the exemplar for Bahá'ís. Though ontologically an ordinary human being and not a Manifestation of God, 'Abdu'l-Bahá had a unique position in the annals of world religious history. In addition to being a perfect human being, a spiritual exemplar, 'Abdu'l-Bahá was the first to believe in Bahá'u'lláh. He then took it upon himself to devote his entire life to serving his father and to taking care of the tactical and strategic affairs of the Bahá'í community as an assistance to Bahá'u'lláh.

Following Bahá'u'lláh's death in 1892, 'Abdu'l-Bahá discovered that Bahá'u'lláh, in His will, had designated him as head of the Bahá'í Faith, as Center of the Covenant, as well as the perfect Exemplar of the Bahá'í life. Not too long thereafter, 'Abdu'l-Bahá began to welcome Western Bahá'í pilgrims to visit him.

In 1912–1913 after being released from bondage as a prisoner of the Ottoman Empire, 'Abdu'l-Bahá undertook a remarkable journey in which he traveled to Europe and then to America, where he spent 239 days traveling from New York to San Francisco and back. During the course of this memorable sojourn, 'Abdu'l-Bahá met with high and low alike, but the focus of his travels was to meet with the Bahá'í communities across the breadth of the country. Wherever he went, he spoke about the glad tidings of the new revelation and explicated in detail many of the principal features of the Bahá'í revelation. These remarkable talks, recorded in several volumes, were sometimes formal and erudite, sometimes simple and to the heart. He appeared before gatherings as diverse as a mission in the Bowery of New York or the esteemed Unity Church in Oak Park, Illinois.

So it is that the art of living the Bahá'í life, of following this diverse path, can be inferred by studying what 'Abdu'l-Bahá said in these talks and from studying his spirit in motion. In every account of him interacting with others there is a parable, a lesson to be learned. In every glance and gesture was unveiled a glimpse of perfect wisdom. All who met him—and I talked with several over the years—were so transformed by this encounter that for the remainder of their lives they could talk of little else. This was the source of all else they would accomplish, the spiritual fountain from which they imbibe the inspiration for their life's work. This was the quality of the transformative power that emanated from this unique figure.

THE ROAD OVER MY SHOULDER

Were I to reflect on the "milestones" in my life during the decades since the events depicted in the pervious chapter, let alone attempt any sort of evaluation of how I did during what I suppose should be the core of my life experience, I would be no less at a loss for words than I was as a child pitting myself against the standard set by Christ. The standard or *mizán* established by 'Abdu'l-Bahá is so refined, so lofty and rarified, that I can only hope I am yet a work in progress, even if the Chamber of Commerce might portray my present circumstance as a retiree, an American male reclining on a porch to watch his "Golden Years" pass by.

But don't get me wrong. I am happy to be retired from what they paid me for (being a professor), and though I miss the pay, I in no way miss grading papers. I am also eternally grateful to my grandfather who bequeathed me a bit of land, the sale of which provided me with sufficient funds to keep me, my wife, my mother-in-law, my youngest son, the dog, and the chickens with a sufficient supply of groceries. What is more, now that I have completed all the work assigned me by "others," I can spend the entirety of my working hours exclusively on that which has been my true vocation all along—thinking, writing, and teaching about this path revealed by Bahá'u'lláh, trekking along toward that horizon that indeed "fades for ever and for ever when I move."

Yes, I am well aware, as everyone on the Bahá'í path, that for us there is no point of "retiring" from anything. Life is never winding down. One following this endless trail does not try to find entrancing distractions to disguise an uncomfortable truth—that he or she is merely waiting for death—because the journey toward death never ceases to be ever more exhilarating and expansive. As a dear Bahá'í friend mentioned to me a few days ago, it seems we chose this path only yesterday.

In the small Bahá'í community in which I now reside in Plant City, Florida, there is a lady my age with MS who is confined to a motorized wheelchair. There is an elegant, refined, and humorous ninety-two-year-old woman who works as a volunteer at the hospital. My mother-in-law is ninety-one, tutors others about the Bahá'í Faith, and drives every week to nearby Lakeland to spend quality time with her elderly sister-in-law who is too frail to visit her. There is my wife who devotes every spare minute doing amazingly creative work to help coordinate the systematic teaching of all in our "cluster"[10] who want to learn about this Gospel and to assist others to teach it to all who will listen.

These four women of strength, character, and resolve in no way feel that any part of their lives is finished, that they have come to a stopping place, or that they have completed the job of preparing for whatever may be the next milestone in their lives. So why should I, who am more than two decades the junior of two of them, feel or behave any differently than they?

I suppose in the midst of such a life and surrounded with such enduring vitality, I find it odd and possibly even vain to think of my life as something that could or should be reviewed at this time, as if it has been completed, as if I have learned and accomplished anywhere near all that I need or want to do.

I have no trouble recalling any part of it. The milestones in my life would not be any clearer had they occurred yesterday, nor would they be any more pertinent to who or what I am. And in spite of the gradual increase in the percentage of my relatives, friends, and colleagues who have passed on, I find it hard to believe that a half-century has occurred since the events of the previous chapter took place, since I took as my own that new *mizán* during Christmas break in Atlanta in 1959.

For five decades I have studied, have taught, have married, have had children, have written books, had operations, have gotten well, have had more operations, have retired, have bought a fine tractor with a front loader, have endured the loss of a father, a mother, and

---

10. A "cluster" is a term designated to an area containing various Bahá'í communities that coordinate their efforts in various critical activities for the secular community: providing children's classes, devotionals, and study circles for teaching others about the Bahá'í concept of spirituality as expressed in daily life.

a brother so that from my nuclear family, I alone survive. I am the last to recall the stories of the early days in Commerce, Georgia, as my mother and her sisters grew up in that small country town. I am the last in my family to be able to pass along the tales of Dad's days growing up on a farm in Franklin, Tennessee.

I have also realized to my dismay that should I neglect this charge of passing these stories along to my progeny, our family history would evaporate, as if this rich parade of families and lives, of wars and loss, of doing without, of sharing unconditional love all never really happened.

I suppose what is most surprising, though it should not be, is that here and now, in this place during this tumultuous time, I am living more contentedly, more existentially than ever before. I have few goals imposed on me from outside this old ranch house. I certainly do not dwell on nostalgic recollections of what no longer exists or what no longer works as well as it once did, or on how the quality of life in my part of planet Earth has deteriorated.

Since I began following this path fifty years ago, I became an Assistant Professor of English literature, then an Associate Professor of English literature, then a full Professor of English literature, and I am now a Professor Emeritus of English literature. But all that was mostly to buy groceries and make house payments so I could do what I really wanted to do—study the Bahá'í Faith and write about what I discovered along the way, about twenty books worth so far.

I never was and never really wanted to be a serious academic. I did what some might consider to be a bit of academic stuff—an academic book or article or presentation here and there. But it was never my goal to be considered a scholar, not in any traditional sense. I enjoy thinking, reflecting, inventing, and I use writing as a tool to force myself to examine thoughts in a systematic way. If my writing happens to assist others in doing the same thing, that's a bonus.

Writing gives me the opportunity to think about complex problems and figure out ways to solve them, like understanding death, for example. Because for me it is by studying and reflecting in a methodical way (even as John Wesley was characterized as doing with his entourage, his so-called "Methodists") that I can best keep myself from slipping on the rocks or becoming too distracted from paying attention to the signs along the path. And the prospect of even more "ventures"—what my son John and I used to call our forays into the woods back in the mid 1960s—is what keeps me excited about this life, even if the next big milestone may be associated with a gravestone (onto which I intend to have carved, "I'm really feeling quite better!")

So these were my milestones—becoming a Bahá'í, graduation, marriage, another graduation, children, another graduation, divorce, books, another marriage, more children, more books, grandchildren, more books, promotions, more books, retirement, and more books. And being in relatively good health and with the prospect of further adventures, what's to fear about death, especially if I am assured that this transition will be felicitous, a welcome relief, an ascent to something more grand, more enjoyable where all I have accomplished or will accomplish will become fulfilled and take on a more expansive meaning?

RATIONAL RESPONSES TO FEARS ABOUT DEATH

As I have said several times already, according to everything I sincerely believe and hold dear, death is merely a birth into a more expansive and enjoyable reality, a reality my essential self already occupies. My rational mind has memorized and relies upon an array of wonderful passages from the Bahá'í writings assuring me that this is so, that death is not to be feared but to be welcomed as a release from the constraints and suffering of what 'Abdu'l-Bahá and Bahá'u'lláh sometimes call this "dust heap" of a world:

Be not content with the ease of a passing day, and deprive not thyself of everlasting rest. Barter not the garden of eternal delight for the dust-heap of a mortal world. Up from thy prison ascend unto the glorious meads above, and from thy mortal cage wing thy flight unto the paradise of the Placeless. (Bahá'u'lláh, Hidden Words, Persian no. 39)

When the human soul soareth out of this transient heap of dust and riseth into the world of God, then veils will fall away, and verities will come to light, and all things unknown before will be made clear, and hidden truths be understood. ('Abdu'l-Bahá, *Selections from the Writings of 'Abdu'l-Bahá*, no. 149.3)

In fact, in a delightful analogy 'Abdu'l-Bahá compares the feeling of being released from the constraints of this life to the sense of exhilaration a bird might feel in being freed from its cage:

To consider that after the death of the body the spirit perishes is like imagining that a bird in a cage will be destroyed if the cage is broken, though the bird has nothing to fear from the destruction of the cage. Our body is like the cage, and the spirit is like the bird. We see that without the cage this bird flies in the world of sleep; therefore, if the cage becomes broken, the bird will continue and exist. Its feelings will be even more powerful, its perceptions greater, and its happiness increased. (*Some Answered Questions*, p. 228)

Why is it, then, that only now do I consider how the art of living is inseparable from the art of dying and that increasingly I feel I am not yet prepared for that "release"? After all, early in our discussion we noted that the art of living and the art of dying are theoretically one-in-the-same process. Bahá'u'lláh notes this axiom when he states point blank that the central purpose that the Manifestations of God sacrifice Their lives to provide us spiritual education and enlightenment is to prepare us for that second (or third) birth:

> The Prophets and Messengers of God have been sent down for the sole purpose of guiding mankind to the straight Path of Truth. The purpose underlying Their revelation hath been to educate all men, that they may, at the hour of death, ascend, in the utmost purity and sanctity and with absolute detachment, to the throne of the Most High. (*Gleanings,* no. 81.1)

Since I am admittedly concerned about death, and, in all candor, I do not at the moment wish to attain it, I must presume I have not yet accomplished my life's purpose and have not as yet completely mastered the art of living well.

I am pretty sure I would unhesitatingly give my life on the spur of the moment to save another or to uphold my beliefs. Yet clearly I have not yet perfected the art of living, else I presume I would be ready and eager to "ascend, in the utmost purity and sanctity and with absolute detachment, to the throne of the Most High." Certainly, if I had attained absolute detachment, I would not spend hours scouring the internet for good prices on a Prius. Neither would I be so eager to make regular visits to Grandpa Johnson's Barbeque to consume large quantities of collard greens and pulled pork.

How detached and spiritual can I be when I still maintain hopes of getting back into shape, of trimming down, of firming up my abs? I sometimes even consider buying a suit to look smart in case I am called upon to accept some grand award. Were I really finished with the process of living, then it seems I would be ready, willing, and able to welcome that silly old grim reaper when he knocks at my door in the middle of the night or some afternoon while I am reading in my easy chair.

But after all these years I think I have finally figured out what bothers me, and it's not the usual sort of fear. I don't believe in hell, other than as a spiritual or mental sense of remoteness, and I don't really fear punishment or retribution, because I really do believe that so long as I desire it and strive for it, God will forgive me my foibles and assist me in overcoming them, if not here, then in a more refined environment, and I certainly plan on desiring it for all I'm worth.

Or to put it another way, I have no doubt that whatever I am made to endure after this earthly period of gestation, that future experience will have as it sole objective my further benefit and development. Certainly I do fear nonexistence. I have done enough research and had enough convincing empirical evidence to rest assured that my consciousness, my "essential self," is not dependent on its connection with physical mechanisms for its continuation after its dissociation from what remains of my mortal frame when the time comes.

LEARNING ABOUT DEATH IN MADRID

What I do fear, I think, is something like the trepidation and dislocation I felt my junior year in college, which I also remember as if it were yesterday. It seems that my sophomore year at Vanderbilt I decided, for reasons I have entirely repressed, to spend my junior year studying abroad in Spain at the University of Madrid. I had to be a Spanish major to do this, so temporarily I became a Spanish major, even though I had not done all that well in Spanish. I certainly had no conversational experience.

In fact, I clearly recall that on some level I was really quite nervous and intimidated about going by myself to a foreign country. But I was proud and stubborn, and determined to see my plan through because having professed my plans to friends and family, I could not back down, especially after I had mustered my best rhetorical skills to convince my father that it would actually be cheaper to attend the university in Spain than it would be to spend a year at Vanderbilt. I may have mentioned something about it being a real boon to my education, though I don't know how I could have managed that.

I am almost positive that there were major road signs I missed that would have saved me from what I was about to undergo, but I missed them or ignored them. They would have read something like "Caution: Do Not Go to Spain, John!"

I was able to conjugate the most common Spanish irregular verbs, but I had never had the opportunity, or had never taken the opportunity, to practice Spanish in conversation. I could not understand someone telling me what time it was, let alone comprehend the totally distinct vocabulary and idiomatic expressions of street Spanish, especially Castilian Spanish. Nevertheless, without someone sensible to stop me, I found myself on a plane late one night in July from New York to Madrid.

Like everyone else on board, I took great joy in watching the sun come up as we headed east over the Atlantic. I was more or less oblivious to the fact that I had just lost a night's sleep, that I had not slept much at all the night before, and that I was actually going to a country where people did not speak English, at least not any better than I spoke Spanish.

I had with me only what I carried in one suitcase because my steamer trunk with all my clothes, portable typewriter, books, and toilet paper (unknown in Spain at that time) had been shipped over a month before and (so I was assured by the shipping company) would be there waiting for me.

It was a gloriously beautiful summer morning when the plane set down, some three weeks before school was to start. Unknown to me at the time, my wonderful trunk had been retained in Customs in Barcelona and would not arrive until late October. Nevertheless, after I got off the plane with my blond crew-cut and single suitcase and two changes of clothes, I felt ready to head-off into the unknown.

Since there was no one there from the university to greet me (as I had been told there would be), I took a city bus into the downtown area. The bus did not go to the university, but I was told that probably a taxi could take me there. As the bus bumped and jostled along on the cobbled streets and the *tranvía* tracks, I was already beginning to feel tired. I was also starting to detect a noticeable sense of isolation.

I had never been out of the country by myself before. I did not know anyone else in this land. I did not know what the money was worth. For some reason, my entire Spanish vocabulary would not come to me, except useless phrases like "clean the eraser" and "brush your teeth." I tried to construct something to say to the taxi driver, but all that would come to me were odd words for "overcoat," "lawyer," "shoe lace," and "watch band."

The taxi driver could tell I was an American, or else German—my blond hair allowed me the grace of not necessarily being typed as an American. I appreciated this because the *Madrilleños* hated Americans since the young men from the Tarajon Airforce base were forever driving around in their cars (which the local populace could never afford), coming into town, honking horns, getting drunk, and molesting the extraordinarily beautiful Spanish ladies.

Finally I tried, "*Tengo que irme a la Universidad de Madrid*" ("I have to go to the University of Madrid"). Simple enough, one would think. How many University of Madrid's could there be, right?

As it turned out, there is no University of Madrid, at least not in the mind of the taxi drivers or anyone else who goes anywhere in Madrid. So he took me to some old solitary building, a private secondary school in the middle of the city, and assured me this was the only school he knew about. I naturally believed him, paid him a bunch of pesetas, and he quickly left with his biggest tip of the day.

I went inside, but absolutely nobody in this place, only a couple of whom spoke broken English, considered this establishment to be the University of Madrid. They suggested I try going to *La Ciudad Universitaria* (The University City) to see if someone there could help me. Naturally I believed them and hailed another cab.

I tried as best I could to pronounce "*La Ciudad Universitaria*," though I couldn't remember where the accent went in *universitaria* and the *Ci* in *Ciudad* is pronounced with a voiceless *th* sound. Nevertheless, he seemed immediately to know where I wanted to go. "*Ah, sí señor.*" And off we drove, and drove, and drove until we had gone all the way to the other side of the city of Madrid. I could tell this because there were no more buildings, and we came to a street whose sign read "*La Calle de Limite*," a phrase I quickly translated as having something to do with the city limits!

I asked if he were sure we were going to "*La Ciudad Unversitaria*" "¿Esta seguro?" ("Are you sure?") I queried. He assured me we were on target. And by golly, before long I saw students on bicycles and motor scooters riding down this wide parkway toward a vast area in which clumps of quite impressive buildings were widely set apart, as if . . . as if this were a city! Yes, I thought, this might indeed be the "University City!"

"*Señor,*" he queried, "*¿A cual Facultad?*"

"*¿Como?*" I responded, as I would so often respond in the coming days. He repeated the same sentence very slowly and very emphatically.

¿Quisiera ir a cual Facultad? I wasn't totally stupid. I knew that *facultad* had something to do with faculty, or so I thought. I presumed he wanted to know what department I needed to find.

"*La Literatura*," I responded, though it wasn't really a literature department. I needed the "Year in Spain Program" for New York University, but I knew he would have absolutely no idea what that was. Besides, I dared not say anything about New York or I might find myself being driven back to the airport.

By the grace of *Dios*, he dropped me off at what seemed to him the best building for someone wanting to study about literature, *La Facultad Filosofía y Letras* (the Faculty of Liberal Arts).

I thanked him, paid him a week's worth of tips, and went inside. Here surely I could find someone who spoke English, who knew where the University of New York program office was. Possibly I could even discover where I was supposed to stay. Perhaps I could also get some food, because it was now afternoon and I had not eaten since the night before. More than anything else, I wanted something cold to drink.

I walked down the echoing hall with my suitcase in hand, and *Dios* was kind—the office for the program was right before me! A small paper sign said as much. But, alas, the program director was not there, the lady at the desk informed me in the little English she knew. She said she did not have any idea when he would return or what I should do.

"Possibly morning time," she said. "*Very seek*," she said with a thick accent. "*How you say, hiz wife very seek*." I nodded my head in sympathy.

"*I know!*" she said as she watched my haggard and bewildered expression. "*You estay here*."

"Where?" I asked, hoping she did not mean in her office. She went on to explain through a series of frenetic gestures, tiny hand drawn maps, and her own special form of hieroglyphics, that there was a dorm not far away. I could lug my one suitcase there and stay for the night until the director returned in the morning.

This was fine with me. Doubtless the dorm would also have a bit of food, something cold to drink, and a bed. So I walked and walked and walked until a half hour later I arrived at the dorm she described. A man at the desk spoke decent English, and I was able to explain my situation, whereupon he gave me the key to a room on the second floor—after I paid him an unspecified amount of pesetas that he benignly extracted from my open hand.

I climbed the two flights of stairs, found the right door number, and entered a large white room with two single beds. Its large windows were open and a nice breeze was blowing in. This would be fine for the night, but first there would be food, and the man at the desk said that I could eat at the cafeteria downstairs—for only a few pesetas, if I hurried.

I put my bag on one of the beds, scampered down the stairs because dinner was ending soon, grabbed a plate, and filled it with what seemed to be some sort of pan fried fish. I sat down at the one table that had an empty chair where there were four students, all Spanish, all paying absolutely no attention to me, engrossed as they were in eating and talking in a language I could not understand.

That was fine. I wanted food and a sip from the tall pitcher of ice tea that was sitting prominently in the middle of the table. The last thing I needed was to try to formulate coherent sentences. I nibbled at the fish, which was replete with tiny bones that stuck in my throat when I tried to extract tiny flecks of meat. So I immediately bit off a sizeable portion of bread, poured myself a tall glass of the tea, which unfortunately had no ice. Nevertheless, I hoisted the glass to my parched mouth to wash down the fish bones, took an ample swig, and swallowed hard before the iced-tea colored liquid registered, first on my palate, then my esophagus, then in my gut. This was *not* iced tea!

This was wine! This was not even good wine! This certainly was not even cold wine! I know not what color my face turned as I forced myself not to wheeze or cough or give any other grossly overt signs of my state of shock, dismay, and discomfort. Furthermore, as a new

Bahá'í, I did not know whether it was the better part of abiding by my religious convictions to spit out the remainder of the alcoholic beverage into my napkin, or simply close my eyes and swallow hard.

I swallowed hard and realized that the particularly wretched part of this was not that I had unwittingly partaken of a substance forbidden by my Faith. My mouth, my throat, my entire being had been eagerly awaiting the comforting, cooling, quenching feel of iced tea streaming down my gullet and into my dry tummy, and now these tender organs were receiving instead a gulp of harsh, nondescript warm amber-colored wine.

I looked around to be sure the students weren't staring at me, took a few more bites of bread, then left to go upstairs to my room. I was still hungry, but I would wash up, change shirts, and rest. Food could wait. But before I could get my suitcase open, there was a knock on the door, and a young woman dressed in a white uniform opened up. She had come to change the sheets.

"*Buenas tardes* (good afternoon)," she greeted me with a smile. Wonderful, I thought. Something I can understand.

"*Buenas tardes,*" I returned.

"*Hace mucho calor,*" she said in one breath with a Castilian accent so that *hace* was pronounced *áhthey.*

"*¿Como?*" I replied with a smile.

She repeated it again, pointing outside this time. On the third time I finally realized she was telling me that it was very hot. Lord, the simplest and most common of idioms, the very one we had practiced a thousand times, and I had not understood it. "*Sí*" I responded in a subdued tone of hollow victory. "*Sí, hace mucho calor.*"

Fortunately for me, she did not attempt any other communication. I suspect she realized I was a dunce. I certainly did.

When she left, I walked over to the other bed where my one suitcase lay full of my stuff, my clothes, all my things from America, my little bit of home away from home. I clicked the lock with glee, opened the lid, and there were my clothes, my shirts, my socks, my underwear, all MY stuff! But as I lifted up a fresh shirt, I realized immediately that something was sadly wrong. Everything was completely and totally sopping wet!

My head dropped as I let the lid fall back down. I fell back on the bed and tried to imagine how the baggage handlers had managed such a feat. I thought seriously of crying, but I was afraid that, once having let go, I might not ever stop. I walked to the window and leaned on the sill. The sun was just setting even though it was 9:00 pm. I scanned the huge campus of the University City. I wondered what my parents might be thinking. I wondered what my friends at Vanderbilt might be doing. I remembered the niceties of my two-room attic apartment in Nashville. More than anything else, I wondered just what I was doing in Spain! What had I been thinking? Why had I wanted to come all the way to Spain for a year anyhow?

It was bad being so lost, but it was so much worse that nobody knew I was lost. I could converse with no one. I had only a small portion of my "stuff" and what little stuff I had was soaked. Was it conceivable, I wondered, was it at all possible that somehow, by some convoluted mastery of rhetorical prowess, I could call my father and convince him that the entire idea had been a horrible mistake and that I needed five hundred dollars to take the next plane back home?

This one day in my life hardly represents the most grueling tragedy in my life—not by a long shot. Neither was this the worst sense of despair and displacement I have experienced—not by any stretch of the imagination. To those who have experienced serious tragic losses of loved ones, of entire homes or villages, this story is vain and silly, a clear demonstration of how sheltered my life had been relative to that of the majority of people in the world. In fact, since Bahá'ís believe that we are never tested beyond our capacity, I would suspect that Bahá'u'lláh knew my capacity was pretty meager at that time and was proceeding to train me incrementally in bite-size portions.

The point is that this event, together with the months that followed, became for me an important point of reference, a symbol of the fragility of my sense of self. It became a touchstone for me the rest of my life any time I was tempted to have any illusion about having personal power, resilience, and fortitude. But for the purposes of this discussion about the art of living and the art of dying, it serves to call to my mind the sort of "torpedo vision" that Socrates speaks of, that recognition of truth we have when everything we have been learning about a concept suddenly comes together and makes complete sense, the way Copernicus must have felt as soon as he came up with his heliocentric theory.

So while thinking about death, about waiting for death, about the art of dying and how it relates to the art of living, I have come to realize that my trip to Spain informed me more about my residual fear of death than anything I had read or previously considered.

Not that I feared Spain as a country. I had never been there, though I knew a bit about its history and culture. I did not fear the Spaniards, especially after being in Spain for a while and realizing how much love they would shower upon an individual, regardless of what their preju- dices might have been against the Americans from the air base. What I feared that day was what I would fear about any journey to any place where I might be totally dislocated, some place where I have never been before, where I must go without any remnants of the things and people with which I am familiar, where I cannot communicate, and where I do not know the expectations of the culture, and where, most important of all, I am totally alone.

When I had initially considered the trip, going it alone in a for- eign country sounded so heroic, very much like the actions of a

Hemingway hero. I would be a macho loner character in a novel that I myself might write. Instead, my initial experience that first day seemed as if I had embarked alone on a trip to Mars or the remote land of Togalonga, if there really were such a place. Such a journey would be fine if I packed well, had with me a cadre of special friends and companions, and had some idea of how to survive once I got there. Most of us would enjoy that and would pay big bucks for a vacation there.

But what if, in the middle of the night without any warning, we were suddenly kidnapped and taken alone and unprepared to some unknown land, like what the Tom Hanks character experiences in the movie *Cast Away* when his plane crashes and he is washed ashore alone? We might think—as I did when I first saw the movie—that there would be no reason to be afraid or panic.

We would relish the quiet, the salt sea air, the untrammeled white sands, the plentiful seafood, the spectacular sunsets, and, most of all, looking up in the night at the vast starlit heavens to marvel at God's beauteous creation. Surely we would befriend strange creatures, swim with porpoises, or hold onto the back of a sea turtle as he took us on a gentle tour of a coral reef. We would have a genuine Disney experience!

But no, this of course wouldn't be the case at all. And the truth is that what I fear about death is not the dying but the leaving, being instantly wrenched from my home and loved ones and books, being totally and completely on my own. Of course, I know this is not so, that in that realm will be all those familiar souls who have passed on before me—father, mother, brother, cousins, friends. But I suppose I will in this stage of my life be forever imprinted by the experience of going to Spain that day, that fear and sense of isolation I felt when I realized I was without family and friends and would need to figure out how to do everything entirely on my own.

ALBERT HATCHER BIDS FAREWELL TO HIS LITTLE FAMILY

Another experience that allowed me to realize this fear that many of us have, of leaving others and being completely alone, was my father's death. When Dad lay dying in a blank and pale green cubicle that hospital rooms seem decreed to be, he had a look about him different from any I'd ever seen on his face before.

We would be talking about whatever came to his mind: The story about his father irately scolding his statuesque wife when grandmother Jeanie invited the ladies' bible study class over during hog killing time; the story about grandfather riding on the back of a stallion behind his father (who had fought in some of the bloodiest battles of the Civil War) as they trotted to a clan meeting in the earliest days of Reconstruction in Arno, Tennessee.

Then in mid-story his visage would screw up into concentric wrinkles of anguish so intense that his entire countenance became an emblem of sorrow, like an ancient Greek mask of tragedy. It wasn't physical pain that carved this expression into his countenance. He knew he was dying, whereas Bill, Mom, and I had naively acceded to the false hopes with which the doctors and nurses daily plied us, probably to ease their own burden, not ours.

Later, I would look back in anger at their denials about the gravity of his speech, mocking the wisdom and courage with which he summoned us together that night just in time to bid us farewell before the cancer attacked the meningies of his brain and, like the flicking of a switch, bereft him of lucidity and the pure will that such a moment requires.

He strained to gain control as Mom and Bill and I sat on the edge of his bed, not really expecting any weighty pronouncements. We had been coming in shifts so that he was never without one of us by his side. But this particular night he had explicitly requested that all of us be there. I think it was the first thing he had commanded in his role as titular patriarch while he lay in that hospital bed—all else had been meek requests to have his legs rubbed or that he be helped to the bathroom to brush his teeth.

He lay there, propped up, looked at the three of us one at a time— mother by his right shoulder, me sitting on the end of the bed, and Bill standing at his left shoulder. He opened his mouth, his face calm, and nothing came out but air. Then his face suddenly contorted into that look of grief as he tried his best to speak. Words emerged, but in a weak and reedy, almost childlike whisper. "It's just that . . . I don't want to leave you."

It was the last thing we expected. We had presumed that he, like us, had fallen prey to the foxfire of hope that had been perpetrated on us, that the occasional moments of delusion were psychological reactions, when the simple fact was that the man knew he was losing it, that his control of his conscious mind was quickly fading, that his ability to determine his own thoughts could be measured in minutes.

He said nothing more, nor could we. We melted as one in hugs and tears and wrenching sobs. We tried to console him, to tell him there was hope, because we believed it. He had responded so well to chemo for two years, and he still looked great at seventy-six. He still looked distinguished, handsome, dignified, refined in his silk pajamas. He did not look like an old man, a sick man, certainly not a dying man.

But he knew the truth, and had he not called us together that night, there would never have occurred another opportunity to bid us farewell. He would have occasional moments of lucidity afterward, but very few. There was no more need to guess what his rambling and incoherent sentences meant, what deep secret pain or longing or guilt lay hidden in the recesses of his well-lived life. Our family doctor, E. Van Buren, Dad's aging Sigma Chi fraternity brother from his days at Emory, knew well the truth and he told it to us simply and plainly, as a friend or brother *should* do. The cancer had entered the brain and nothing could stop it—no sudden regimen of high powered vitamins, no exotic herbs or potions. He had lived "the good life." Now it was over.

11

THE ART OF DYING

Dying
Is an art, like everything else,
I do it exceptionally well.
I do it so it feels like hell.
I do it so it feels real.
I guess you could say I've a call.
—Sylvia Path, "Lady Lazarus"

What was noble and instructional about my father's dying, calling us together like that, was that he left this life as he had lived it, letting his actions reveal his character and speaking only when he had something worthwhile to say. He had never talked much about religion or philosophy. He loved sports, and my mother and I agreed he probably would have been happier as a coach rather than as the Atlanta branch manager for Equifax.

He had a superb mind, and he had been a superb athlete in his youth. He had a chance at semipro baseball, but he always took the path that was safer and more secure. I believe this was partly because he was a child of the depression, partly because he grew up on a farm where affluence was perceived as vain sacrilege, but mostly, I suspect, it was because he had an incredible sense of responsibility to his family and even to the more metaphysical aspects of loyalty to "the company."

I had always assumed he was simply a bit compulsive because he seemed insecure about any sort of disorder in his life. But what could be any more disordering than dying? And yet here he was, still being careful to floss his teeth, to look neat and "proper" in his pajamas and robe, assembling us around him, and delivering his laconic farewell to us. I might have thought in such circumstance he would have revealed some indication of being afraid of this transition he was about to undertake, but he had no fear, only a constant, deathless, faithful love I feel even now every time I gaze at his face in the picture over my desk.

THE CAT AND I

For me, his death will always be foremost in my mind as I search for clues about nobility as regards the art of dying. I suppose it was because of this nobility and the fact that he never really got old or looked like what I would even characterize as "elderly" or "aged" that at his funeral I was inconsolable. How could someone die who still looked healthy and fit, who was still such a pillar of strength and unity for his family?

I have cried like that only a couple of times in my life, where all my private grief and secret sorrows have become untapped and poured out indiscriminately beyond my personal control. The entire day I was oblivious to anyone or anything else, only the stream of ceaseless tears.

Strangely, the first time I recall experiencing this same sort of purgation occurred because of a cat. I was teaching at Virginia Polytechnic Institute in Blacksburg, Virginia, in 1964, and I was living in a small apartment complex. One afternoon my paper grading was interrupted by noisy children outside. When I peered out the back window, I saw some children having a great time letting a stray kitten they had found tumble down the slide. They giggled as the frightened, malnourished creature tried desperately to grab onto the slick tin with his tiny claws, only to slide backward again and again.

I ran out, immediately rescued the kitten, and appropriately chastised the heartless children, who promptly scattered. I took the kitten in my hands and noticed that it still seemed bewildered and ill. I instantly recalled the Chinese proverb about being eternally responsible for any life you save. Here I was with a skinny stray kitten in my hands and no place to put it or take it.

Paper grading had to be set aside. My life was now altered until the responsibility for the kitten was either permanently mine or until I could find somebody else to remove this burden from me. I had no alternative except to begin this path I had just chosen by first taking the cat to a vet. I wrapped the virtually weightless creature in a towel, and off I went, driving carefully so as to calm this abandoned and bewildered animal.

After a brief examination, the vet concluded that the kitten had a rather severe upper respiratory infection but might survive with a hefty dose of penicillin, which I immediately agreed to underwrite. He cleaned up this tiny bit of life, gave it a shot, and placed it back in the towel for my care.

As I carried it to the car, I no longer cared what would be the ultimate outcome of the kitten's future. For now I felt it was sufficient that I had followed the moral imperative. I had done my duty, and I was simply basking in the existential joy of the appreciative look in the eyes of this tiny being whose life I had saved.

As I drove home with the kitten in the towel by my side, I felt a bit ennobled by my selfless act of salvation, but more than that was unalloyed love, a love that I had almost forgotten about in what had become my routinized life of teaching and grading stacks upon stacks of tedious and abominably written papers. I glanced at the kitten frequently, and it glanced back.

About ten minutes into our return trip, the cat began to act a bit strange. Its head began to weave back and forth. Then the kitten's eyes seemed to dilate as it struggled desperately to stand, only to roll over on its back. It then began to shiver.

I stopped the car, picked up the frantic kitten, tried to cradle it, to reassure it, but within a minute it began to seize. I had no idea what to do. I just watched, waiting for the seizure to stop. Finally, the kitten stopped trembling, but it felt limp. I felt for its heart, but there was no beating. I tried a few gentle compressions to see if I could get the tiny pump going again, but the rest was silence. It lay motionless staring out at nothing.

It had been allergic to the penicillin, the vet informed me after I returned to the clinic to see if the kitten could be revived. The vet in his kindness and appreciation of my humanity agreed to "dispose" of the remains, and I was left with nothing but a small white towel, stained with tears and bits of grey and white kitten fur.

I got in the car emotionless. I drove mechanically until I neared the apartment. Then I began to feel emotion well up from my belly to my throat as if a balloon were being inflated inside. Something about the complete and utter helplessness of this creature and my unwitting contribution to its death, combined with the unremitting image of the last expressions in its eyes as it looked to me, its savior, for an answer: "What's happening to me? Something's horribly wrong! I am dying and I don't want to die!" it had seemed to be imploring me in its last gasps of life.

All of this somehow synthesized with a thousand unconscious pains that I had endured and stored up within me, sorrows that I had forgotten or had never adequately understood or commemorated. There was no one to call who could possibly understand why this was such a tragedy. There was no one who could share what I was feeling, why, amid all the tragedies engulfing the world, anyone should think the death of a stray kitten should merit the uncontrollable flood of sorrow that came rushing forth from my heaving sobs.

It was not vain of me to give way to this grief—I frankly had no way to prevent it. I cared not what I looked like trying to steer a car through flowing tears, with my chest heaving up and down rapidly as I tried to breathe in rapid gulps. There was no philosophical consolation or logical perspective that could placate me, because nothing of what I was feeling was a considered response. There was only emotion, only sorrow and grief in its purest form, even as I would, some seventeen years later, have the same sort of purgation at my dad's funeral.

Only now do I think I know why I grieved so or why that pure grief was similar to what I felt the day we laid my father to rest. Both the kitten and my dad were so unobtrusive in this world where only the garish din of the famous and infamous garners public attention and concern.

But there was something else I gleaned from these two deaths. In both deaths I discovered my own isolation, my own secret pain and self-induced loneliness. That desperate look in the kitten's eyes as it felt itself falling irretrievably from this world was like the look in Dad's eyes when only he, struggling to articulate the ineffable, felt himself falling.

And that look of meek and humble candor, that moment of pure clarity, was what I so longed to have for myself. To be able and willing to share, without guile or pretense, what was in my inmost secret heart. That kitten, my lovely father, they were both sharing this with me—the slings and arrows of misfortune, whether being tossed about by outrageous children, or Dad's sense of multiplying cancer cells gnawing away at his conscious mind inducing the loss of all conscious control.

I knew what they felt, but I could explain it to no one who could understand. Like them, some part of me wanted to be bundled in a soft blanket and receive in my goblet but a drop of the wine of unconditional love.

But I would get up again after these moments of uncontrollable sobbing. I would get back on the path again, and, by the grace of God, I would find someone who understood how Faulkner was wrong—that the basest of all things is not to be afraid, not exactly. Being afraid is the natural course of things. It is entirely unavoidable and acceptable. Even Francis MacComber in that short part of his "happy" life was afraid—he simply decided to ignore the fear.

No, the basest of all things is to be lonely, utterly alone and in despair. And it matters not whether the despair is because of the loss of a kitten or the loss of a father or the loss of love. It matters not whether the despair is real, or whether it results from some chemicals out of balance in the brain.

My brother once told me of a conversation he had with someone who at the time was his best friend—he always maintained a very discrete circle of very close associates who had in common the single virtue that they thought and felt deeply about life, and they played chess relatively well.

My brother posed to this friend the following hypothesis: Suppose you were totally happy but completely crazy—say, you live in a mental asylum. Would you accept such a bargain? The friend thought long about his answer. "So I'm completely crazy but totally happy?" he repeated. "Yes," Bill responded, "you are ecstatically happy at every moment of your existence, but you are totally insane."

The friend finally answered that since the purpose of life is to be happy, if he were totally happy—and obviously he would be oblivious to the fact that he was insane—he concluded, "Of course I would accept such a bargain. One would have to be crazy *not* to accept it! Wouldn't you?"

Bill's answer was quick and firm. He would never accept such a bargain. For Bill the purpose of life was to learn the truth about reality. This objective was for Bill more important than being happy, that if forced to choose, he would always sacrifice happiness for truth.

And so throughout his life he did just that, sacrificing his time, and sometimes material well-being, to teach some of the brightest minds what he believed to be the truth. But this choice often came at a cost, and part of the cost was burning himself out so that he died at age seventy when he might have lived another ten years or so, had he devoted himself to living "easily, decorously."

ARTISTS AND THE ART OF DEATH

Here again we discover the inextricable relationship between the art of living and the art of dying. But we also discover that there are life experiences far worse than death or dying. For Bill, living an illusion or a lie was worse than death, or, from his perspective, it was choosing a living death.

For me, what seemed worse than death was being imprisoned in myself, loveless and isolated from a listening ear or a caring heart, a dear one with whom to commiserate. So I wrote poems and studied those who, like me, had found in art a means whereby the astounding power of inner grief and solitude could be unleashed in sensibly perceptible images.

Not that all artists are, or even must be, depressives and lonely. Not all art derives from neediness. But most art, I would venture to theorize, derives from an inner longing—or even from some kind of desperation, a relentless drive to communicate what ordinary language cannot.

Interestingly, for a good number of those whom we set apart as the seers, the visionaries among us, it is this repository of raw emotion that we sense and respond to. We can see it in the swirls of Van Gogh's brushstrokes, in the stone-become-skin of Michelangelo's David, or in the lavish sensuality of alliterative synaesthesia in Thomas's "Fern Hill."

So it is that I used to characterize the artists among us in my university lectures as being like unto kinesthetic receptors for the human body politic. I would further propose to my students that one very pragmatic value the artists have for us is their ability to reflect to us detailed information about our collective circumstance. They inform us about how we are doing in relation to what we say we are trying to achieve and about where we are in space and time in relation to our collective humanity. Perhaps most important of all, they remind us of what our common goals might be.

In our presently disjointed and disintegrating society, this feedback is as essential as clean air and decent water. Unfortunately, it has become the case since we emerged from the stages of our tribal selves that these same artists, who once assumed a lofty status when they sang for us our personal and collective histories, have been relegated mostly to decorating our homes or public parks. Or they are viewed as quaint rebellious children trying to hold up a mirror before us to convince us we are acting foolishly. But we will have none of it. It is they, we respond, who are out of touch with our reality.

Whether the artists are trying to remind us of what we already know on some subliminal or repressed level of consciousness, or whether they are enlightening us about something we have ignored or missed or never understood correctly, these sensitive souls are not among us merely to ornament our lives, though they may delight us, nor merely to arouse our passions, though we may well respond with passion to what they have to tell us about ourselves. The best of them, as Yeats affirms in "Sailing to Byzantium," whisper in our ears about what has passed, is passing, or is to come.

They may tell us we are completely insane, or, more politely, that we are working against our own best interest. But among them, especially, it seems, among some modern poets who indulge in exploring the interior of themselves for our benefit, are the so-called confessional poets. And among these confessional poets are a number who seem bent on the art of dying, or at least who devote a significant portion of their art portraying their preoccupation with the desire to achieve nonexistence, or another sort of existence.

Whether we believe they have come upon truths so painful that they prefer leaving this life over enduring in a world that is out of kilter, or whether they are simply too delicate or maimed to withstand the onslaught of inner angst, they really do want to die. They aren't simply drawing attention to themselves. They want to end their lives and they feel it important to let us know what that desire, together with the sundry emotions that constitute the engine of that desire, feels like, possibly so that others who experience the same emotion will not be so totally isolated, inadequate, pathetic, or guilty.

Immediately we may think of Sylvia Plath, who in 1963 stuck her head in a gas oven; or John Berryman, who in 1972 jumped from a bridge in Minneapolis; or Anne Sexton, who in 1974 turned on the car motor in her closed garage. If we are equating the art of living with the art of dying, then surely something is amiss here. There has even been a rather revealing study comparing and contrasting the characteristics of the work done by poets who committed suicide with the work of their contemporaries, also confessional poets, who did not.[11]

What the research concludes is not that the poets who committed suicide were more in touch with and dismayed by the deterioration of society than were other contemporary artists, but rather that from the beginning, these personalities demonstrated a preoccupation with themselves. This research also notes that even the language the

---

11. Titled "Signs Of Suicidal Tendencies Found Hidden In Dead Poets" and published in the peer reviewed journal *Psychosomatic Medicine*, this research was supported by a grant from the National Institute of Mental Health, National Institutes of Health.

suicidal poets employ seems to allude to their sense of being unable to communicate their inner turmoil to others—an odd dilemma for artists whose medium is language, especially highly nuanced language at that. So possibly we cannot learn what we need to know about the art of dying from those artists who opted out, except that they were in such desperate need of some human communication or companionship that they felt they were incapable of obtaining it in this life, or else that their emotional turmoil derived from some physiological pathology, and not from shattered illusions about the human condition.

THE LOST ART OF DYING WITHOUT DESPAIR

So it is that the artist provides us with important information about ourselves. Or, in the case of the more depressive confessional poets and depressive artists in other media, they teach us much about the anguish of despair, even if they do not seem seriously practiced in the art of dying. For example, it is obvious from the rhetorical tone of Plath's sarcasm that she does not seriously consider herself our mentor in this regard. She describes her own psychic interior, not platitudes about man's inhumanity to man.

While most people die from some final disease, even if the disease is ironically categorized as a "natural cause," perhaps we can discover something more worthwhile about the art of dying from the observations among those who approach this transition not as a calculated escape from physical pain, but as the inevitable next stage in life's journey. What exactly do the dying have to teach us? What have they encountered that might bring us solace and sagacity regarding this lost art?

I call this a "lost" art because it is really only in the modern age that we have come to view death as alien, inappropriate, or unnatural. I have already mentioned the best-selling book *The Last Lecture* in which Randy Pausch, in a very unpretentious and useful account of his own path to his approaching death, sets down for us the noble strategies he devised as a response to death and dying. Certainly his is an artful response in every sense, the proof of which is that were it not, we would hardly consider as inspirational matter the autobiographical thoughts of someone who has but six months to live and who is in the process of experiencing his body being ravaged by insatiable cellular tumors.

In my own reading and study, I have concluded that in those cultures that remain somewhat close to nature, whether as simple farmers or as members of what remains of extant tribal communities, likewise seem to approach death—whether their own or that of friend or family—with a degree of acceptance, wisdom, and ritual calculated to deal artfully with this point of transition. Thus, for the purposes of our exploration of the journey to the milestone of death, I think it useful to converse with those undergoing this same sort of process that Pausch endured so nobly, though there is one important blank page in Pausch's account. He forthrightly acknowledges that he has declined portraying the relationship between his religious beliefs and his coming to terms with his imminent demise, but not because such a relation is not relevant:

> Many, many people have written to me about the matters of faith. I've so appreciated their comments and their prayers.
>
> I was raised by parents who believed that faith was something very personal. I didn't discuss my specific religion in my lecture because I wanted to talk about universal principles that apply to all faiths—to share things I had learned through my relationships with people. (*The Last Lecture,* p. 186).

For Pausch and probably for most people, the art of living can be discussed publically and often, but the art of dying is most often an entirely private thing. Likewise, for Pausch and for others, the relationship between religious belief and the more practical affairs of science and daily living are two distinctly different arenas of thought and practice.

On the Bahá'í path of life, science and religion are integrated and inseparable. In fact, one of the principal doctrines of the Bahá'í Faith is the essential unity of science and religion. This principle does not imply some external imperative that scientists and religionists *must* become more amicable, have luncheons, or go out for coffee together, even though they might well find these shared activities appealing.

Rather what is intended by this belief is that reality is one integrated creation, regardless of which dimension we are discussing. Reality has an outer, visible, physical aspect, and it has an inner, invisible, metaphysical aspect. In other words, the existence of these two "dimensions" is not indicative of two distinct realities. Neither does this principle imply that we come to understand or gain access to these twin experiences separately or independently, any more than we should segregate our spiritual life from our family life and our vocation, or even from our avocations. All aspects of our existence are components of a single and indivisible experience.

This is the true meaning in Bahá'u'lláh's principle of the unity of science and religion, that reality is an integrated system, and that the "spiritual world is like unto the phenomenal world. They are the exact counterpart of each other" ('Abdu'l-Bahá, *Promulgation of Universal Peace*, p. 12). Therefore, science concentrates on studying discrete parts of the material aspect of reality, and religion and religious philosophy concentrate on studying the entirety of reality including that which is metaphysical. But reality itself is one.

What is even more relevant to our examination of the twin aspects of dying (physical pathology and spiritual philosophy), is that each area of study can inform us about the essential verities governing the other. Every relationship or law we discover operant in the physical aspect of reality is analogous to a comparable relationship or law at work in the metaphysical aspect of reality.

For example, Pausch's area of scientific expertise was studying how to construct a "virtual reality." What scientifically based study could be more relevant than coming to understand the motive inherent in the Creator's fashioning of a physical dimension to His Creation? If it is our inherent objective to dramatize or manifest in our daily life the progress and condition of our inner life, then surely the relationship between reality and some attempt to mimic that reality would lead to the realization that this physical part of our existence is doing precisely the same thing with regard to the spiritual part of our existence.

In actuality, even as Socrates himself sets forth in his aforementioned Allegory of the Cave, the entire dimension of physical reality is only a virtual reality, not reality itself. It is, as it were, a show where we play make-believe in order to understand and become practiced in the art of performing well in the "real" world, which we will enter upon our death, or our second (or third) birth: "Know thou that the Kingdom is the real world, and this nether place is only its shadow stretching out. A shadow hath no life of its own; its existence is only a fantasy, and nothing more; it is but images reflected in water, and seeming as pictures to the eye" ('Abdu'l-Bahá, *Selections from the Writings of 'Abdu'l-Bahá*, no. 150.2).

LUNCHEONS WITH LELAND

While we will discuss more pointedly later in an examination of suffering and grief the question of why some are struck down tragically and all too soon, while others are not, I think it apt at this point to examine the perspective of those who, like Pausch, have been given a death sentence, but who are also trying nobly to come to terms with their religious beliefs. And certainly Bahá'ís, even while affirming belief in the continuity of the essential self, must, like everyone else, come to terms with death as an unexpected and uninvited interruption in their attempt at systematic development. For while I have no doubt that Pausch's own faith assisted him daily and more especially at the end in coming to terms with his imminent departure from this dimension, few religions other than the Bahá'í Faith offer a consolation that is both life-affirming and totally rational.

I am not concerned here with those who wonder "Why must I die?" I think we have pretty well established that we are all going to die. We often hear this question or consider it when something happens to us that does not seem warranted. The question usually comes on the heels of discovering that there's something wrong. For example, my friend Mike, who has been my barber for thirty-five years, is presently trying to qualify for a lung transplant as a result of inhaling Agent Orange, a chemical defoliant used by the troops when he was fighting in Vietnam. His solution, he tells me when I ask how he is doing: "Big John," he says with a slap on my shoulder, "one day at a time, one day at a time."

He really means this, and he lives this. He gets the most he can out of each day as he fights the bureaucracy of the Veterans' Administration to qualify for new organs. Whereas so many in similar situations who learn about a life-threatening health problem feel guilty, that they could have eaten better, smoked less (or not at all), or exercised more. But then we immediately think of friends and family who smoked more, drank excessively, exercised less, and yet have no health problems whatsoever.

This is when the "Why Me?" question most often arises, when we feel that we have no important responsibility for the ills we are made to endure. This question is obviously most poignant when it involves terminal illness. For example, there is my dear Bahá'í friend Leland, who is most probably at the end of his life, and he is confronting death head on, trying to understand the art of dying.

A while back Leland learned that his recent difficulty breathing and being short of breath is the result of his having contracted mesothelioma, a form of cancer that results from exposure to working with asbestos. Once diagnosed, it is most common with those suffering from this form of cancer to die within six months to a year. Leland recently asked to have a conversation with my wife Lucia and me to discuss the fact that that he may have no more than about nine months to live.

Now Leland is, for the most part, just an "ordinary" American. His father was Mexican, and his mother was African American. Leland has done everything from working in a Ford factory to owning a hardware store to helping his stepson set up a fish farm. But in addition to being an "ordinary" guy, Leland is also one of the most thoroughly studious Bahá'ís I know. He is extremely well versed in what all the Bahá'í texts have to say about death and dying, and yet he felt that a frank, no-holds-barred, sit-down talk about death and what he was feeling regarding his own upcoming transition might help him consider how best to approach the art of dying.

We sat down at our kitchen table here in the country where the only sounds are roosters crowing, cattle lowing, and Molly the collie dog barking. Our first luncheon began by establishing what we understand or think we understand about death. First, all three of us agreed that each of us is dying and that while he may have no more than a fixed number of months to live, either Lucia or I could "pass away" before he does for any number of reasons.

I gave him a copy of Pausch's book, because in it Pausch acknowledges that knowing that within a year he would be dead from his pancreatic cancer gave him a distinct advantage over those who are hit by "the proverbial bus," the sudden and unexpected death that so many face. His forewarning enabled him to undertake rational and orderly preparation for this event, including an assessment of his life, which is in part what his lecture itself is all about, assessing how he had been able to accomplish the majority of his childhood dreams.

Pausch also acknowledges that one of the underlying purposes in his agreeing to do the lecture was to leave a videotape of his talk as a legacy for his young children so that they might understand something about this man who was their father. Furthermore, with this knowledge (or foreknowledge), Pausch and his wife could move closer to her family so that she cold be assisted in raising their young children after Pausch had died.

Leland discussed this perspective at length, because he said it helped him overcome, to a certain extent, his natural depression about having to leave this life when he happens to be one of those special souls who dearly loves life, who is full of life, and who enjoys nothing more than sharing that love with others.

This realization turned out to be a "breakthrough" for Leland in his determined preparation for his forthcoming transition—the idea that even though he is condemned to death, so are we all, except that he now has the advantage of knowing that he must not put off systematically preparing right now, while the rest of us will probably put off any sort of focused preparation and, subsequently, may leave unexpectedly with all our affairs in a mess.

A few weeks later, Leland called to say he was coming by for another chat, and we happily agreed because we found that we were learning at least as much from these discussions as was Leland. We may have been his sounding board, but he exemplified to us nobility of spirit, clarity of vision, and a fearlessness about trying to understand this incredible transformation he would most likely undergo before too long.

So it was that the second luncheon began, and during the course of our meandering conversation, the three of us received another insight or "breakthrough" that was a source of comfort and even delight. We came to realize during our discussion that the Bahá'í writings clearly imply that the afterlife experience will be specifically tailored to him as an individual. This was a lot more reassuring than the bifurcated view much of our society has inherited from the Christian and Muslim traditions of a "pass-fail" afterlife. From the Bahá'í point of view, the afterlife is *real* life, not merely an eternal assignment based on one's performance here.

Stated the way that seemed to mean the most to Leland, even as God has designed only one Leland and only one "Leland life" during the entirety of His infinite creation, this same God must also be also fully capable of designing a singular afterlife experience geared to the assistance and benefit of this same soul.

Leland understood quite clearly that according to the Bahá'í teachings there is a very explicit relationship between this life and the next, that one's performance here does affect one's initial experience in the afterlife. And he also was fully accepting of the fact that he could have done better. What thrilled him was the idea that he would pick up where he leaves off, that his experience there would be precisely geared to what would assist him in the continuation of his existence, not merely his relegation to some fixed status based on the results of a life review.

It was a month or more before Leland called again. He had begun radiation and chemo treatment and found it hard to drive, but he insisted that he come to our place to talk. And not unpredictably during our third luncheon, Leland experienced a third and, for Leland, perhaps his most powerful realization about the art of dying. He came to understand that according to the Bahá'í writings, God is entirely and inevitably benign, that God is not unpredictable or capricious, not constrained by some predetermined laws whereby we must be judged. Expressed more appropriately, we three came to appreciate that there really is no mystery about God in this sense, no guess work about what God will do, at least insofar as overall purpose is concerned. By definition, God will inevitably do what is best for us. What is more, God will always make available to us His mercy, His forgiveness, and His grace so long as we sincerely seek His assistance.

This last realization was perhaps assisted by a story I shared during our conversation about a course I had given at Louhelen Bahá'í school. The students and I were talking about several passages in the Bahá'í writings that speak about the progress of the soul after this life. Specifically, we were discussing the extent to which we will have sufficient free will after death to bring about positive change in our condition, especially if we should die in a condition of "sinfulness," despair, or faltering faith.

One student in the course offered a scenario in which someone had lived a decent life, but at the last minute had lost faith and died in a state of fear and consternation. "What would God do with such a person?" the student asked. The question was a good one because Bahá'u'lláh remarks in one place about the possibility of some last-minute conversion or, alternatively, a last-minute loss of faith. This passage seems pointedly devised to inspire vigilance and constancy in pursuing one's spiritual development:

> He [the "true seeker"] should not wish for others that which he doth not wish for himself, nor promise that which he doth not fulfill. With all his heart should the seeker avoid fellowship with evildoers, and pray for the remission of their sins. He should forgive the sinful, and never despise his low estate, for none knoweth what his own end shall be. How often hath a sinner, at the hour of death, attained to the essence of faith,

and, quaffing the immortal draft, hath taken his flight unto the celestial Concourse. And how often hath a devout believer, at the hour of his soul's ascension, been so changed as to fall into the nethermost fire. (Bahá'u'lláh, *Kitáb-i-Íqán,* ¶214)

"That is a frightening consideration," I remarked after we read the passage together; "the idea that we could work all our lives in the service of others and the promulgation of God's teachings, and then suddenly lose our faith with our dying breath!" I paused, and considered what Socrates might do by way of some logical strategy for getting the student to end up articulating the answer to her own question.

"Tell me," I asked, "Are you afraid of God?"

"Aren't we supposed to be?" she answered. And she quoted a passage from the writings of Bahá'u'lláh: "Fear ye God, and turn not away disdainfully from His Revelation. Fall prostrate on your faces before God, and celebrate His praise in the daytime and in the night season" (*Gleanings,* no. 15.5).

"And what is it about God that we are supposed to fear, do you suppose?" I asked.

"I'm not sure," she answered in perfect candor.

"Well, surely it's not God's love, or His mercy, or His forgiveness."

"Of course not," she laughed along with the rest of the class. "But I suppose that none of us know if we have done sufficiently well to merit His . . ." and she paused. That was the big question. At what point would God stop being merciful and loving and forgiving and become a strict judge who might deem us unworthy?

"Look," I said, "we are given the impression in the Old Testament that God is a pretty rough character, like a tribal chieftain, right? He is jealous, vengeful, even at times capricious, or so it seems. He overreacts. He'll smite down an entire tribe because of what we might consider some trivial transgression. I mean, turning a woman into a pillar of salt because she looked the wrong way, that does not sound like a God you want to decide your fate, am I right?"

"Exactly," she responded. "That's precisely what I mean. Besides, doesn't Bahá'u'lláh repeatedly state that 'God doeth whatsoever He pleaseth'?"

"Over and over again," I responded. "I think I understand your concern. It sounds like a pretty reasonable apprehension. In other words, you would prefer to deal with God the Father, the loving Father that Jesus describes, rather than God the jealous Lord of creation."

"What do you mean?" she asked, a bit puzzled.

"Well, Jesus talks about God as a loving Father who is about to sacrifice His only begotten Son to atone for all our sins. You'd rather be judged by that God, I guess. Because the God in the Qur'án also seems a lot like the God of Moses—He condemns infidels and talks about hell and retribution a lot more than Christ does."

"Hold it!" said someone in the class who formerly followed the Jewish faith. "What about the Psalms of David? In Psalm 23 God is portrayed as a loving shepherd who protects us, his sheep. You know, 'Thy rod and thy staff, they comfort me.'"

"Interesting," I said. "The rod is used for smacking the sheep when they stray from the path, while the staff with its crook is used to rescue the sheep who have gone astray or fallen into some crevice. And yet both the retributive act and the act of salvation are portrayed as the acts of a loving shepherd."

"This is nuts," said the woman who had asked the question to begin with. "We are all in agreement here that there is only one God and that He is changeless!"

"Good point," I said. "Then let's assume that these different images of God are simply different points of emphasis, different perspectives from different cultural and historical points of view. So let's temporarily set aside these biased images and construct God from what we ourselves have discerned to be the attributes of this Deity as depicted in the Bahá'í Writings."

So the class and I proceeded to begin quite a long list of the attributes of God. He is kind, loving, forgiving, omnipotent, omniscient, a kind parent, a perfect teacher, a guardian of humankind. He creates not out of need, but in order to fashion a being capable of receiving and willingly benefitting from the beauty of creation itself and from the love and bounty He has to bestow.

On and on we went, but nowhere was there in this anything to be worried about or fearful of. There was no capriciousness, no irrationality, no unpredictability, no anger management problems, not over the long haul.

"Enough," I said after a while. "Since the attributes of God are infinite and our class time is not, let's presume we have a pretty good idea of what God is all about, how He operates and reacts in any given situation."

"So why should we fear Him?" said the woman who set the whole dialogue in motion.

"We shouldn't," said another woman, who was elderly and who, until now had been quiet. She spoke with a thick Persian accent, and had come to the United States only recently. "What we fear is ourselves should we turn away from God, because this we can do if we are not careful. Believe me, I know this. I have seen this with my own eyes."

The class went silent. With the continued persecution of the Bahá'ís in Iran, we could only imagine what she had witnessed during her life as a Bahá'í. At last I felt the need to bring closure to our discussion about God, but before I could speak, the woman with the original concern said, "But what about the idea that 'He doeth whatsoever He willeth'?"

"Tell me this," I asked, "Would this God we have described ever do anything that was not for the benefit of humankind or that was intended to be detrimental to any human soul?"

"No, of course not."

"So we need not fear that God would ever do anything to harm us. God will always will that which is for our best interest, our ultimate benefit, right?"

"It only makes sense."

"Because God will do whatever is logically best to achieve the ultimate objective of assisting and educating us."

"He's perfect, isn't He," she responded.

"Then let's return to your individual who has lived a life of service and selflessness but who, for whatever reason, loses his or her faith at the hour or the moment of the soul's ascent. How would a rational, loving, and forgiving God respond to such a soul? Or let's put the question in more personal terms. What would *you* do to such a soul if you were God for a day?"

"I'd forgive him," she said instantly. "*I* would shower that soul with love and forgiveness. After all, the person lived a good life and served humanity." In her tone and inflexion was the clear indication that what *she* would do might be different from what she inferred this omnipotent Deity might do.

"And do you think God less good, less 'Godlike' than you?" She laughed out loud at first, but then returned to the rest of the passage.

"But what about the 'nethermost fire?' Why would God cause them to fall into the deepest fire?" she continued.

"Hold on. You added something there. The passage does not say that God 'causes' them to fall. Their own doubt and sudden loss of faith brings about this descent. Furthermore, what does Bahá'u'lláh say that symbolic terms like 'Satan' and 'hellfire' represent?

"The self," offered the formerly Jewish class member. "The insistent self. Allusions to Satan and the Satanic symbolize our own vanity and selfish desires. And the fire represents the agony, the spiritual and emotional pain of what it feels like to be remote from God."

"There's one more catch to this," I concluded. "Notice that the passage does not say that this person who has lived a good life will stay in such a condition. After all, if God is like the good shepherd, should we not presume if one has fallen into the fire, the staff would be quickly lowered down to the temporarily distraught and frantic soul to rescue it?"

This account struck a chord with Leland, even as the exchange in class had with me. Like so many insights about complex questions that occur in any class, a great deal of enlightenment that a teacher acquires derives from the need to formulate answers to difficult questions. This is perhaps the major ancillary benefit of teaching—the teacher invariably learns more than the students. Or stated another way, when you try to articulate something you *think* you know, you discover that you begin to comprehend things a whole lot better. And if you do not, the class will inevitably let you know about your failure.

THANK GOD FOR LIFEGUARDS

But it was not the sudden and unexpected discovery of Leland's condition that alone brought about this need on my part to think about death in relation to my own future. As I mentioned earlier, so many friends and colleagues, those who are my age or slightly younger or older, have been dying of late, or else are presently in the process of going through the final stages of death. So many friends and family have been plagued with suffering of one sort or another that I feel the need to come up with answers for them and for me, because I am officially a senior citizen, an old person, an elder, a codger.

And it seems I am destined to remain such so long as I continue to associate with this aging temple that has been so capably reconstructed by the skilled hands of competent surgeons. It was a few weeks ago that this fact of my existence became inescapably obvious to me.

I was swimming my laps as part of my attempt to become young again, or at least avoid looking quite so codgeresque. I had just finished swimming my usual forty laps, whereupon I began my so-called sprints. I would swim as hard as I could from one side to the other, then make my way back with a sort of floating breast-stroke, intermixed with bouncing my toes off the bottom of the pool.

"Are you OK, sir?" called out the young blond lifeguard from her perch atop the lifeguard stand. My first instinct was to ask her why she thought that someone who could swim forty laps and then do sprints might be in trouble, but I have of late attempted not to be so sarcastic with people. Also, I realized that had I been in trouble, she probably would have noticed, instead texting her friends or listening to her iPod.

That pleased me—the idea that she took her job seriously and, should I have been in trouble, she would have come to my rescue. "I'm just fine," I responded in a pleasant enough tone.

"I just don't want you to drown on me," she commented gaily.

"I assure you," I answered, "my desire not to die on you far surpasses your own."

She giggled and I tried to flex whatever muscles are still capable of flexing as I climbed out of the pool to demonstrate that I wasn't as old as I looked, or that I looked younger than I am.

Anyhow, a few days later she gave me the *coup de grâce*. Once again I was swimming my laps and once again the same young lady was watching over me. I did my usual forty laps. I then did a few sprints, and climbed out of the pool, whereupon she summoned me to the lifeguard stand as I was toweling off.

"Excuse me sir, could I ask you something?" she said in a soft voice so no one else could hear—this was going to be personal. I took a few steps closer. I dare not share the sort of accolades my vain imaginings had concocted.

"Go right ahead," I responded.

"Just how old are you?" she asked.

"I'm sixty-eight," I replied, in a somewhat nonplussed tone.

"Well, I just wanted to say that I really admire you." My shoulders drooped and my muscles unflexed.

"Thanks," I said despondently, and I turned and slouched toward the dressing room, realizing that her admiration could only mean that she was stunned that someone who looked as old as I could possibly still swim forty laps. It was several days before I returned to the pool. Fortunately, she was not on duty.

12

AGING AS A
TRAINING TECHNIQUE

An aged man is but a paltry thing,
A tattered coat upon a stick, unless
Soul clap its hands and sing, and louder sing
For every tatter in its mortal dress,
Nor is there singing school but studying
Monuments of its own magnificence;
And therefore I have sailed the seas and come
To the holy city of Byzantium.
—W. B. Yeats, "Sailing to Byzantium"

So that was it. With the most subtle of indirection, the young blond nineteen-year-old paid to guard my life at the pool had pronounced my age, even as four hundred years before Shakespeare in *As You Like It* had catalogued the sixth of the seven ages of man. I don't think I yet qualify for the seventh and final stage, or "last scene" as it is called in the play:

> Last scene of all,
> That ends this strange eventful history,
> Is second childishness and mere oblivion;
> Sans teeth, sans eyes, sans taste, sans everything.
> (Act II, Scene vii, Lines 163–66)

I still have most of my real teeth, however alloyed they may be with various combinations of base and precious metals. I may be childish at times, but quite aware of that behavior, even as I have always been.

THE FEAR OF ALFS

And yet do I even want to endure until that seventh and final stage? I saw my mother's compatriots at the ALF (Assisted Living Facility) gradually turn from folksy, to forgetful, to mumbling and palsied fixtures wheeled from room to room. At the end, they would be placed in front of huge TV screens to which they were oblivious. At dinner time they would be spoon-fed like infants.

My father and brother never had to endure such indignity, nor did Mom, other than having to watch sadly as her friends and companions one by one traverse this final threshold. And yet, how strange of us to disdain what God has wrought. How dare we disparage any stage of life ordained by the natural course of things, especially a stage that serves as our final detachment from whatever fondness or glee we might still derive from this physical world?

Yes, it is painful to see these once noble visages and keen minds bereft of all they once held dear. But by what possible right should we deride or ignore this final scene, especially should we live long enough to endure it ourselves? All the Manifestations of God have forbidden self-slaughter for a reason, so euthanasia is not an option except when machines are doing our living for us.

Perhaps we admire the people who live through this last stage of life with all important faculties in tact, but do we then turn away in contempt or disrespect from those who, through no fault of their own, have lost those faculties and whose lives are reduced to waiting for their turn to ascend?

Surely as a natural course of things, this final stage also has something noteworthy to bespeak, some vital lesson for us to learn if we have the humanity and patience to sit among the aged at this last station, to provide them a bit of companionship and love as we hold their hands in patient surveillance.

When I first came to Florida more than forty years ago, I took note of what were then only a few of these incredible new buildings, these Assisted Living Facilities. In my young mind, they stood out as modern monuments to human ingenuity and cruel and heartless commerce. At the time I never dreamed that anyone I knew—my mother, for example—would willingly choose such a destiny. And so it was in mocking condescension that I wrote the following poem:

THE AWFUL WONDERS OF THE SUN BAY TOWERS DEVELOPMENT FOR SENIOR CITIZENS

I am told that there is, neatly
on the wall of each cubiculum
in the looming white
monument to mercantility
rising before me, a door two
feet square, coal-bin-hatch
size, stainless steel, hinged at
the top, connected to a chute
so when pains come tingling
up the arm, one simply leans
forward from the waist, then
it's zoom down the slide to the
basement and plop in the red
velvet box on rollers tripping
the lid shut—the momentum

carrying the whole assemblage
(me inside) into the back of a
dark waiting Cadillac, station-
wagon shaped, motor running.

But as I watched the occupants at my mother's facility dodge the children on Sunday when grandchildren and great grandchildren would weave in and out of the walkers, canes, and trembling limbs, I realized that the walls were there to ward off danger, not to box in these elders among us. For twelve years after my father's death, Mom had kept house for herself, by herself, and at eighty-two she was ready and deserving to let others assist her with the mundane chores of living, but Florida was too hot for her taste and Quebec too cold, so living with either me or Bill was not an option, especially since all her friends at St. Mark Church still lived in Atlanta.

THE FOREWARNING OF POETS

I have not yet reached and probably will not reach such an age where I will need to be relegated to a senior home and have someone take care of me, though I will not disdain it should this prove to be my fate. I suppose that my being officially classified as a "senior citizen" is not the end of anything but the beginning of my winding down, however much I refuse at present to lose a step, unless it is taken from me by force.

I will drive my tractor and use my chain saw and trim the pasture and till the gardens until I no longer find it joyful to do so or until I become a danger to myself or others. I joke with fellow elders about getting in touch with my "inner codger," and share stories about the strangeness of being grandparents. Occasionally I turn once more to those poets whose pithy insights have foretold the milestones of my past to discover what wisdom or catchy lines they have forged in their studied lives and well-honed craft about this stage of life. What crumbs and clues to mark the trail might they have left behind about the imposed detachment that is the art of aging?

Most days, my morning mirror tells me all I want or need to know—that the lifeguard's nervous query about whether I am just resting between laps or am struggling to stay afloat is probably warranted. Yet, instead of benefiting from associations with those like me waiting to board the last train, society seems to have settled on an aggregate contempt for us. It is certainly understandable why as a society we have done this—the fear of death and dying.

We would rather not accept the fact that at some point all of our lives, at least on this physical plane, will inevitably come to an end. We would rather think that through careful diet, regular exercise, and skillful surgeons, we can look and feel much the same in old age as we did in youth. We can even sign up for spare parts if some major organs malfunction or become irreparably damaged—hips, knees, heart, liver, lungs, etc.

We may gaze at the flawless beauty of some starlet and feel certain that age will be powerless to conquer that luminescent glow, those shining locks, that silken skin, those bright young eyes. True, in youth we may try to seduce such a creature by terrifying her with some *carpe diem* lines about the brevity of youth and the specter of aging, as did Waller with his memorable verse, but we apply it as a gambit of seduction, not because we recognize the stark truth underlying the vain ploy:

> Go, lovely Rose-
> Tell her that wastes her time and me,
> That now she knows,
> When I resemble her to thee,
> How sweet and fair she seems to be.
> Tell her that's young,

And shuns to have her graces spied,
That hadst thou sprung
In deserts where no men abide,
Thou must have uncommended died.
Small is the worth
Of beauty from the light retired:
Bid her come forth,
Suffer herself to be desired,
And not blush so to be admired.
Then die-that she
The common fate of all things rare
May read in thee;
How small a part of time they share
That are so wondrous sweet and fair!

The most famous of these attempts to caution reluctant young maidens about the brevity of this time of youth and beauty when they can conquer hearts with but a smile or a glance is Marvel's "To His Coy Mistress." Here the speaker proclaims that were time not an indomitable foe, he would spend eons wooing the fair maiden, but the fact is that if she withholds herself, she will waste all the beauty and charm that are hers for so brief a span. The most gruesome but effective bit in his argument goes thus:

But at my back I always hear
Time's wingèd chariot hurrying near;
And yonder all before us lie
Deserts of vast eternity.
Thy beauty shall no more be found,
Nor, in thy marble vault, shall sound
My echoing song: then worms shall try

That long preserved virginity,
And your quaint honour turns to dust,
And into ashes all my lust:
The grave's a fine and private place,
But none, I think, do there embrace.

These cynical cautions about life's brevity penned by English cavalier poets in the middle of the seventeenth century would not work today. The foundational premise of the poem would not be believed: that the fair maiden cannot conquer age. Instead, we have become convinced by television ads and drugstore periodicals that with special emollients and skillful surgeons, with exotic juices from berries gleaned from treetops in South America, the fair maiden actually can retain that youthful shape and hue. The bags under her eyes can be trimmed, the hair dyed, the breasts made more fulsome and shapely than anything nature wrought.

When we see the airbrushed pictures of many of these famous women in their forties or fifties, we too may be inclined to agree. We agree so long as we do not by chance discover a picture of these once ageless beauties in a state of inevitable decline, when sutures and creams, when nips and tucks no longer sustain the outer miracle of that all too brief a span.

The fact is that we cannot defeat laws of nature regarding aging any more than we can defeat the law of gravity. If we jump, we will fall. If we live, we will age. This fact was demonstrated painfully to me recently while scanning the Web on the subject of aging.

I recently came across a picture of Bridget Bardot, possibly the most adored and seductive icons of female sensuality and natural beauty from my youth. I had remembered her as an inviolable beauty, a flawless nymph who, I was certain, would ever remain impervious to time. But there she was at age seventy-two, but a few years older than I, only looking worse off. The life guard would not have let this woman in the pool without a signature on a liability release.

Side-by-side was another picture of her at the peak of her pulchritude—confident, coy, untouchable. There was some slight resemblance in the eyes and mouth. Otherwise, the picture of her older self looked as if someone had taken the youthful face and stretched it beyond its capacity to rebound so that the skin seemed to drip from her once prominent cheeks and once firm neck and chin. The fire of life had been held beneath that glorious face so that it had melted into a Halloween caricature of a visage that once might have indeed launched a thousand ships.

POETS REFLECT ON THE "END TIMES"

Anyone familiar with poetic considerations of aging, of death and dying, is well aware of Dylan Thomas's poetic plaint "Do Not Go Gentle into that Good Night." The poem begins with the aphorism that someone who is aged should not meekly accept the fate of becoming decrepit, should not approach death with hushed acquiescence:

> Do not go gentle into that good night,
> Old age should burn and rave at close of day;
> Rage, rage against the dying of the light.

In particular, the speaker is trying to encourage or coerce his father (who, we infer, is sinking peacefully into death) to fight manfully against entering this "good night." In truth, we can presume the poem says more about the speaker than about the father.

Perhaps the speaker fears death, or else he is unable or unwilling to accept his father's departure. For whatever reason, he chides the dying man for his meek compliance with what the speaker seems to think is an unnatural response to entering the "dark night" of death—which is a "good night" only in the sense that it is a farewell (a "good night") to his son.

So it is, after a series of examples of those who have refused to accept passively the diminishing of their vitality, the speaker pleads with his father to do the same—not to accept his decline submissively, but to rage against death:

> And you, my father, there on the sad height,
> Curse, bless me now with your fierce tears,
> I pray.
> Do not go gentle into that good night.
> Rage, rage against the dying of the light.

In a noticeably different response to aging, the speaker/persona in Yeats's "Sailing to Byzantium" is himself an aging man who also makes distinctions between two categories of those who are "aged," but not between those who struggle against aging and dying versus those who succumb. Instead, the speaker distinguishes between those who allow themselves to become intellectually and spiritually stagnant in old age versus those who strive relentlessly to attain a spiritual and intellectual ascent that belies the insignificant outer appearance of their dwindling physical self:

> An aged man is but a paltry thing,
> A tattered coat upon a stick, unless
> Soul clap its hands and sing, and louder sing
> For every tatter in its mortal dress,

This metaphor for the physical aspect of an aged man as a "tattered coat upon a stick" is, for me, one of the more powerful images in all of poetry, being at once visual and visceral, and yet so accessible and compact. Yeats' image of the aged physical self stands in stark contrast to the latent capacity still available if the real "self" of the person—the "essential self" or "soul"—would but "clap its hands and sing."

This pithy image is a provocative allusion to one's ability to acquire and express wisdom through art or some other sensibly perceptible idiom. The "tatters" of the physical self in this figurative image represent the strife, pain, and turmoil the body has endured, the outer scars of life on the physical self that signify those milestones of learning achieved by the inner self.

There is so much more to learn from Yeats' insightful thoughts expressed in his beguilingly simple language. In particular it is important to note the speaker's conclusion about what he intends to do as a result of observing in the very first line how "That is no country for old men":

> Nor is there singing school but studying
> Monuments of its own magnificence;
> And therefore I have sailed the seas and come
> To the holy city of Byzantium.

Here the speaker observes that the best opportunity for a soul to understand what is worth singing about and how to "sing"—to express what it has learned—is by studying the masterpieces of the past that serve as "monuments" to the magnificence of the capacity of the human soul to discover the important truths of life and subsequently to express these verities through some artistic medium. To me it seems that the speaker desires to escape from a materially/sensually oriented life and discover an environment where voices of wisdom harkening to the spirit and the soul of humanity will be heard and heeded.

This art, these enduring monuments of the human soul that Faulkner alludes to in his Stockholm speech, represent, among other things, the work of those poets who address the matters of the human heart, and Byzantium, whatever precise symbolic value it may represent for Yeats, alludes to such an environment—one, I suspect, that is yet to be born or created. In this piece, then, age is capable of bringing with it wisdom, learning, and such powers than can be acquired solely through life experience, but only with the effort and perseverance sufficient to escape the bonds of a sensually oriented society.

And yet, such wisdom is imparted only to those aged ones who have first been attentive to the wisdom that the "monuments" of the past have to impart. Even then, the poet or spiritually advanced human being of whatever artistic capacity must combine that vision with a determination to escape from those forces of moribund doctrines. The artist must discover or forge a space (real or metaphorical) where such wisdom will have a fit audience that is receptive to this knowledge, capable of building upon that storehouse of wisdom, and determined to do so.

One of the most familiar poems dealing with aging in an affirmative tone is Tennyson's memorable "Ulysses." In this dramatic monologue, the figure of Ulysses, having long since returned from the battle in Troy and his meandering adventures through the Mediterranean, has now become thoroughly bored with his tenure as king. He longs to return to a life of adventure and discovery. He does not enjoy the routine duties of governing his island people in Ithaca, nor does he feel he is particularly good at it. Therefore, he decides to turn over the kingship to his son Telemachus and venture out with his fellow aging mariner-warriors (codgers all) to dare one last challenge—this time to sail beyond the Pillars of Hercules, the Straits of Gibraltar, what the Achaeans believed to be the divinely imposed boundaries of the world.

At the end of this grand soliloquy, he speaks in a tone that doubtless would have pleased and consoled Thomas' despairing speaker in "Do Not Go Gentle." He confesses that he and his men are indeed old, that they do not now have the strength they once had. But he vows that they can still accomplish something that has never been done before, or at least die trying (which, alas, they do, according to Greek mythology). But Ulysses does rage against the dying of the light—the approach of the end of his life—and a most poetic rage it is:

> My mariners,
> Souls that have toiled, and wrought, and thought with
>   me—
> That ever with a frolic welcome took
> The thunder and the sunshine, and opposed
> Free hearts, free foreheads—you and I are old;
> Old age hath yet his honor and his toil;

Perhaps we should end with this piece—it is so upbeat, so encouraging, especially to those who share this spirit of adventure, this unconquerable will to survive and strive and conquer. But because of the Bahá'í perspective, which coalesces all points of view into what I consider to be a most hopeful yet practical solution to aging and its emotional indices, I think it helpful for us to conclude the examination of what the poets have to tell us about aging with a delightfully crass and cynical poem, also penned by Dylan Thomas.

It is another dramatic monologue, this time narrated by a dying man. But unlike Ulysses, this man is no longer able to venture out, and he resents the fact that he must be bedridden and die such a placid and wimpy death when he has spent his entire life devoted to being a bawdy, brawling, beast of a man, a man who, having blasted the world with his boorish and crude devouring of life, now finds himself all tidy, clean, and flat on his back.

He rages, all right. He rants and howls, but not against the "dying of the light." We come to doubt that he has ever received much "light" in the first place. He is furious that he must, in the end, endure what he considers the indignity of having to experience such a simpering demise when he has lived such an arrogant, roaring life. He would have preferred to die, we infer, in a drinking bout or in a rowdy brawl at the local pub.

The poem is wonderfully structured so that each successive stanza represents another age in the chronology of the "Old Ram Rod's" progression through the years, a bit like Shakespeare's ages of man. Thus, by the next-to-last stanza, age has bereft him of his manhood and, in fear of damnation, his apprehensive soul has turned to religion, though clearly he hates himself for this weakness, the surrender of himself to all he would have formerly ridiculed and disdained.

In the last stanza, he pronounces the final tones of his cynical contempt for his own weakness and ignoble demise:

> Now I am a man no more no more
> And a black reward for a roaring life,
> (Sighed the old ram rod, dying of strangers),
> Tidy and cursed in my dove cooed room
> I lie down thin and hear the good bells jaw—
> For, oh, my soul found a sunday wife
> In the coal black sky and she bore angels!
> Harpies around me out of her womb!
> Chastity prays for me, piety sings,
> Innocence sweetens my last black breath,
> Modesty hides my thighs in her wings,
> And all the deadly virtues plague my death!

This is pretty pessimistic and frightening stuff. No hope, no nostalgia, just a hollow rail against dying, and not even against the dying of any "light," if light symbolizes a bit of enlightenment, and not merely the life force that might sustain some degree of mortal existence. This boorish character hasn't acquired any enlightenment, nor do we suspect he has ever desired any.

He has indulged himself in existential chaos and machismo. Nevertheless, he is memorable, even if not admirable. Perhaps he can take some pride in representing for us symbolically something like the very last scene in the very last Rambo movie that will ever be made.

AGING AS DIVINELY ORDAINED TRAINING

Having surveyed some of the poetic responses to aging and various takes on the meaning of the deterioration of the metaphorical self that comes with age, we are ready, I feel, to examine what I have found to be a simple yet remarkable and precious gift that aging has to give us, if we are, like Yeats's aged man, attentive to its call. Indeed, I would deign to propose that we can discern in this perspective both the wisdom in this climactic phase in our creation, and the love inherent in the Creator's design of this inescapable and outwardly ignominious departure.

The Bahá'í paradigm has already been implied throughout our discussion, but it is worth illustrating it here in graphic form for two important reasons. The first of these is the relationship of this paradigm to the aforementioned Bahá'í concept that our earthly existence is designed by God precisely to prepare us for our future existence in a metaphysical environment. Consequently, one of the most important lessons we must learn is how gradually to extract the spiritual lessons available in this physical or gestational stage, while simultaneously to become ever more detached from bonds and fetters of materiality.

The trick is that these twin processes must occur simultaneously and in a reciprocal fashion. The more we aspire to intellectual and spiritual development, the more we must gradually cease to rely on physical and sensual experience as an end in itself. As we have already noted, the physical classroom, when utilized properly, has the value of providing us with a laboratory wherein we can put into practice our newly acquired spiritual powers and capacities:

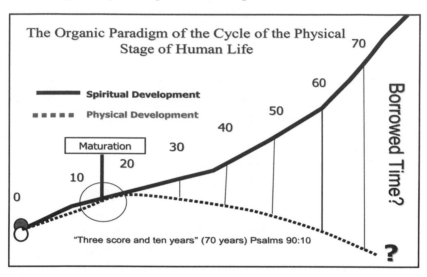

The Organic Paradigm of the Cycle of the Physical Stage of Human Life

— Spiritual Development

■ ■ ■ ■ ■ Physical Development

Maturation

Borrowed Time?

"Three score and ten years" (70 years) Psalms 90:10

In this graph we can observe that spiritual development and physical development are more or less in sync until approximately age fifteen, designated in Bahá'í law as the age of maturity. According to this perception of human development, when we reach this age, we are responsible for our own conduct, presumed capable of making some major life decisions.

But more to the point, it is not too much longer after physical maturation that our physical self attains the peak of its potentiality, somewhere in our early twenties. From then on, our capacity or potential for physical exploits diminishes, even though we may maintain or even improve our physical conditioning individually. But as we see on the graph, it is around this same time, at the apex of physical capacity, that our mental and spiritual capacities (expressions of our inner strength) are just beginning their ascent. Indeed, it is our hope, if we have any serious aspirations about life, that over time we will become ever more capable of assembling the information we accumulate at every stage of our journey. In addition, it is our further hope that we will become ever more proficient in assembling this learning into increasingly complex and creative insights into the meaning of life itself.

Of course, we should not infer from this assertion that the brain as a physiological organ is itself increasingly more capable. Like the rest of the body, the brain achieves maximum capacity around the age of maturity. But as with the other physiological capacities, the more intricate application of body parts to intellectually or conceptually related activities can undergo marked acceleration way past the peak of physiological development.

For example, the dexterity of a master violinist, weaver, painter, or pianist rarely demonstrates the zenith of power until sometime around middle-age or later, even though examples of child prodigies may show the raw or latent capacity already inherent. But the synthesizing of sheer physiological capacity with the mental or spiritual aspects of such arts and crafts requires something more than brute strength. It requires depth of feeling, a willful synthesis of nuance, a fusion of experience, a subtlety of vision. This complex blending of physiological or neural training of muscles, nerves, and memory with the wisdom and vision that generally awaits life experience is what most often marks the peak of an artist's accomplishments.

Naturally, these observations are gross generalizations. We can counter such observations with stories of the early genius of a Mozart. Likewise, we can offer hope for later development with equally encouraging stories of late-bloomers like poet Wallace Stevens. But the point is that insofar as spiritual and mental preparation for birth into the metaphysical stage of our life is concerned, where no dexterity or physical prowess is required or even usable, there is no limit in this life to the useful stages of ascent we can attain.

Stated axiomatically, except in cases where brain disorders seem to limit or shut down inner development during the physical stage of our lives, the capacity for spiritual development in this life is endless. Furthermore, as Bahá'u'lláh has noted, even in those cases where there is injury or illness regarding the body or the mind, the soul itself is not impaired nor is its ascent necessarily encumbered. To repeat a passage we cited earlier, "That a sick person showeth signs of weakness is due to the hindrances that interpose themselves between his soul and his body, for the soul itself remaineth unaffected by any bodily ailments" (*Gleanings*, no. 80.2).

Of course, aging and the field of gerontology are, generally speaking, newly emerged concerns for our modern age. The average lifespan in the year 1900 was forty-seven. The average lifespan is now seventy-five. Consequently, problems resulting from the physiological deterioration of the aging brain are only recently becoming intensely studied. Compared to other amazing advancements in scientific exploration of reality, our understanding of the human brain is still at the very earliest stages of exploration and development.

But as I discussed at some length in chapter four, the more science examines this most complex creation in all of physical reality (the human brain), the more viable is the theory that human consciousness is nonlocal—not resident in or dependent on a physical organ.

Over time, and not all that much time at that, the study of the interplay between physics and metaphysics will doubtless vindicate completely this understanding of the human reality. For now, we can accept it or not based on our individual study and experience. My own experience is that "I write, therefore I get published," an axiom that is decent enough for me to accept that I am thinking. Furthermore, I refuse to give credit for my thinking to the random firing of a bunch of neurons that reside in some specialized lobes of my brain, though I may take my royalties and buy some brain food (smoked salmon is good) as a token of appreciation to my lobes.

DETACHMENT: READY OR NOT!

The relationship of this paradigm to the Bahá'í concept of human purpose—spiritual preparation for a birth into a metaphysical environment—is extremely enlightening as regards our creation, particularly as regards the notion of our being made in the image of our Creator. As we view the graph above, what we are actually viewing is the manner in which the essential self begins gradually to escape the bonds of physiological constraints and, ultimately, to escape physiological association altogether. Or stated from the Creator's perspective, our relationship to physical reality is specifically designed to extricate us by degrees from attachment to our lower or physical nature.

Most of us may have recognized that the most bountiful knowledge seems to emerge from some of the more aged exemplars of wisdom. We certainly do not discount or disregard their amazing insights about reality because they happen to no longer be physically elegant or dexterous. For example, I remember listening to a talk given by Hand of the Cause of God[12] Shu'á'u'lláh 'Alá'í shortly before he passed away in 1984. At 95, he was wracked with age, barely there at all—truly a "tattered coat upon a stick" until I heard his soul clap its hands and sing.

---

12. "Hand of the Cause of God" is a title given certain individuals who were appointed by Bahá'u'lláh and later by Shoghi Effendi to protect and propagate the Bahá'í Faith.

Two men carried him to the stage and set him down in a chair before a crowd of several thousand. His face was drawn and withered. His dark and deep set eyes seemed unfocused and his aspect bewildered. We might have expected some hazy recollections of the highlights of his noble life or some anecdotes about the adventures he had as he served the Bahá'í Faith throughout the world. Then he began to speak.

First we were astounded that such a mighty a voice could emanate from such a slight frame. Sentence by sentence we became increasingly mesmerized by his mental acuity. We were amazed by his frank wisdom as he explained the significance of the present time in which we live and the relationship of our brief lives to the ultimate destiny of humankind on our planet.

This was not a meandering reminiscence by some relic of the past. One by one this incredible man catalogued the indices of a society in decline. Then, with equal fervor and eloquence, he filled our hearts with expectation about the glorious future that could be ours, but only if we were willing and able to take upon ourselves the responsibility that we as American Bahá'ís have been mandated in the authoritative Bahá'í texts. If we would but plant the seeds of faith in the rich soil of the hearts of waiting souls, if we would but shoulder that single burden, world reformation would soon emerge from the most unexpected peoples and places.

The incredible thing was that as he spoke and as we became by stages astounded, then entranced, then inspired, and then empowered, we no longer paid any attention whatsoever to the physical dimensions or the age of this magnificent man. He became his voice, and that voice seemed to originate from some other realm. The years seemed to melt away from his eyes, and his countenance seemed to glow with power and authority. The slight frame that had seemed so lamentably frail and shattered, gradually assumed a stature that the mightiest potentate might envy.

I will never forget that experience, that firsthand empirical evidence of how a physical apparatus so maimed by age, so tattered by life, could yet be employed by so grand a spirit as a vehicle for spiritual power and inspiration and insight. Afterward, I never required further proof of the non-locality of the soul. Instantly I understood how the divinely ordained process of aging can, if we allow it, peel away bit by bit our attachment to things of this world, whether it be our vanity about ourselves or our appearance, or whether it be our reliance on the trivial pursuits that distract us from the path we are fashioned by God to follow.

Consequently, whenever I view this graph of human reality in this physical stage of our existence, I see a wondrous and felicitous change occurring instead of the loss of all I hold dear. I see the spirit ever ascending even as, stage by stage, the physical or metaphorical self declines and, in the end, becomes incapable of channeling that spirit, which is then released to pursue its intended goal without physical encumbrance.

This, for me, is what is meant by the concept of "detachment" as discussed at length in the Bahá'í texts. In the beginning of our journey, the term may refer simply to proceeding with moderation in our use of physical reality to learn spiritual lessons, to be *in* this world but not *of* this world. In later stages, the term assumes more complex and more profound meaning. It can allude to monitoring carefully how attached we are to the things we possess and to assessing regularly the *mizán* we use to prioritize our daily life.

In old age, *detachment* may well allude to the very subject of this book, preparing ourselves spiritually for the final milestone in our physical experience while not distancing ourselves from the requirement that we always express our virtuous inner character with outward action so long as we are able.

The path toward detachment is thus a thoroughly subtle path in this respect—not being ashamed to aspire to accomplishments, to become the best that we can be in every sense, and yet always taking stock of how what we accomplish relates to our ultimate destiny as human souls. At all times we may sense the elastic pull of the things of this world. That is why when I see the graph, I always imagine that those vertical lines that mark the decades are like elastic cords attempting to restrain the soul from its ascent, like the literal bonds and ties of earthliness.

Finally, aging as a divinely created process trains us in the most subtle art of striving for selflessness. For while we retain throughout our lives a sense of ourselves as individual consciousnesses working from within the bone-shell of our skull, our objective, according to the Bahá'í teachings, is to strive to become ever more inclusive in our sense of self. Repeatedly Bahá'u'lláh reminds us that ultimately our most joyful moments are experienced as we work in concert with other souls striving for the same objectives.

We are trained in this from the outset, that we cannot be happy if a member of our family is troubled or in pain. As we develop, that circle of self expands until we lament and are discomfited if anywhere within our kind there are those without, those who are hungry, those who must endure a single day without clothing or shelter or love.

This is a type of selflessness that is not abnegation of the self, not the abasement or denial of self, but the ultimate joy and fulfillment of self. It is characterized by a sense of belonging, of being integrated into a larger social "self." It is the same category of joy we may become initially introduced to by such simple exercises as singing in a chorus, playing on a team, and all the myriad ways we give to ourselves by the act of giving ourselves to others.

A recent uncomplicated but possibly profound experiment demonstrates the scientific fact of this process. A group of individuals were given a certain amount of money. Half of the group were told to spend their money on themselves, and half were told to spend their money on someone else. When tested after the experience, the group that spent the money on someone else was significantly happier about their experience than were the members of the other group. The "givers" spent their money more freely and easily, and their sense of joy and felicity was determined to be significantly greater than that of the "keepers," who fretted over what to get, and later had a bit of buyer's remorse as to whether or not they had received the best "stuff" for the money they were given.

Aging has the capacity to teach us these kinds of lessons, about this process of achieving a healthy sort of selflessness. As our physical self deteriorates and our desire to exalt ourselves becomes strained and unrewarding, we are better able to appreciate the value of being part of an enterprise larger and more encompassing than our personal agenda, status or acquisitions.

It is doubtless for this reason that the elderly in the Bahá'í Faith are never relegated to some ancillary or subordinate role. There is no age at which a Bahá'í cannot participate in electing administrative institutions or in serving on these same bodies. Likewise, in teaching and learning within the Bahá'í community, there is no distinction made between the youngest and the oldest members. There is no segregation according to age or any other external and circumstantial considerations.

In the final analysis, then, aging is truly an ingeniously constructed divine gift because it forces us to consider little by little what we might otherwise choose to ignore, that however much we may want to keep things the way they are, or to hang on to the things of this world—including our own bodies—we are programmed to let go by degrees. Aging is a carefully designed exercise that constantly urges us with increasing insistence to attend to that part of our selves that is most important, the essential part of our selves that will endure and continue its endless journey toward fulfilling its capacity to become ever more refined, ever more complete and joyful.

13

EVEN MANIFESTATIONS GRIEVE

I have, O my Lord, offered up that which Thou hast given Me, that Thy servants may be quickened, and all that dwell on earth be united.

—Bahá'u'lláh, *God Passes By*

When I was little, I believed in Santa Claus. This was back in the 1940s when Santa Claus was more believable. He was not quite so crass, more akin to the jolly elf of mythology than a mercantile creation. If you've seen Jean Shepherd's wonderful movie *A Christmas Story*, then you get the idea.

But this was not an isolated belief in metaphysical figures of love and goodness—it was part and parcel of my entire system of belief, including Christ, the afterlife, ultimate justice, and the first law of thermodynamics. In simple terms, I believed what all children believe until they learn otherwise—that reality makes sense, that life is good, and that in the long run we all will get what we deserve.

The idea that Santa Claus did not exist would have been much harder for me to accept than that Christ did not exist. I had persistent empirical evidence that Santa Claus existed, whereas I was taking other people's word that Christ had existed two thousand years ago.

And even though, like Santa Claus, Christ was supposed to be nice to everyone and gave them rewards (healing, happiness, and so on), he had never come down my chimney.

Each Christmas morning I would wake up to tangible evidence of Santa's visit. There were presents that only a metaphysical being could have known I desired. There were cookie crumbs and a half-full glass of milk that I had left especially for him. Who else could have consumed this?

There was simply nothing in my life more magical, more anticipated, or more spiritual than this one visitation from an actual being from the realm of spirit, a being who left demonstrable evidence of the capacity of divine beings to intervene in our lives and to perform acts that, according to the laws of the physical world, would be impossible.

I still remember the incredulous laughter of my big brother when Mother felt it time to inform me that my deeply held belief was a hoax. I know I was older than most children who still held on to the belief—probably about five or six. And I remember very clearly how much I cried and how much this news mangled my worldview.

I had believed this myth with my whole heart, because I had evidence, because it made sense, and because I was reassured that it was true by the two people whom I trusted more than any others in the world—Mom and Dad. I knew they would never do or say anything to hurt or deceive me. But after the sad news, I had to wonder what else they may have told me that was also a ruse.

Did Christ really die on a cross? Did He really rise from the dead? If so, where did He go? Was heaven a real place? If so, where was it? Was there an actual Satan and a hell? If God was in charge of everything, then how could He possibly allow some evil spirit to deceive trusting souls and ensnare them in his wicked clutches for eternity?

All this made far less sense and was far less credible than a beneficent spirit who lovingly bestowed on innocent children a token of his love—

exactly what they wanted and had prayed for, or something close to it—close enough to indicate that he was aware of their wishes and desires.

THE SPIRITUAL MEANING OF THERMODYNAMICS

My recognition that Santa Claus was not real, and my subsequent questioning of some of the teachings of my church, is associated in my mind with my discovery of the first law of thermodynamics, a law that, in its most straightforward sense, is all about justice, and, ultimately, about dying, death, and grieving. Let me explain.

One Christmas I got a new bicycle, except that it wasn't new. It was my brother's old bicycle repainted and with new tires. By this time I was somewhat over the deconstruction of Santa Claus, and I had even managed to segregate that parental myth about Santa from both the trust I had in my parents and my more serious beliefs in God and Christ, primarily because in my dreams and interior world, the concept of justice and logic still reigned supreme.

However, I still had a few major misconceptions that had to get worked out. For example, I could accept the idea that the world was round, but I had presumed we were living on the *inside* of the globe, on the bottom, where the dirt and trees were, as opposed to the top of the globe which was colored blue. So naturally I often dreamed of venturing out some day on my bicycle and pedaling to the seam where the shell-like sky rounded down to meet the edge of the dirt. I wondered what it might feel like, that sky stuff. This theory, while a bit silly to most contemporary scientists, nevertheless explained for me the logical relationship in everything I observed, no less than did Ptolemy's geocentric universe to the thinkers of his day—and for everyone else for some thirteen hundred years afterward.

What I further formulated a couple of years later was the idea that energy could not be created—it could change form, but it could not come from nothing. This theory I came upon during that Christmas when I learned to ride the new bike I had inherited from my brother via my Santa Claus father.

Dad was an incredibly expedient teacher, if not always a subtle one. He taught me to ride my bike in exactly half an hour. He took me to the top of the hill on which we lived on Homewood Avenue. In his defense, it was not a very large hill. Dad then put the bike in front of him in the middle of the street with me on it as he held on to the seat from behind. He then aimed the bike more or less downhill after showing me how I could turn the front wheel from one side to the other, and, before I knew it, gave me a hefty push and let go.

The fact that I hit a telephone pole at the bottom of the hill in no way impaired the joy I had felt speeding down and having a brief sense of the way the thing worked. Not only could I go faster by churning my feet on the pedals, but I could keep mostly upright by turning in whatever direct I started to fall. Unfortunately, the last turn happened to be in the direction of the hard wooden pole (the "Bump" syndrome again), but after Dad straightened out the handle bars, I was up and back at the top, ready to go again.

I pushed the bike to the top, and went down again, only this time on my own. By the end of the day, I was able to determine the direction I would go sufficiently well that I ventured going up the hill on the bike. The first time was a failure. I couldn't muster sufficient energy, and the bike fell down with me on it under the screeching tires of a station wagon coming over the hill from the other direction.

The driver, a nicely dressed lady, suddenly put her hands to her face, then shook her head slowly from side to side. Wherever she is right now, she is probably still shaking. The point is that over time I began to appreciate how much more energy it required going up the hill than it did going down the hill.

A few days later when Mom was driving me home up the same hill, I noticed that by simply pushing a pedal on the car, she could make the 1946 Pontiac sedan go *up* the hill without seeming in the least exhausted. Somehow, this was not right. Why should she be able to accomplish the same task so effortlessly in a large car when I had to push as hard as I could on the bicycle pedals over and over again to go up the hill on my much smaller bicycle?

Immediately I theorized that somehow, somewhere, all this had to equal out—there had to be justice. Nothing so large could simply go up the hill without someone somewhere paying the price for the bounty of this power. In short, I realized that something can't come from nothing, especially where energy is concerned.

This realization about the transfer of energy, which I later understood in greater detail as I investigated the mechanics of the internal combustion engine when I made model airplanes, tied in neatly with my worldview about justice, Santa Claus, and God. The harnessing of goodness would necessarily bring about good results. It could be no other way. Goodness or love, I sensed, was a force, a kind of energy, whereas evil was not a force—it was a lack of force, a lack of goodness or love.

The more I meditated on this theory of energy and goodness or love, the more I became convinced that there had to be equilibrium—things simply had to work out the way they should. How could they not? Those who performed acts of goodness through their love of others would themselves become recipients and beneficiaries of that energy, even as my forward motion on the bicycle came from the energy of churning my legs. Likewise, Dad's car moved up the hill because of the exploding gaseous vapor at the top of the cylinder heads.

For the luxury of this power, Dad paid money for gas to be poured into the tanks. He also paid money for the construction of the car with its engine capable of transforming explosions into the downward thrust of the piston rods, which turn the crankshaft, which turns the drive shift, which the differential changes into the rotary motion of the wheels.

I remember at a science fair seeing what was purported to be a perpetual motion machine, a turning wheel composed of marbles in various segments of a clear plastic wheel so that as one marble dropped down, the wheel turned, bringing the wheel around and another marble into place so it could drop. The man in charge of the display explained that it was an illusion, that there was no such thing as perpetual motion, because that would require a result without a cause, an engine without effort.

The corollary of this principle likewise rang true and clear in my mind, that without energy from some source outside an engine, whether my bicycle or Dad's car, or the fake perpetual motion machine, all action and motion would cease. The consequence of this with my theory of justice was that without some source of goodness, badness or injustice would automatically occur. Without Santa Clause (whom I knew now to be my father), there would be no decorations, no presents, just another day. The fact that Christmas commemorated the birth of Christ was mostly incidental, though I did enjoy putting together the little hand-carved German crèche that my mother stored so carefully in a box with straw and thin tissue paper so that the legs of the camels and sheep would not get broken, though at least one bit the dust every year.

Anyhow, my thinking about this process did not stay on this theoretical geophysical plane very long at all. It quickly morphed into the more practical and commonplace concept of human notions of reward and punishment. I don't mean justice in the sense of theories of penology. I mean that I came to believe that ultimately good people were rewarded for their goodness, that people who perpetrated iniquity would suffer the consequences of their perverse deeds, and that everything had to turn out for the best in the end.

Not only did all my Methodist church training confirm this theory with vivid tales from both the Old and New Testaments (mostly the Old Testament where God is more proactive), but it was also manifested in the so-called Hollywood "code," especially when it came to the movie stars of Westerns, such as Gene, Roy, the Durango Kid, and my favorite exponent of justice and revenge, Lash LaRue, the master of the bullwhip.

Logic and love—these seemed to be the inseparable parts of any divine paradigm of reality. I still hold onto this axiom. The Saturday morning Western movies with Gene Autry and Roy Rogers (and Dale Evans and Trigger), helped me in applying this theory. These cinematic portrayals of law, order, disorder, justice, and redemption always tied things together pretty neatly, except that Gene was always left alone, never with the girl—naturally it was different with the case of Roy and Dale.

But when I started watching the more realistic movies about the real life battles of World War II, like *Guadalcanal Diary*, I realized that any time there was a young blond kid (like me), he would almost always get killed early in the movie, and yet the movie went on as if he had never existed.

This made no sense. Where was justice? Where was goodness? Sure, we could assume the dead soldiers were walking across the celestial sky as the credits started to role, but they were still quite dead. And, as I mentioned earlier, the Protestant view of heaven never appealed to me whatsoever. Where was justice in depriving these people of the ability to play, to get married, to have children, and just to . . . be?

THE SUFFERING OF THE INNOCENT

It was not all that far along in my life that I began to recognize a problem that seemed to undermine both my theory of justice and the ability of my religious beliefs to respond meaningfully to blatant injustice. I gradually became aware of common injustices in the world, such as the suffering of the innocent, the death of children, car accidents, plane crashes, and, of course, the ever-present "acts of God" such as earthquakes, tornados, floods, and other "natural" disasters. While insurance policies may find this term a fitting description of acts for which we ourselves are not responsible, for me it has always been an obvious misnomer since I could not imagine that the God I knew and loved would intentionally perpetrate such heinous events.

This problem about the injustices present in the world remained in the back of my mind for a long time, but I soon became distracted with girls, high school, sports, and such. When my interest in solving this problem of injustice and suffering finally reemerged, it was called "theodicy"—a philosophical area of discussion that considers how one can have a belief that God is benign and omnipotent, yet unwilling to intervene to set things right in this world.

The question remained, then, how could God and His creation exist simultaneously with persistent injustice, whether manmade or the result of the arbitrary misfortunes of the changes and chances—the accidents—of this life. The question had become increasingly interesting to me the more I endured some of the whips and scorns of time over the first two decades of my life, and I was in need of a consolation of philosophy to help me endure and prosper amid a life that was becoming progressively more chaotic and totally unromantic. It was in the midst of this angst that I turned to poetry, both as a writer and as a student.

One of the first great literary theorists, Aristotle, describes the purpose of the dramatic genre of tragedy as the "purgation" or "catharsis" of the emotions of pity and fear. While there are a number of interpretations about what he means by "catharsis," one obvious implication is that we do well to *exercise* and thereby *exorcise* these emotions, to stay in touch with our humanity, and to be wary of those events that instigate them.

That he selects these particular emotions of pity and fear as collateral components of our response to viewing something tragic is also fairly apparent. We pity the consistently tragic moral choices of the hero that lead him or her to a downfall, because these are, by and large, not really bad people. For the most part, these tragic figures are noble at heart and have great potential, but it seems they are addicted to some fatal passion, some lower aspect of "self" that consistently overrides good judgment. Sometimes they are simply addicted to "the insistent self" that entices them to focus too much attention on personal well-being rather than on moral principles and spiritual development.

The fear we experience as we watch the tragic fall of these characters occurs because we realize—if we are attentive to the subtlety of their fall—that we too are liable to the same sort of tragic choices. At the very moment of viewing the play, we may be on the brink of experiencing precisely the same fate, because these character flaws are not obvious, except in retrospect. In fact, if the playwright has done an effective job, we may wish to run home and make lists to review all our present actions to see if there is some unhealthy pattern among the choices we are presently making. Perhaps we are a tragic figure in the making, but, like the characters in the plays, we are blind to our own foibles.

Exercising emotions similar to those experienced with tragic loss and the agony of lamentation is also an integral part of a particular genre of lyric poetry, the elegy. In fact, American poet Edgar Allen Poe remarked, when discussing those subjects that are most emotionally evocative among subjects for the expression of grief in the lyric mode, that the most poignant theme a poem could express is the untimely death of a young girl.

Whether or not we agree with his theory, it is easy to discover among the better known lyric poems about grief a number of memorable examples that would seem to support Poe's observation. Like the tragic genre, these verses can also help us have a catharsis of pity and fear, especially if we, like the parents in these poems, have given a ransom to fate by having children of our own.

The most powerful of these poems, however, are not always narrated from the point of view of a parent—the ones who are doubtless the most distraught—but from the perspective of someone who has enough emotional distance to observe the grief and to frame the irony of death in poetic form. I suspect this technique of employing a more objective perspective than the parents might have is the assumption on the part of the poet that the distraught and overwhelmed mother or father would be so destroyed as to be incapable of expressing any neat comparisons or catchy image of the conflagration of their internal chaos.

In the case of Theodore Roethke's "Elegy for Jane," for example, the narrative point of view is the teacher of a young girl who has died after being thrown from a horse. Though observing that he has no implicit "rights" to be the elegist (being unrelated to the child), he nevertheless recalls those characteristics that distinguished his young student from the other children, those special qualities that seemed to make her death all the more ironic and tragic and unacceptable:

Elegy For Jane

I remember the neckcurls, limp and
    damp as tendrils;
And her quick look, a sidelong pickerel smile;
And how, once startled into talk, the light syllables leaped
    for her,
And she balanced in the delight of her thought,
A wren, happy, tail into the wind,
Her song trembling the twigs and small branches.

The shade sang with her;
The leaves, their whispers turned to kissing,
And the mould sang in the bleached valleys under the rose.
Oh, when she was sad, she cast herself down into such a
    pure depth,
Even a father could not find her:
Scraping her cheek against straw,
Stirring the clearest water.
My sparrow, you are not here,
Waiting like a fern, making a spiney shadow.
The sides of wet stones cannot console me,
Nor the moss, wound with the last light.
If only I could nudge you from this sleep,
My maimed darling, my skittery pigeon.
Over this damp grave I speak the words of my love:
I, with no rights in this matter,
Neither father nor lover.

The dominant impression of the child's vitality is expressed in terms of the quick and lively movements of spritely birds—a wren, a sparrow, a "skittery" pigeon. Other images likewise speak to the unpredictable mood swings and motions of this energetic personality.

The poem requires little explication. It captures wonderfully what has been lost. It asserts that no consolation is available to account for how one endowed with such tender charm and extraordinary delight could suddenly vanish from existence.

Of course, from a Bahá'í perspective, this sense of the impossibility of such an occurrence—the instant nonexistence of such animated liveliness—is a valid inference. This young child's lively spirit, the energy that surrounded her bright personality, would continue to exist and even flourish, but not in the physical realm.

This is where my idea about the continuation of energy began to confirm for me more precisely what my intuition had informed me about the second law of thermodynamics. Somehow, somewhere, that energy must still exist and thrive. It must be so, and our hearts can countenance no worthy consolation that does not somehow confirm this law of reality.

The exact same sort of ironic perspective is conveyed by poet John Crowe Ransom in another elegy for a deceased young girl in "Bells for John Whiteside's Daughter." In this piece the speaker is a next-door neighbor in a rural setting who is accustomed to viewing the adventures of the little girl chasing her geese in the yard. But now he has come over to view the child in her casket, "primly propped" and in a "brown study" (with an uncustomary serious countenance), an aspect so totally alien to the vivacious character he has watched from his window. He, too, finds this deathly change incredible and untenable:

Bells For John Whiteside's Daughter

There was such speed in her little body,
And such lightness in her footfall,
It is no wonder her brown study
Astonishes us all.
Her wars were bruited in our high window.
We looked among orchard trees and beyond
Where she took arms against her shadow,
Or harried unto the pond
The lazy geese, like a snow cloud
Dripping their snow on the green grass,
Tricking and stopping, sleepy and proud,
Who cried in goose, Alas,

For the tireless heart within the little
Lady with rod that made them rise
From their noon apple-dreams and scuttle
Goose-fashion under the skies!
But now go the bells, and we are ready,
In one house we are sternly stopped
To say we are vexed at her brown study,
Lying so primly propped.

Certainly the idea of the geese lamenting her absence is one of the more deft touches of this fine poem. But the "vexation" felt by all who see her so still, so prim and proper in her funeral dress, derives from the sudden vanishing of all the wonderful images of delight and vigor with which she adorned the country setting—the "speed in her little body," the "lightness in her footfall," her "tireless heart" and her scattering the "lazy geese" from their "noon apple-dreams."

There's nothing new for us in this poem, no great insight or message in either piece. These are emblems of bewildering grief, perhaps not the same degree or power of grief as the parents are experiencing, but nonetheless they are attempting to exorcize some of the most power-ful emotions we fall prey to. How can a life that was at one moment so alive, so full of dimension and beauty and possibilities, vanish so suddenly and irretrievably from our presence? How can such vitality and energy evaporate?

HOW PARENTS GRIEVE
No one knows the emotional sense of ironic loss more than parents who have lost a baby to SIDS, a child to some rare form of cancer, a youth to an auto accident, or a young adult to war or to some form of senseless violence that plagues our contemporary world. It is needless

to recite here the catalog of possible tragedies that may await even the most careful among us—drive-by shootings, sexual predators, exotic drugs, depression and suicide, and on and on.

"We are sorry for your loss," the detectives say on the TV shows immediately before interviewing the bereaved parents. And the actors portraying grieving parents may shed a tear or two, possibly hang their heads in feigned sadness, but no writer or actor can approximate the blaring horror that would actually be displayed in real life, ear-piercing sirens of grief, with heaving chests gasping for air as wave upon wave of disbelief is interspersed with attempts to awaken from a nightmare that will not stop, not now, not in the morning, not ever.

"We know this isn't the best time to ask you questions," the TV detectives will say, and the fake parents will calm down, just minutes or hours after the tragedy and rattle off reams of facts, statistics, names, and places—all to help solve the mystery within the hour-long time slot.

Real life parents in the same situation would wave off such queries. They would wave off life itself if they could, jump from this life and this consciousness if they could. And when, if ever, they escape from this dark and lonely cave of sorrow, they know that in dreams and unguarded moments, visions of the lost child, the martyred youth, the dutiful soldier will forever be an appendage to their conscious life.

In several instances in the Bahá'í writings, 'Abdu'l-Bahá offers impressive tokens of consolation derived from the divine logic of the Bahá'í paradigm of life, love and logic that confirms my early instincts about physical laws of thermodynamics being parallel to metaphysical laws about the same process.

In a touching letter written to grieving parents, 'Abdu'l-Bahá assures them that their son has not really died, that instead, he has been freed from the trials of this life. And yet, while bestowing on them the consolation that their son is still alive in the heavenly realm, he acknowledges the validity of their "sorrow and grief":

O ye two patient souls! Your letter was received. The death of that beloved youth and his separation from you have caused the utmost sorrow and grief; for he winged his flight in the flower of his age and the bloom of his youth to the heavenly nest. But he hath been freed from this sorrow-stricken shelter and hath turned his face toward the everlasting nest of the Kingdom, and, being delivered from a dark and narrow world, hath hastened to the sanctified realm of light; therein lieth the consolation of our hearts. (*Selections from the Writings of 'Abdu'l-Bahá*, no. 169.1)

However, his further consolation is neither vague nor conveyed in such broad and philosophical strokes. 'Abdu'l-Bahá states that there is a divine wisdom in this seeming injustice (that spiritual version of the law of thermodynamics again), and he bestows on them a remarkably powerful and effective poetic image of a gardener transplanting a tender shrub that it may grow more fully and bear its fruit:

The inscrutable divine wisdom underlieth such heart-rending occurrences. It is as if a kind gardener transferreth a fresh and tender shrub from a confined place to a wide open area. This transfer is not the cause of the withering, the lessening or the destruction of that shrub; nay, on the contrary, it maketh it to grow and thrive, acquire freshness and delicacy, become green and bear fruit. This hidden secret is well known to the gardener, but those souls who are unaware of this bounty suppose that the gardener, in his anger and wrath, hath uprooted the shrub. (*Selections from the Writings of 'Abdu'l-Bahá*, no. 169.2)

The power of this analogy is twofold. First it attempts to explain that the child's death is not an arbitrary or unnecessary event—that there is a divine wisdom in what the parents or others may perceive to be blatant

injustice or the apparent "wrath" of the gardener. However, it is important to note here, as other Bahá'í texts likewise confirm, that the nature
of this wisdom will most probably remain veiled to the parents during
this life. In fact, in one discussion Bahá'u'lláh notes that among those
things we cannot understand in this life are, first, the suffering of the
innocent, and, second, where God's will ends and our own begins.

Secondly, the analogy of the gardener explains that there is not only
a hidden justice in this seeming injustice, but that there is a very specific
purpose involved. Somehow this act will redound to the benefit of the
youth and enable him to "bear fruit"—to make the most of the nascent
capacity with which he has been endowed, a fulfillment that could not
have occurred in any other way. Had the youthful plant been made to
remain in association with its earthly form, the development of that
soul would have become hindered and root-bound.

'Abdu'l-Bahá's major point here, I sense, is that this "hidden secret,"
which the gardener alone is presently privy to comprehending, not
only enables justice; it also brings about a bounty for the youth that
otherwise would not have been possible, or at least would not have
been accomplished as well. In short, this theory is not merely asserting
that God can redeem this misfortune or make something good come
from a tragic circumstance. He is asserting forthrightly that could the
parents but understand the divine wisdom in this event (as they will
be able to do in the continuation of their lives in the spiritual realm),
they would appreciate that this was not "unfortunate" at all, but the
best of all possible outcomes for the ultimate destiny of the child.

This is the sort of justice I had in mind in my early youth, exactly
what I meant when I thought I had invented the first law of thermodynamics, even though I did not at the time realize that Gottfried
Leibniz had posited a similar theory in the seventeenth century—that
everything turns out for the best. Of course, it is a pretty inescapable conclusion for anyone who believes in God. If God exists and

is loving, forgiving, all-powerful, and all-knowing then how could it be otherwise? There has to be justice in the long run, however veiled from us it may temporarily be.

THE CONSOLATION OF RELIGIOUS PHILOSOPHY

Later in my life, while working on my PhD, I realized that Boethius had said precisely the same thing in his *Consolation of Philosophy*, which he wrote in 524 CE while awaiting his own execution for something he didn't do—a great motivator for trying to figure out how there can be divine justice in a physical world ostensibly run by heartless and often ignorant people. About a decade later I would begin the journey of writing a series of books explicating how the Bahá'í teachings advance these concepts of love, logic, equality, and justice even more plainly.

The point is that this letter penned by 'Abdu'l-Bahá to these bereaved parents is no palliative, no "sorry-for-your-loss" hallmark card sort of consolation. He gives them a very plausible explanation for what has happened, and he then exhorts them to attempt to "attain utmost patience, composure and resignation" until such time as they are apprised of the love, logic, and justice underlying this seeming injustice.

However, 'Abdu'l-Bahá is not callous in his letter. He certainly does not tell them to be elated. His comfort for them is that they will in time understand the meaning of this act, even if not in this lifetime. He does not chastise them for grieving, but this assurance at least assuages any temptation they might have to ponder how a loving God could allow such an event to occur.

This realization, if the parents can fully grasp it, helps them to appreciate that they really grieve for themselves, for their separation from the child, however temporary and temporal that separation might be. But 'Abdu'l-Bahá also gives them a specific exercise to practice so that their sole recourse is not simply to wait for time to assuage their pain. They can assist their son by praying for his spiritual progress.

This is a particularly powerful exercise inasmuch as it accomplishes two tasks at once. First, it points the parents in the direction of the most important conclusion they can reach—that their son is still alive, still in progress, even though they are temporarily prevented from communicating directly with him or sharing the joy of observing that progress firsthand. Second, it enables them to continue the work they had begun by way of assisting in the child's development. They can still have a direct influence on his continued development and ascent as a human soul.

In another letter, this one to a grieving mother, 'Abdu'l-Bahá similarly expresses understanding about the incredible weight of grief, but he also assures her that her son "hath not been lost but, rather, hath stepped from this world into another" and that she "will find him in the divine realm. That reunion shall be for eternity, while in this world separation is inevitable and bringeth with it a burning grief" (*Selections from the Writings of 'Abdu'l-Bahá*, no. 171.1).

Even more interesting in the advice 'Abdu'l-Bahá gives in this same letter is the following exhortation: "Therefore be thou not disconsolate, do not languish, do not sigh, neither wail nor weep; for agitation and mourning deeply affect his soul in the divine realm" (*Selections from the Writings of 'Abdu'l-Bahá*, no. 171.2). This statement actually presents us with another axiom about such unfortunate deaths and our part as parents in grieving—that the soul of the child is aware of the parents' sorrow and that excess of grief on their part will actually impede the felicity of the child's soul in its ability to make progress in its new environment. The child will feel the weight of the parents' pain and lamentation.

Finally, 'Abdu'l-Bahá offers what are probably the most profound statements regarding this most egregious of griefs—the lamentation for a child or for someone who, through no fault of their own, suffers from emotional, physical, or mental handicaps. These consolations are stated in the forms of axiomatic verities regarding such conditions and, like the previously mentioned statement of Bahá'u'lláh regarding the fact that no physical or mental condition can impair the soul itself, are articulated succinctly and with a tone of authority and certitude.

Regarding the eternal "condition of children who die before attaining the age of discretion or before the appointed time of birth," 'Abdu'l-Bahá asserts that these infants are "under the shadow of the favor of God" and that, inasmuch as they are undefiled by any "impurities of the world of nature," they will become the "centers of the manifestation of bounty, and the Eye of Compassion will be turned upon them" (*Some Answered Questions*, p. 240).

EVEN MANIFESTATIONS GRIEVE

The Prophets are superbly human, even in their grief and sorrow. We can and should study them and their responses to reality in order to gauge how we ourselves should respond. And since the Prophets or Manifestations lament, we are forced to infer, therefore, that grief and sorrow are not signs of weakness or loss of faith. Rather these all-too-human emotions are essential and valuable parts of the human experience. Therefore, if we are tempted to infer from the previous passages in 'Abdu'l-Bahá's letters to grief-stricken parents that the certitude of eventual reunion should suffice to placate the maimed heart of those who grieve, we need only to recall the lives of the Manifestations to conclude that we are wrong.

In attempting to come to terms with the validity and reality of grief, professional grief counselors have tried to develop systematic processes for assisting those who are bereaved. This process is partially accomplished by recognizing that grief is not a single event or a single emotion, nor is it consigned to a set period of time. It is a process whose progression will vary according to each individual situation, but it can be usefully plotted according to relatively predictable stages of (1) denial, (2) anger, (3) bargaining, (4) depression, and (5) acceptance.

And yet as grief counselors who employ this and other schematics of grief will readily admit, the final stage of "acceptance" is not necessarily synonymous with resignation, nor does it signal a permanent reconciliation to loss. Grief is not so clean and simple as this paradigm might be taken to indicate.

Nowhere is this fact more apparent than in the accounts of the Manifestations Themselves who, though exemplary human beings and perfect in Their patterns of response to the tribulations of life, are inundated with grief in those circumstances where those near and dear to Them undergo agony, torture, or death. Two examples from Bahá'í history will suffice to make the point, especially since Bahá'í history, unlike the history of earlier revelations, is recent enough to be authenticated and to have been accurately recorded.

The first example concerns the life of the Báb in the summer of 1849.[13] The Báb had been confined for nine months in the remote mountain prison of Máh-Kú from July of 1847 until April of 1848. He was then moved to the prison fortress of Chihríq where He would remain for two years until His execution in Tabríz on July 9, 1850.

These three years (1847–1850) were a tumultuous period for the Bábís in Persia. Over twenty thousand Bábís were cruelly slaughtered. But probably the most storied attack on the followers of this new revelation was the seven-month siege by government troops on a

---

13. The Báb (1819–1850) was the Herald and Forerunner of Bahá'u'lláh, but also a Manifestation in His own right and founder of the Bábí religion.

makeshift fort the Bábís had constructed to defend themselves at the shrine of Shaykh Ṭabarsí.

It was here that the first to believe in the Báb, Mullá Ḥusayn, the Báb'ul-Báb ("the gate of that Gate," a title given to Mullá Ḥusayn by the Báb), was killed, along with many others. Then, after seven long months of starvation and subsisting without any supplies, the beleaguered young Bábís, most of whom were students and hardly equipped to endure the attack, agreed to leave the protection of their fortress on the promise made on the Qur'án by the Prince on May 10, 1849, that should they surrender, they would be safely conducted to their homes.

Once they walked out of the fort, they were instead openly attacked by the soldiers, killed or sold into slavery, except for Quddús, the young Bábí leader. He was taken to his native village of Bárfurúsh. There he was handed over to the mullás. Five days later he was tortured in a grotesque manner in the village square. As the Báb would later discover, Quddús was paraded through the streets in chains, his clothes torn from his body. Then, bareheaded, barefooted, he was set upon with knives, finally being dismembered with an axe, and the parts of his body thrown into a fire. But before Quddús was execrated by the howling mob, he spoke out in a loud voice begging God to forgive his attackers, saying, "Forgive, O my God, the trespasses of this people. Deal with them in Thy mercy, for they know not what we already have discovered and cherish. I have striven to show them the path that leads to their salvation; behold how they have risen to overwhelm and kill me! Show them, O God, the way of Truth, and turn their ignorance into faith" (quoted in *The Dawn-Breakers*, p. 411).

Quddús was extremely dear to the Báb. It was he whom the Báb had chosen to accompany Him on His pilgrimage to Mecca and Medina in October of 1844. Quddús, together with Bahá'u'lláh and Táhirih, had planned and carried out the historic Conference of Bada_sh_t in June of 1848.[14] Consequently, when the imprisoned Báb learned in July of 1849 about the slaughter of His followers at the fort at _Sh_ay_kh_ Ṭabarsí and the subsequent heinous and cruel desecration and mutilation of His beloved Quddús, the Báb was immersed in sorrow.

Though a Manifestation of God and having no doubts about the glorious destiny awaiting Quddús and these other faithful souls in the world of the spirit, the Báb could neither write nor dictate for six months: "The deep grief which he felt had stilled the voice of revelation and silenced His pen. How deeply He mourned His loss! What cries of anguish He must have uttered as the tale of the siege, the untold sufferings, the shameless betrayal, and the wholesale massacre of the companions of _Sh_ay_kh_ Ṭabarsí reached His ears and was unfolded before His eyes!" (quoted in *The Dawn-Breakers*, p. 411).

Though the particular events surrounding the sorrow of Bahá'u'lláh are hardly as dramatic on the surface, it must be remembered that this painful event experienced by Bahá'u'lláh on June 23, 1870, occurred after eighteen years of incalculable privation, hardship, and torture. Bahá'u'lláh had been incarcerated in the Síyáh-_Ch_ál with chains so heavy He forever bore the scars. After His release in 1854, though still suffering illness from this imprisonment, He had been made to go on foot in the midst of a harsh winter across the mountains of Hamadán into exile in Baghdad.

After further exile to Constantinople and then to Adrianople, He had been poisoned at the hands of this same half-brother so that

---

14. Ṭáhirih was the only female among the Letters of the Living. A renowned poet, she was an indefatigable teacher of the Bábí Faith. The Conference of Bada_sh_t was called by Bahá'u'lláh ostensibly to consult about how to free the Báb from captivity, but His true intention was to announce that the Bábí Faith was a new revelation from God and that the Báb was a Manifestation equal in rank to Muḥammad.

He nearly died and His hand forever shook. Finally, He and His family, together with a few other followers, had been exiled to the wretched prison-city of 'Akká in August of 1868, where they were confined in the stench-filled barracks cells. There they endured the most pitiful of conditions imaginable—little food, foul water, cold stone floors and walls, and putrid air that rose up from the sea water in the mote below.

While Bahá'u'lláh and the holy family endured these conditions for more than two years, it was in June of the second year that a particularly grievous tragedy befell Bahá'u'lláh. His twenty-two-year-old son Mírzá Mihdí fell through an unguarded skylight one evening at twilight as he paced along the roof engrossed in his evening devotions. He fell onto some wooden crates that shattered and pierced his ribs and caused him to die some twenty-two hours later.

Mírzá Mihdí, also titled "The Purest Branch," had been a loving and dutiful son. He had been imprisoned with His father since the days in Baghdad, serving to assist his beloved father in any way he could. As Bahá'u'lláh grieved beside his dying son, Mírzá Mihdí requested that his life be accepted as a ransom to God for those who had been kept back from visiting Bahá'u'lláh so that they might at last be allowed to attain His presence, a request that Bahá'u'lláh readily granted.

The extent of the grief this experience caused Bahá'u'lláh is evident in one line from a prayer He revealed in honor of this precious son: "I have, O my Lord, offered up that which Thou hast given Me, that Thy servants may be quickened, and all that dwell on earth be united." He then addresses his departed son with this assurance: "Thou art the Trust of God and His Treasure in this Land. Erelong will God reveal through thee that which He hath desired" (quoted in *God Passes By*, p. 188). The body of Mírzá Mihdí was then washed in the presence of His sorrowing father and prepared for interment.

THE CONSOLATION OF A BAHÁ'Í BURIAL

There is no Bahá'í formula or ritual for grieving, no explicit prescription for purging of sorrow and surmounting the grief from the loss of a loved one. The most obvious consolation is straightforward—the belief that the death of a loved one, even if the result of injustice or if considered premature from an earthly or personal perspective, has not in any way deterred the felicity or progress of the essential reality of the deceased, the conscious rational soul.

Where it may be a traditional observation with many belief systems to note that the departed has passed beyond this "veil of tears" and will no longer be made to suffer the trials and tribulations of this life, such observations seem hollow and leaden to one who does not simultaneously understand that, in reality, the departed soul is not actually deceased, but has been temporarily removed from the observation, presence, and companionship of the bereaved. Yet the absence of further worldly affliction on the part of the deceased is, by itself, not much consolation to those left behind.

It is in this sense that the Bahá'í attitude toward the death of a loved one begins from an entirely distinct point of view. The sorrow and grief are no less real, but these emotions and the actions associated with them are recognized as having two fundamental purposes. The first purpose is to memorialize or honor the decedent, to pay homage to the contributions this soul has made to the spiritual progress of humankind. The second purpose is to provide an occasion for those left behind to share expressions of sorrow for the loss of the companionship of the one who has been born into the next and more felicitous and expansive stage of existence. Obviously this response and these purposes are as important and valid for one who has died as an infant as it is for one who has died of old age.

So it is that our certitude or faith should never be called into question, by ourselves or by anyone else, simply because we grieve. Our sorrow is not an index to our confidence that life goes on beyond the veil. In this context, it is well worth noting before we conclude our assessment of the Bahá'í attitude about the art of dying how Bahá'u'lláh has provided explicit guidance for dealing with this time of transition on the part of those who are left behind. But as with all of the laws of Bahá'u'lláh for this Dispensation, there is very little in the Bahá'í approach to funeral and burial services and procedures that is ritualistic or formulaic. Like all Bahá'í laws regarding administrative procedures and personal, familial, and community life, the laws regarding interment are culturally neutral and adaptable to various types of memorial services or commemorative trappings.

The core laws regarding such matters as preparation of the body of the deceased and burial and interment are few in number, but of physical, spiritual, and emotional significance for all cultures and climes.

For example, one law is that the body should not be removed more than one hour's journey from the place of death to the place of burial. If we examine this restriction in terms of what has taken place in some cultures where a body will be transported from place to place for purposes of commemoration, we can appreciate that the law might derive in part from the attempt to deter the spread of disease.

This aspect of the law becomes a bit more obvious when it is considered in conjunction with the Bahá'í law that the body of the deceased not be embalmed, unless so required by local law. Likewise, the requirement that the body not be embalmed would seem to have both a spiritual and a physical component. Symbolically, allowing the body to return to the dust from which it comes demonstrates the Bahá'í principle that the important life associated with the body is elsewhere, that the physical temple is a vehicle through which the soul can express itself.

However, both this law and the law forbidding removal of the body more than an hour's distance might bear some relationship to the exhortation that the burial take place as soon as possible. While in places where refrigeration of the body is possible, this period may extend to several days, but here again we can discern a probable confluence of spiritual, physical, and emotional exigencies. Naturally, these laws are not intended to discourage whatever memorial services the family or community might want to arrange later.

Another law would seem to be almost entirely spiritual in nature, though the integration of the dual aspects of all laws would seem to make such speculation unwarranted. Bahá'u'lláh has forbidden cremation. The reason for this law might well have something to do with the notion in so many cultures that consigning something to the fire is a symbolic gesture of disdain and disrespect, even as was the case with the earthly remains of Quddús.

But in an interesting philosophical perspective on this law, 'Abdu'l-Bahá has observed that burial is preferable because the decomposition of the body complies more completely with the natural law of decomposition. 'Abdu'l-Bahá states, "Now, if you consign this body to the flames, it will pass immediately into the mineral kingdom and will be kept back from its natural journey through the chain of all created things" (*Wisdom of Burying the Dead*).[15]

Another law regarding burial of the dead has to do with preparation of the body, and this too, we might infer, has practical, emotional, and spiritual applications. After being cleansed (usually by members of the family), the body is wrapped in a shroud of silk or cotton, and on the ring finger of the right hand, a burial ring is placed containing the following inscription: "I came forth from God, and return unto Him,

---

15. 'Abdu'l-Bahá further states, "Another point remains, and it is this: that in case of contagious diseases, such as the plague and cholera, whether cremation of bodies with lime or other chemicals is allowable or not? In such cases, hygiene and preservation is necessarily more important; for according to the clear Divine texts, medical commands are lawful, and 'necessities make forbidden things lawful' is one of the certain rules." ('Abdu'l-Bahá, *Wisdom of Burying the Dead*).

detached from all save Him, holding fast to His Name, the Merciful, the Compassionate."

As with so many laws, the option with regard to material indicates Bahá'u'lláh's concern that the poor not be prevented from partaking in this or in any other Bahá'í ceremony or activity. Consequently, there is no preference as to whether the body be wrapped in the more expensive silk or the more affordable cotton. Likewise, while usually the Bahá'í family prepares the body by washing it and wrapping it, there is no explicit requirement that the family itself carry out these procedures. Obviously in some cases this procedure would cause a strain on the sensitiveness of the family beyond what some could be expected to endure.

Bahá'u'lláh ordains that the casket itself be comprised of crystal, stone, or hard wood. Here again the various choices indicate Bahá'u'lláh's awareness that these laws must be capable of being implemented by all people in various economic and cultural conditions. In effect, He has allowed anything from the simplest to the most exquisite casket for the body. The theme here, as with all else concerned with this process, is reverence, dignity, and an attempt to understand what has occurred regarding the continuation of the soul. It is, as it were, as much an educational exercise for the bereaved as it is an opportunity to honor the departed.

The final requirement for Bahá'í burial is entirely spiritual in nature—the Prayer for the Dead revealed by Bahá'u'lláh must be read at the funeral. This special prayer is used only for Bahá'ís over the age of fifteen (designated the age of maturity), and is recited by one believer while all present remain standing:

> O my God! This is Thy servant and the son of Thy servant [if
> the departed is female, then "Thy handmaiden and the daughter of
> Thy handmaiden"] who hath believed in Thee and in Thy signs,

and set his face towards Thee, wholly detached from all except Thee. Thou art, verily, of those who show mercy the most merciful.

Deal with him, O Thou Who forgivest the sins of men and concealest their faults, as beseemeth the heaven of Thy bounty and the ocean of Thy grace. Grant him admission within the precincts of Thy transcendent mercy that was before the foundation of earth and heaven. There is no God but Thee, the Ever-Forgiving, the Most Generous.

The one reciting the prayer then repeats six times "Alláh-u-Abhá" ("God is Most Glorious"), and then repeats nineteen times each of the following verses:

> We all, verily, worship God.
> We all, verily, bow down before God.
> We all, verily, are devoted unto God.
> We all, verily, give praise unto God.
> We all, verily, yield thanks unto God.
> We all, verily, are patient in God.
> —Bahá'u'lláh

CONCLUSION

If I had a choice, perhaps I would chose to die like the "virtuous men" described by John Donne at the beginning of his famous poem "Valediction Forbidding Mourning." I would pass on peacefully, quietly, unobtrusively, privately:

> As virtuous men pass mildly away,
>   And whisper to their souls to go,
> Whilst some of their sad friends do say,
>   "Now his breath goes," and some say, "No."
> So let us melt, and make no noise,
>   No tear-floods, nor sigh-tempests move;
> 'Twere profanation of our joys
>   To tell the laity our love.

But if I should be destined to live on into that final seventh stage Shakespeare so disparages, that time of being truly aged, perhaps oblivious to self, I really won't mind. If I am truly demented, I will also be oblivious to my piteous state, and that stage, while possibly abhorrent to my loved ones to behold, will all pass swiftly in my mind, like a dream from which I will awake as if it had been the twinkling of an eye.

Should this fate befall me, even those who know me truly and love me unconditionally will sense that lurking somewhere near that ragged coat upon that stick is a soul that is the source of my true self, either resting or else watching and waiting in appreciation, but careless of the body's winding down to its last turn.

So I am about as prepared for death as I think I am going to get. My will is in order. I have created a hefty "Death File" to show Lucia where everything is. And I am, like Ulysses, in the midst of setting out again full force, if not to venture out past the Pillars of Hercules, then surely to some place else equally forbidding and beauteous, like Milford Sound in the south island of New Zealand where I can look up one more time at the incredible hanging gardens on the side of Mitre Peak, watch the crested penguins, the fur seals, the bottlenose dolphins at play, and the sun setting over the Tasman sea between the sheer rock sides of cliffs carved out by glaciers eons before the Maori first glimpsed God's handiwork.

Or if not New Zealand, there's a bright orange Kubota L3130 tractor sitting in the back with its bright orange front loader waiting to do its work. And Molly the collie is waiting to prance along beside me, sniffing out raccoons, opossum, foxes, and squirrels. And always the kestrel is sitting atop the lightning rod waiting to slice through the morning air to find some delectable breakfast mouse in the field.

I sincerely look forward to being once more in the presence of my loved ones who have blazed the trail ahead—Mom, Dad, and especially Bill, who enabled me to discover the Bahá'í Faith and whose conversations with me through the years have been so mutually beneficial. I would hope that he and I can continue where we left off, conversing about what he's discovered, even as we were doing the day before he passed.

I also hope I can finally discover from Chaucer if my theory about the unity of *The Canterbury Tales* is correct. But even more important to me would be the honor of learning from Ṭáhirih if the work Amrollah Hemmat and I have done by way of bringing to light and translating her poetry has pleased her, even as sensing the proximity of her spirit during our work has been so immensely pleasing to us.

But what I have learned more than anything else in my life's journey and in this rehearsing of bits of it is that I can forget about preparing for death. It's a needless waste of time. There is simply too much to be done here and now regarding what is taking place on earth during this critical stage of human development, this turning point in the history of planet Earth.

The Bahá'í community worldwide has a mandate from Bahá'u'lláh to inform others about the rather important news—that God has spoken again through another Manifestation who has revealed a method for forging a spiritual kingdom, a planetary commonwealth, a milieu so refined and so capable of infinite progress that this earthly environment will gradually become an ever more wondrous place for the spiritual training of souls like me.

This work will be quite sufficient to prepare me for whatever awaits me, because whatever awaits me will necessarily be designed for my ultimate benefit, even if it starts off with some painful recollections of things that I should not have done, things I should have done, and things I could have done much, much better.

Bahá'í
PUBLISHING

AND THE BAHÁ'Í FAITH

Bahá'í Publishing produces books based on the teachings of the Bahá'í Faith. Founded over 160 years ago, the Bahá'í Faith has spread to some 235 nations and territories and is now accepted by more than five million people. The word "Bahá'í" means "follower of Bahá'u'lláh." Bahá'u'lláh, the founder of the Bahá'í Faith, asserted that He is the Messenger of God for all of humanity in this day. The cornerstone of His teachings is the establishment of the spiritual unity of humankind, which will be achieved by personal transformation and the application of clearly identified spiritual principles. Bahá'ís also believe that there is but one religion and that all the Messengers of God—among them Abraham, Zoroaster, Moses, Krishna, Buddha, Jesus, and Muḥammad—have progressively revealed its nature. Together, the world's great religions are expressions of a single, unfolding divine plan. Human beings, not God's Messengers, are the source of religious divisions, prejudices, and hatreds.

The Bahá'í Faith is not a sect or denomination of another religion, nor is it a cult or a social movement. Rather, it is a globally recognized independent world religion founded on new books of scripture revealed by Bahá'u'lláh.

Bahá'í Publishing is an imprint of the National Spiritual Assembly of the Bahá'ís of the United States.

For more information about the Bahá'í Faith,
or to contact Bahá'ís near you,
visit http://www.bahai.us/
or call
1-800-22-UNITE

OTHER BOOKS AVAILABLE FROM
BAHÁ'Í PUBLISHING

HERITAGE OF LIGHT
THE SPIRITUAL DESTINY OF AMERICA
Janet A. Khan
$17.00 US / $19.00 CAN
Trade Paper
ISBN 978-1-931847-73-5

An examination of a fascinating religious community and a penetrating look at the spiritual destiny of America

Heritage of Light is an accessible description of the American Bahá'í community and a penetrating look at the spiritual destiny of America. This exploration traces the historical and spiritual connections that link the American Bahá'ís with the early Bahá'ís of Iran, who displayed an unparalleled staunchness of faith and heroism in the face of unspeakable brutal persecution and oppression. The author's examination of the writings of the Bahá'í Faith, along with extensive historical and archival records, demonstrates the unique role assigned to the American Bahá'ís and to the American nation as a whole in the development of a unified global society and the eventual inauguration of a world civilization.

ILLUMINE MY WORLD
BAHÁ'Í PRAYERS AND MEDITATIONS FOR PEACE
Bahá'u'lláh, the Báb, and 'Abdu'l-Bahá

$14.00 US / $16.00 CAN

Trade Paper

ISBN 978-1-931847-65-0

A heartwarming collection of prayers designed for people of all faiths during times of anxiety and chaos in the world

Illumine My World is a collection of prayers and meditative passages from the writings of the Bahá'í Faith that will help bring comfort and assurance during a time of growing anxiety, chaos, and change in the world today. As financial and religious institutions crumble and fall, as the tide of refugees from countries torn by civil strife continues to grow, as the oppression of women and minorities are brought to light more and more in so many parts of the world, readers can take comfort from these soothing passages. The prayers included specifically ask, among other things, for protection, for unity, and for assistance from God. Individuals from all religions will find strength and assurance in this inspiring collection.

MIND, HEART, & SPIRIT
EDUCATORS SPEAK
Heather Cardin

$18.00 US / $20.00 CAN

Trade Paper

ISBN 978-1-931847-66-7

Real-life stories from teachers who share their passion for shaping the lives of young people today.

Mind, Heart, and Spirit: Educators Speak is a collection of real-life stories from a diverse group of educators on a wide range of issues such as how to deal with difficult students, the role of parents and religion in a child's education, and the similarities and differences in educating children in different cultures across the globe. Filled with interesting anecdotes and personal accounts, this is an intimate, sometimes frustrating, sometimes exhilarating insight into the experiences of all these educators as they have struggled to overcome various challenges in educating children. Their passion for teaching and their devotion to their students come shining through and offer a glimpse of the important role that Bahá'í education—with its emphasis on unity, tolerance, and diversity—can play in shaping the lives of young people today.

MARRIAGE
A FORTRESS FOR WELL-BEING
Bahá'í Publishing
$15.00 US / $17.00 CAN
Trade Paper
ISBN 978-1-931847-63-6

Valuable insight about applying spiritual principles to the practical realities of the marital relationship

Marriage: A Fortress for Well-Being offers valuable insight for every couple, whether married or in preparation for marriage, to apply spiritual principles to everyday needs. Redefining marriage as the basic building block for world peace and unity, the book explores issues such as dating, how to prepare for marriage, the purpose of marriage, conflict resolution, interracial marriage, raising children, divorce, and more. By taking an in-depth look at what the Bahá'í writings say about marriage, the book examines the institution in light of God's purpose for humanity and provides guidance for building spiritually founded marital unions. Coming at a time when modern social conditions are forcing a reexamination of the institution of marriage, the book offers sound advice, encouragement, and tremendous hope for the future. This new edition has a foreword by Elizabeth Marquardt, author of *Between Two Worlds: The Inner Lives of Children of Divorce,* and an affiliate scholar at the Institute for American Values.